MW00772699

RAISING HER VOICE

RAISING HER VOICE

*African-American
Women Journalists
Who Changed History*

Rodger Streitmatter

THE UNIVERSITY PRESS OF KENTUCKY

Copyright © 1994 by The University Press of Kentucky
Scholarly publisher for the Commonwealth, serving Bellarmine University, Berea College,
Centre College of Kentucky, Eastern Kentucky University, The Filson Historical Society,
Georgetown College, Kentucky Historical Society, Kentucky State University, Morehead State
University, Murray State University, Northern Kentucky University, Transylvania University,
University of Kentucky, University of Louisville, and Western Kentucky University.
All rights reserved.

Editorial and Sales Offices: The University Press of Kentucky
663 South Limestone Street, Lexington, Kentucky 40508-4008
www.kentuckypress.com

PHOTO CREDITS: Maria W. Stewart (woodcut, which appeared with Stewart's essays in the
Liberator, reprinted by permission of the Houghton Library, Harvard University). Mary Ann Shadd
Cary (reprinted from Elizabeth Lindsay Davis, *Lifting as They Climb* [Washington: National Association
of Colored Women, 1933]). Gertrude Bustill Mossell and Josephine St. Pierre Ruffin (reprinted from
G.F. Richings, *Evidences of Progress among Colored People* [Philadelphia: George S. Ferguson, 1897]). Ida
B. Wells-Barnett (reprinted, by permission, from Wells-Barnett's *Crusade for Justice: The Autobiography
of Ida B. Wells,* edited by Alfreda M. Duster © 1970 by The University of Chicago Press). Delilah L.
Beasley (reprinted from Beasley's *The Negro Trail Blazers of California* [Los Angeles: 1919]). Marvel
Cooke (courtesy of Cooke). Charlotta A. Bass (by permission of the Southern California Library
for Social Studies and Research). Alice Allison Dunnigan (courtesy of Robert Dunnigan). Ethel L.
Payne (courtesy of Payne). Charlayne Hunter-Gault (courtesy of MacNeil/Lehrer Productions/Bruce
Lawrence).

Library of Congress Cataloging-in-Publication Data

Streitmatter, Rodger.
    Raising her voice : African-American women journalists who changed
history / Rodger Streitmatter.
        p.   cm.
    Includes bibliographical references (p.) and index.
    ISBN 0-8131-1861-1; 0-8131-0830-6 (acid-free)
    1. Afro-American journalists—Biography. 2. Afro-American women—Biography.
3. Journalism—United States—History—19th century. 4. Journalism—United States—
History—20th century. I. Title.
PN4872.S66   1994
070'.92'273—dc20   93-35932
[B]
ISBN-13: 978-0-8131-0830-8

This book is printed on acid-free recycled paper meeting
the requirements of the American National Standard
for Permanence in Paper for Printed Library Materials.

∞ ✪

Manufactured in the United States of America.

 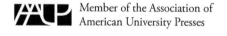

Member of the Association of
American University Presses

CONTENTS

I dedicate this book to TOM GROOMS.
On so many occasions and in so many
ways, he cleared my mind.

ACKNOWLEDGMENTS

When I submitted my first manuscript to a scholarly journal, my research skills were at such an elementary level that any editor in her right mind would have summarily rejected the manuscript. Fortunately, Susan Henry, then editor of *Journalism History,* assiduously avoids being of the "right mind." I have benefited immensely from Susan's daunting intellectual timber as well as her personal commitment to making the world better. Without her, neither that first manuscript nor this book would ever have been published. I thank her.

My second scholarly mentor has been Maurine Beasley. Maurine's integrity, dedication, support, and energy provide a model to which I continue to aspire.

Much of the material in this book originated as conference papers and articles in scholarly journals. Among those persons whose contributions I want to acknowledge, therefore, are dozens of individuals I cannot name because their identities are masked behind the blind review process of the American Journalism Historians Association, History Division of the Association for Education in Journalism and Mass Communication, Institute for Massachusetts Studies, *Journalism Quarterly, Journalism History, Howard Journal of Communications,* and *Afro-Americans in New York Life and History.* Fortunately, the reviewers know who they are, just as I know how much I have gained from them.

In addition, I am indebted to Bernell Tripp for generously sharing her research on African-American journalists with me and to Jerry Baldasty and Barbara Cloud for their friendship, their standard of excellence, and their willingness to critique my work.

On my own faculty in The American University's School for Communication, I thank my colleagues Barbara Diggs-Brown for working with me on the Marvel Cooke chapter and Sanford J.

Ungar and Laird Anderson for providing unwavering support and encouragement.

I very much appreciate the financial support that Dean Ungar and Betty Bennett, dean of the College of Arts and Sciences, have provided for my research. The District of Columbia Community Humanities Council also has supported my work through two grants that produced public exhibits about Alice Dunnigan and Ethel Payne.

Fern S. Ingersoll of the Women in Journalism Oral History Project of the Washington Press Club Foundation has been an invaluable resource and friend, both through the rich materials she has produced for scholars and the professional standards she has exemplified.

Marvel Cooke, Charlayne Hunter-Gault, and the late Ethel Payne graciously granted me the time to interview them in order to bring more depth to the manuscript. Robert Dunnigan allowed me to rummage through his garage for photographs and other material about his mother.

Much of the information contained in this book could not have been unearthed without the assistance of the individuals working in a long list of research insititutions around the country, from the Moorland-Spingarn Research Center at Howard University to the Rare Books and Manuscripts Division at the Chicago Historical Society. Above all others, I thank Sarah Cooper of the Southern California Library for Social Studies and Research for going far more than the extra mile to help illuminate the life and work of Charlotta Bass.

Finally, I thank Chris Delboni, Kim Gazella, and Marles Streitmatter for critiquing the manuscript during its final stages, and Matt and Kate for accepting the very strange fact that their father prefers working at the computer to doing most anything else in the world.

INTRODUCTION

One afternoon in the summer of 1989, I went to the Martin Luther King, Jr., Library in Washington, D.C., in search of material on a man named William W. Price. I was researching Price, the reporter who transformed the White House into a news beat, and was having difficulty locating original sources. The librarian dutifully went into the closed stacks to see what she could find for me. When she reappeared with a book in hand, I smiled anxiously as she announced: "I'm sorry, sir. I couldn't find a single thing on Price . . . but I did find this book about Alice Dunnigan, the first black woman to cover the White House." I thanked her and accepted the book she handed me, but my smile had turned plastic. I wanted material about a white man of the 1890s; she had given me a book about a black woman of the 1940s. A lot of help she was. I thumbed quickly through Dunnigan's autobiography, then left.

But after finishing the article on Price, I couldn't shake the image of Alice Dunnigan grinning up at me from the cover of her life story. I mentioned Dunnigan's name to a fellow journalism historian who has published as much about American women journalists as anyone in the country. My friend said no one had documented Dunnigan's contributions. I did not yet know it, but I had begun the odyssey that would culminate in this book.

Researching Dunnigan's life and work went smoothly until I attempted to place her contributions into the larger context of African-American women journalists. There was no such context. It was impossible to place Dunnigan because journalism historians, like historians in general, have not fully examined the lives and contributions of African-American women. When I referred to the standard history of American journalism, I found a description of the career of only one black woman, Ida B. Wells-Barnett—whose life was compressed into seven lines.[1] Nor were histories of the African-American press of much help. When I looked at the standard in the field, I found that the descriptions of women of both the nineteenth and twentieth centuries were limited to a dozen pages.[2] Histories of women journalists were somewhat more helpful, containing descriptions of several African-American women. The scholars who described these women, however, also acknowledged the inadequacy of their research. In her book *A Place in the News: From the Women's Pages to the Front Page*, for example, Kay Mills wrote of black women working for the black press: "The experiences of women in that segment of the press should be the subject of another book."[3] This is such a book.

The picture I paint is not always a pretty one. Each portrait is a case study of the triumph of the human spirit, but each is sketched against the backdrop of a society rife with prejudice, injustice, and hatred. It is precisely because of these factors that American historians have, until recent decades, largely ignored women of African descent. The chroniclers of this country's evolution—most of whom have been white men—generally have discounted black women as long-suffering victims who not only endured their oppression and degradation but passively submitted to it. Because of the prejudice against these women, they have been perceived as powerless and dismissed as unimportant. Only recently have researchers begun to document that, in reality, many African-American women steadfastly refused to accept their subjugation and, indeed, helped to shape this nation's history. During the last decade, scholars have documented that black women resisted the emotional, physical, and sexual oppression of slavery and that they provided important leadership in the anti-slavery, women's suffrage, and modern civil rights movements.[4]

As my research progressed, I, too, discovered individual African-American women who were anything but passive. The eleven case studies assembled here demonstrate that African-American women journalists, despite racial and sexual discrimination, fought back against their oppression and were at the forefront of major events in American history. From the early 1800s to today, the American woman of African descent has raised her voice in both the black and the white press. The research summarized in this book adds a new chapter to an evolving depiction of the African-American woman as a defiant, strong-minded, and independent individual who refused to be a silent victim.

The women whose stories follow are, in many ways, a diverse group. Just as they broke new ground for their race and gender by contributing to the news media, they also broke the stereotypes of African-American women of their particular eras. Three became penniless orphans at an early age, but two others were wealthy and highly educated women of the aristocratic black elite of Boston and Philadelphia. Geographically, the women represent virtually all sections of the United States—from Minnesota to Mississippi, Rhode Island to California. Likewise, the portraits painted in this book do not glorify African-American women journalists as universally unblemished in their professionalism or their virtue. Some were driven by a noble sense of journalistic mission; others were not.

But they, to a woman, share one characteristic: defiance. Although they were isolated from each other, both by time and by geographic location, they all defied conformance to the limited spheres that the societies of their respective eras defined as those of the African-American woman. Each woman profiled in this book chose not to submit quietly to the oppression with which society attempted to subjugate her. Each woman fought back. Each woman did so by raising her voice through the news media. Each woman became both a journalist and a racial activist, using her position to advocate equality for her race, for her sisters, and for humankind.

Together as well as individually, these women changed history. Many reporters reject the concept of the journalist as agent of change. A reporter simply chronicles the events of the day, such purists argue, and should not shape those events. Stated another way, the argument is that the role of the reporter is to reflect society, not to lead it. Such an argument would not, however, come from a participant in the African-American press. The history of the black press, grounded in a tradition of advocacy, is closely intertwined with the history of black America. Individuals working in the African-American press have been some of the most important leaders of African-American history.

Ida B. Wells-Barnett is one example. By writing scathing editorials for her Memphis newspaper, Wells-Barnett founded the anti-lynching movement in this country. Later she expanded that

movement to Great Britain, and still later she played a leading
role in the American woman's suffrage movement by leading the
first national march to demand voting rights for American wom-
en. Ethel L. Payne is another example. During a White House
press conference in 1954, Payne, a reporter for the *Chicago Defender*, publicly confronted President Dwight D. Eisenhower,
asking him point-blank when he was going to ban segregation in
interstate travel. The dean of the White House press corps cited
Payne's question as the catalyst that moved civil rights onto the
national agenda. Payne, in her understated way, later acknowledged: "I've had a box seat on history, and I've been able to
chronicle some of the major events that have made a change in
society, made a change in the law. My writings may have helped
to influence some of that change."[5]

But the most stunning example of a black woman journalist
who changed history is Charlotta A. Bass. From the moment in
the spring of 1912 when she laid down fifty dollars and bought the
California Eagle at public auction, she and her newspaper became
integral elements in the battle against discrimination in Southern
California. Her first investigative reporting project did not stop
when her front-page story revealed that the Los Angeles County
General Hospital refused to hire black employees. No, indeed. She
appealed directly to the county board of supervisors and demanded that the policy be overturned. Although it is not always
possible for a journalism historian to show a cause-and-effect
relationship between a specific item in the news media and a
historical event, with Bass there is little doubt. In the case of the
hospital hiring policy, Bass persuaded the supervisors to hire
black workers—if, in turn, Bass agreed to interview and select
the candidates. For the next year, Bass wore another hat in addition to that of newspaper editor and publisher; she also became
an employment counselor. Hundreds of her African-American
sisters filed into the *Eagle* office to apply for jobs as nurses aides
at the hospital. Bass made her selections, the women were hired,
and history was made. During the next four decades, Bass became a one-woman tour de force as she led the desegregation of
the Los Angeles Fire Department and Southern California Telephone Company, dealt a body blow to the Ku Klux Klan, and
convinced the United States Supreme Court that restrictive housing covenants were unconstitutional—among other actions.

Because of a plethora of incidents such as these, there is no doubt that the thousands of news stories, editorials, essays, columns, and feature articles written by the journalists profiled in this book had impact on the development of both public opinion and public policy.

It is Bass who gave this book its title. In 1915, she spearheaded a campaign against D.W. Griffith's epic motion picture, "Birth of a Nation," because it depicted blacks as savages. As Bass went up against one of Hollywood's leading producers at the same time that motion pictures were becoming the most important commodity in Southern California, she was not intimidated. In a blistering editorial, she wrote: "As long as the Afro-Americans of this country sit supinely by and *RAISE NO VOICE* against the injustice heaped upon them, conditions for them in this country will grow worse."[6]

The first American woman of African descent to raise her voice through the press was Maria W. Stewart, who helped fire the abolition movement by publishing powerful anti-slavery essays in the *Liberator* beginning in 1832. She was followed by Mary Ann Shadd Cary, whose support of the Canadian fugitive slave movement led her to establish her own anti-slavery newspaper, the *Provincial Freeman*, in 1853. Other nineteenth-century women and the historical movements to which they contributed were Gertrude Bustill Mossell and black America's transition from slavery to self-sufficiency, Ida B. Wells-Barnett and the anti-lynching crusade, and Josephine St. Pierre Ruffin and the African-American women's club movement. Twentieth-century women and the events they influenced were Delilah L. Beasley and the movement toward accommodation and conciliation to white America, Marvel Cooke and the Harlem Renaissance, Charlotta A. Bass and the emergence of Black Power, Alice Allison Dunnigan and desegregation in the North, Ethel L. Payne and the modern civil rights movement, and Charlayne Hunter-Gault and the blight that continues to shroud black America.

These journalists have been on the forefront of change, making history for their nation while simultaneously making history for journalists of their race and gender. As the generations have passed, these women have become increasingly empowered by their evolving journalistic heritage. Charlayne Hunter-Gault, the youngest of the women, spoke to this progress when she described her job as national correspondent for the "MacNeil/Lehrer News-Hour," one of the most prestigious news organizations in the country today. Hunter-Gault said, simply but poignantly: "I have so much *voice* in what I do." [7]

This book illuminates the lives and works of eleven pioneers through the use of a variety of primary sources. Most important among these sources are the journalists' published writings. Analysis of the words these women used and the topics they chose to write about identifies recurring themes in their journalistic work. Many statements from their writings are quoted, in an effort to ensure that the women have the opportunity to speak with their own voices. Most of the articles were found in newspapers preserved at the Library of Congress or the Howard University Library in Washington, D.C., although some of the newspapers were used at or borrowed from other libraries around the country. In addition, excerpts from oral history interviews with several of the women enable the subjects to speak directly to the reader. Of particular use were transcripts of the Women in Journalism Oral History Project of the Washington Press Club Foundation. Sources for the personal lives of the women include such traditional sources as census records and marriage certificates, but the sources also extend to a variety of nontraditional documents. Information about Maria Stewart's early years was found in a claim form she filed in an attempt to receive a pension as the widow of a soldier in the War of 1812. Details of Delilah Beasley's personal life were gleaned from a library researcher's card she completed at the California State Library and from medical records at the hospital where she died. Fragments of Josephine St. Pierre Ruffin's life surfaced in half a dozen documents scattered among four libraries from Massachusetts to Louisiana.

Searching for information about members of a minority group that has been denied its history can be difficult, frustrating, time-consuming—and fruitless. Relatively few African-American newspapers have been preserved, and research libraries contain the personal papers of only a handful of black women. The problem is exacerbated by the invisibility of African-American women; if any journalist's byline was omitted from an article, it was that of the African-American woman. The challenge of locating primary sources has led to the exclusion of journalists from this book who rightfully deserve their chapters. For example, two scholars have identified Sarah Gibson Jones as the only African-American woman journalist working for a newspaper during the Civil War, arguably the most important event in the history of black America.[8] I devoted two months to piecing together Jones's biography and searching for her original newspaper articles in the *Cincinnati Colored Citizen*. I found only two extant copies of the newspaper—one at the Library of Congress and another at the University of Cincinnati. Jones has been excluded from this book, however, because neither copy of the *Colored Citizen* contains any indication of Jones having written or edited any of the articles in it.

To state that primary sources about the journalists described here have been difficult to locate is not to suggest that nothing has been written about these remarkable individuals. Some of the women have been the subjects of previous research. Maria Stewart has attracted a large body of scholarship relevant to her public speeches; Josephine St. Pierre Ruffin has been examined as an organizer of African-American women's clubs. The endnotes to these women's respective chapters identify more than a dozen such works. This book is the first work, however, that looks at Stewart's or Ruffin's words as those of journalists.

This raises another concern in this project—establishing the limits of the term *journalist*. By its narrowest definition, the term applies only to individuals who write, edit, and publish articles about news events. Some of the women appearing in this book do not fit in this little box. Stewart's work for the *Liberator*, for example, consisted solely of essays; she never reported council meetings or fires or legislative issues that are the grist of the news media today. Likewise, the majority of Marvel Cooke's early work during the Harlem Renaissance was in the form of critical reviews that were published in a monthly magazine, and Josephine St. Pierre Ruffin's extant contributions appeared in a monthly publication that could be labeled either a newspaper or a magazine. I have, in short, adopted a broader definition of the term journalist.

This expansion is justified by the fact that, throughout much of American history, both the white and the black press were largely closed to African-American women journalists. The general-circulation newspapers that chronicled the news of the day were a male domain. Women of neither color were written about or allowed to contribute to the writing or editing of the news. Women with a yearning to raise their voices through the media of their day, therefore, had to seek alternative routes. For Stewart, that route was commentary published in the leading abolitionist newspaper in the country. For Cooke, entering the field of journalism meant writing reviews for the magazine that, more than any other publication of its time, was describing the black experience. For Ruffin, providing a forum through which African-American women could speak and be heard by others of their race and gender meant founding her own monthly publication that others could call a magazine but that she called a newspaper. I am of the belief that an arbitrary definition of journalism should not prevent the stories of these determined and resourceful women from being told—even if to do so means expanding the canon of journalism. For the purposes of this book, therefore, a journalist is defined as an individual whose nonfiction work is disseminated in a regularly appearing publication aimed at a broad audience.

At this point it also seems prudent to define the term *feminist*, as this word has been defined and redefined many times. This book adopts a traditional definition of a feminist as a person who advocates and, to at least some degree, demands for women the same rights that have been granted to men, particularly with regard to political or economic status.

Having overcome the difficulties of locating sources and crafting appropriate definitions of journalist and feminist, this book tells the stories of eleven African-American women who, through their published work, helped shape the evolution of their race, gender, and nation. This book is intended for students of American history. Most especially, it is aimed at students of the history of American women journalists as well as students of the history of American journalism, American women, and Americans of African descent. It is hoped that, through the pages of this book, future generations of scholars and students, unlike those of past generations, will learn that black women journalists have been active participants in the life of this country.

The hope that this book will be read by students as well as scholars has defined the style in which it has been written. Each profile begins with a brief summary of the historical event that the specific journalist helped to shape, and the first notes for each chapter guide readers to sources on those events. The bulk of each chapter is written in a narrative style, telling the story of the woman's life and journalistic work. These individual chapters purposely are not steeped in the theory of women's history or the African-American experience. Other scholars may want to examine the details of these women's lives through such prisms, but that is not the purpose of this book. Nor is the purpose of this volume to serve as the final, definitive work on each of its eleven subjects. Instead, this volume seeks to tell these women's stories in a straightforward style that is accessible to students and general readers. This book is not written solely for scholars; it also is written for students of American history who previously have had few sources from which to learn about women journalists of African descent. I leave to future scholars the task of writing the comprehensive, theory-based biography of each woman profiled in this book. Each and every journalist described here certainly deserves such specialized treatment.

This book, I believe, will be particularly useful because the women described in it span a broad spectrum of American history. The first woman was born in 1803; two women are still living. My hope is that this breadth will allow professors to avoid the "add women and mix" syndrome that sometimes has been manifested in the teaching of history. This comprehensive examination of black women journalists during the last two centuries invites professors to integrate the experiences of these women into courses with attention to the context of the women's race and gender.

With regard to providing that context, it may be helpful in this introduction to mention a few broad generalizations that may guide readers who are unfamiliar with major themes relevant to the experiences of African-American women. In particular, as a person begins reading the individual profiles, he or she would be well advised not to assume that the themes dominant in the history of white American women are necessarily valid with regard to the history of black American women. The evidence that there has been a tradition of sisterhood of cooperation and similarity of experience between white and black women is far outweighed by the evidence that there has been a tradition of tension. Some of the privileges that white women have enjoyed have been at the expense of black women; some of the opportunities that white women have fought for—such as being allowed to enter the workforce—are ones that black women would have been only too happy to have forfeited generations ago.[9]

Foremost among these concepts is that African-American women historically have identified themselves first as members of an oppressed race, feeling the pain of racial prejudice more acutely than the pain of sexual prejudice. This priority is fully understandable when framed in such events as the lynchings and bombings that have characterized black America's struggle for human rights. In 1987, Ethel Payne said that every African American is assaulted by the system every day of her life, and, because journalists have the potential of being agents of change, this constant assault shapes a journalist's approach to her work. Charlayne Hunter-Gault spoke even more to the point when she recalled her involvement in the modern civil rights movement, saying: "The overriding issue then had to be racism. The simple truth of the matter: black women were first discriminated against because they were black, then because they were women." Whether it was in the 1830s or the 1990s, racial reform was of paramount importance to each of the journalists described in this book. Each woman was both a racial activist and a journalist—in that order.[10]

Another relevant generalization is that black men historically have been relatively accepting of black women as coworkers. While white women have struggled against employment discrimination from the men of their race, black women have more easily entered the various workplaces. Gertrude Bustill Mossell wrote in 1894: "Our men are too much hampered by their contentions with their white brothers to afford to stop and fight their black sisters." For African-American women journalists, this reality has translated into opportunities for them to work in a wide variety of capacities and to cover a wide variety of topics for the black press.[11]

Economic circumstances of African-American women also are an important consideration to keep in mind. Specifically, the lack of access to education and job training and the discriminatory practices regarding the employment of African-American men have resulted in the majority of African-American women traditionally working outside the home. Because of these realities, African-American women historically have been accustomed to being economically independent and self-sufficient.[12]

Finally, education and religion have been central to the lives of African-American women. Slave women invented underground schools in an effort to ensure that the next generation of the race would be literate; later generations continued the tradition, with many African-American women improving their status by becoming schoolteachers, one of the few professional-level occupations open to them.[13] Slave women maintained religion as part of their lives during a time that most human rights were denied them; just as white women of the eighteenth and nineteenth centuries were considered the moral guides for their people, black women assumed similar roles for their race.[14]

The final chapter of this book revisits these topics as it discusses how these and other factors have enabled African-American women journalists to contribute to the shaping of American history. That concluding chapter synthesizes the material about the subjects of the eleven profiles, responding to the broad question: What have been the recurring themes in the lives and published works of African-American women journalists?[15]

As a synthesis, the final chapter departs from the structure and content, but not the style, of the previous chapters. Such a departure is justified, I believe, because it is this chapter that advances the research on black women journalists to a higher level. Historian Gerda Lerner has identified four stages of conceptualization in women's history. First comes compensatory history, which closes some of the gaps in the historical record by identifying significant women and describing their accomplishments. Next comes contribution history, which describes women's achievements and status in a male-defined society. Then comes a transitional stage that depends on women's own words— typically in the form of letters, diaries, autobiographies, and oral histories—to create new categories by which historians can examine material. The fourth and final stage is one of synthesis in which women's history blends with men's history to create a history of all people that has been enriched by the exploration of women's experiences so that new questions are raised about that blended historical record.[16]

It is with Lerner's concepts in mind that the synthesis chapter at the end of this book has been written. The chapter identifies elements common to the lives and written work of African-American women journalists. The first eleven chapters fundamentally are examples of the compensatory stage and, because much of the research is based on the women's own words through their journalistic work and oral histories, the transitional stage of historical research. The final chapter advances to the contribution stage. It builds on the earlier chapters by identifying and pulling together themes threaded through the individual narrative biographies to suggest how African-American women journalists, as a group, fit into the institution of American journalism, a field that has been and continues to be dominated by white men. Although my attempting to move to Lerner's final stage may be presumptuous, the last chapter tries to move in that direction by identifying and discussing themes that may be worthy of consideration in the reexamination of both white women journalists and the broad topic of American journalists of both genders and all races.

One question I feel compelled to respond to is one that I have been asked in numerous settings and in various tones. I will state the question here in its most accusatory form: "What gives you, a white man, the right to invade the research area of the history of black women journalists?" It seems that responding to this question is part of the rite of passage through which every scholar of my race and gender—and there certainly have been many before me—must experience if he chooses to focus on such a topic. My answer is that in a pluralistic field such as American history, the life experiences of American women of African descent represent legitimate scholarship and that every area of research should be open to every scholar, just as the knowledge we discover should be accessible to every student. As several African-American women scholars already have acknowledged, the lack of research about the contributions that this minority group has made to the American media represents such a huge hole that sensitive black male, white female, and white male researchers must be attracted to this area of scholarship if the hole is to be filled.[17]

Even though some scholars may approach my presence in this subject area with skepticism, I have attempted not to allow those feelings to prevent my research from identifying negative as well as positive traits in the subjects. Although each and every woman profiled here deserves to be described as "remarkable," that does not mean that each has been unflawed by personal and professional warts.

For instance, some of these women became so driven to change society and so sure that they knew exactly how to do so that they became impatient, obstinate, intractable, intolerant of anyone with a position different from their own—to the point that their determination became a barrier rather than a benefit to the causes they cherished. Indeed, their aggressive natures resulted in some of the journalists being banished from their communities and drummed out of organizations committed to social reform.

Others were elitist. The combination of being born into a high social caste and marrying men who reinforced this position resulted in a wide gulf separating these women from the uneducated, lower-class blacks who had been denied the opportunities that accompany wealth and education. Rather than using their journalistic positions primarily to improve the condition of their less fortunate sisters and brothers, these aristocratic women fashioned a style of journalism aimed primarily toward other well-to-do members of the African-American elite.[18]

Still others described in this book were not gifted writers. All of the women successfully bridled the power of the press to contribute to important reform efforts and movements in American history, but they all did not demonstrate the ability to craft graceful prose or to write in clear, effective, grammatically correct language.

Identifying such negative characteristics is not intended to denigrate these women or to lessen their importance. The history of women journalists is a relatively new area of scholarship that is still in its embryonic stages. Much of this scholarship has tended to idolize the individual women whose lives and works have begun to be illuminated. The tendency is a natural one. Because these women previously have been ignored, the temptation is to overcompensate by glorifying them. To do so, however, is to place these women on the pedestal that generations of American women have been attempting to vacate. So, for the last decade, scholars have been calling for more rigorous examination and critical analysis of the lives and works of women working in journalism. Articulating some of the blemishes of African-American women journalists is intended to provide such in-depth analysis.[19]

To explore the full depth of these journalists' personal and professional lives—warts and all—is to accept them as multidimensional human beings rather than to glorify them or to dismiss them as cardboard figures. To examine these individuals critically is to recognize and to respect them as historical subjects worthy of complete and unrestrained study and analysis. Besides, to treat these individuals gingerly would suggest that African-American women journalists have been weak and helpless, in need of protection. They have not. They have been individuals of strength and stamina. Their significance cannot be destroyed by rigorous examination. Regardless of their flaws, these journalists have been strong, defiant women who have raised their voices and, in so doing, have changed history.

1

MARIA W. STEWART
Firebrand of the Abolition Movement

From 1831 when the *Liberator* was founded until 1865 when its singular goal of ending slavery had been achieved, the militant newspaper was a powerful force in the abolition movement. When the *Liberator* ceased publication after the Fourteenth Amendment was ratified, the *Nation* magazine stated: "It did more than any one thing beside to create that power of moral conviction which was so indomitable an element in the campaign." The individual most closely connected to the *Liberator* was its editor, William Lloyd Garrison, but other advocacy journalists also added their fiery words to the newspaper's steady attack on the sins of slavery. One of these largely overlooked voices came from a black woman.[1]

Maria W. Stewart's words were published in the *Liberator* from 1831 to 1833. Garrison showcased Stewart's essays by creating for them a "Ladies' Department"—complete with a woodcut of a black woman in chains—in the *Liberator*, as well as reprinting them as pamphlets. Stewart, a domestic with little formal education, relied on her knowledge of the Bible and the experiences of her own suffering to argue against slavery. Her voice was bold and passionate, fired by the unwavering conviction of religious fervor and personal sorrow. Her words were eloquent. In one essay for the *Liberator*, she wrote: "Methinks I heard a spiritual interrogation—'Who shall go forward, and take off the reproach that is cast upon the people of color? Shall it be a woman?' And my heart made this reply—'If it is thy will, be it even so, Lord Jesus!'"[2]

Opposition to a woman being so outspoken led black men to jeer and throw rotten tomatoes at Stewart. Such violent reaction forced her to leave Boston and to end her work for the *Liberator* after a mere two years, but her brief journalistic career set a standard of defiance that African-American women journalists have fought vigorously to sustain for a century and a half.[3]

Her groundbreaking work as the first journalist of her race and gender introduced themes that continued to define the work of African-American women journalists. Her religion-centered essays argued for the abolition of slavery as well as the end of oppression of free blacks. Stewart believed that African Americans could achieve justice for their race only if they led moral lives; she also believed it was imperative for African Americans themselves to fight for their rights. In addition, Stewart exhorted African-American women to expand beyond their limited role in order to lead the progress of the race.

Maria Miller was born free in Hartford, Connecticut, in 1803. Orphaned at the age of five, Maria was "bound out" as a domestic servant to the family of a clergyman. Her classroom education lasted only six weeks, but she studied the Bible and had some access to the literary world through the minister's personal library. She later wrote: "I was deprived of the advantages of education, though my soul thirsted for knowledge." At the age of fifteen, Maria left the clergyman's home and, for the next five years, worked as a domestic.[4]

When Miller was twenty-three years old, she married James W. Stewart, a forty-seven-year-old independent businessman from Boston. James W. Stewart had served as a seaman on several U.S. Navy ships during the War of 1812, later having been captured and held prisoner in England. When peace had returned, he had parlayed his shipping skills into his own business as a shipping master who outfitted whaling and fishing vessels. After their marriage in 1826, the Stewarts settled into Boston's small African-American middle class.[5]

Their security was short lived. Three years after the marriage, James W. Stewart became severely ill with heart disease. He died in December 1829, leaving his wife a twenty-six-year-old widow. In keeping with a request in Stewart's will, his widow added the middle initial "W" from his name to her own.[6]

Maria W. Stewart then experienced the vulnerabilities of a young black woman of the early nineteenth century. As the widow of a successful businessman, Stewart should have received her husband's substantial estate. Instead, the white executors of her husband's will conducted a series of legal maneuvers that ultimately deprived Stewart of her rightful inheritance, leaving her destitute and forcing her to become a domestic once more.[7]

Stewart sought comfort from God. In 1830 she underwent a religious conversion and publicly announced that she had consecrated her life to God's service. Specifically, she felt called to express herself through the written word, even though her association with literature had been limited almost exclusively to the Bible. So Stewart framed her words in biblical discourse. This journalistic approach was not unusual in the early nineteenth century when many newspaper articles sounded much like sermons.[8]

Her initial written work was in the form of meditations upon the values of morality. Emboldened by reading Garrison's remarks on the power of female influence, Stewart took several of her essays to the *Liberator* office. Garrison later wrote to Stewart of his first meeting with her: "You were in the flush and promise of a ripening womanhood, with a graceful form and a pleasing countenance." Stewart asked Garrison only for criticism and advice, but the abolitionist editor was so pleased to discover eloquent prose written by an African-American woman that he published the essays in his newspaper. He also printed the essays in pamphlet form, promoting Stewart as "a respectable colored lady," and sold the tracts from his office. Stewart's words first appeared in the *Liberator* in March 1831, a year and a half before she made her first public lecture.[9]

Stewart's spiritual fervor was central to all of her journalistic work, but it was particularly prominent in her earliest essays as she established why she was involved in journalism. Early in 1832, she wrote: "God has fired my soul with a holy zeal for his cause. It was God alone who inspired my heart to publish the meditations." [10]

Although Stewart talked of the love of Jesus Christ, her words were not always loving. She often chastised humankind. In the same 1832 essay, for example, she speculated that Christ would not approve of the behavior of many men and women who professed Christianity, writing: "Were our blessed Lord and Saviour, Jesus Christ, upon the earth, I believe he would say of many that are called by his name, 'O, ye hypocrites, ye genera- tion of vipers, how can you escape the damnation of hell?'" [11]

This quotation illustrates Stewart's reliance on the Bible as a literary source. In this instance, she clearly incorporated into her statement a variation of Matthew 23:33: "Ye serpents, ye gener- ation of vipers, how can ye escape the damnation of hell?" Many of her essays were peppered with similar statements from and allusions to biblical verses.

Drawn to religion by the difficulties in her own life, Stewart adopted Christ as her savior and became an evangelist. The jour- nalistic work that was the product of her missionary zeal was part of an evangelistic movement that flourished in northern cities in the 1830s and 1840s. Because of increasingly repressive legislation and unjust treatment by whites, articulate free blacks preached the words and teachings of the Bible as their salvation. [12]

As Stewart's journalistic writing matured, she used the frame- work of spiritualism to discuss various secular issues. Primary among them was the abolition of slavery. The devout Christian built her anti-slavery stance on the Bible. She compared the United States to ancient Babylon, observing that both civiliza- tions were morally corrupt because they sanctioned the sale of the souls of human beings—and that both civilizations were, therefore, doomed. [13]

Stewart was so fervent in her commitment to the abolition of slavery that she publicly stated, as did Garrison, that she was willing to sacrifice her life in order to help end slavery. She wrote: "I will willingly die for the cause that I have espoused; for I cannot die in a more glorious cause." [14]

Stewart did not limit her racial reform efforts to the abolition of slavery but also campaigned for an end to oppressive treatment of free blacks. She wrote: "Tell us no more of Southern slavery; for with few exceptions, I consider our [free blacks'] condition but little better than that." Her own experiences had taught her that emancipation did not guarantee justice. Although she had been born free, she still had suffered at the hands of opportunists. Stewart had learned that abolition was not a panacea for black Americans.[15]

Nor was Stewart willing to listen to the merits of the colonization movement, which would have deported free blacks to Africa. By 1832, the American Colonization Society had been established and more than a dozen state legislatures had approved the society's efforts to ship African Americans to Liberia. Stewart, however, steadfastly opposed the work of the colonizationists, writing: "Their hearts are so frozen toward us they had rather their money should be sunk in the ocean than to administer it to our relief." Stewart preferred fighting for increased rights to escaping from hostile whites. Again dramatically expressing her willingness to become a martyr, she wrote: "They would drive us to a strange land. But before I go, the bayonet shall pierce me through."[16]

Though Stewart praised the work of white abolitionists who organized anti-slavery societies, she believed that the impetus for racial reform had to rise from African Americans themselves. Stewart advocated African Americans following a two-pronged strategy to achieve equality.

First, she urged them to strengthen their own morality. She articulated this theme in the full title of her first essay in the *Liberator*: "Religion And The Pure Principles Of Morality, The Sure Foundations On Which We Must Build." As a born-again Christian, Stewart was convinced that the sinful behavior of her people had led to the downfall of the race and that, therefore, untainted moral behavior would allow African Americans to rise to their proper status once more. She saw her responsibilities as a journalist to be serving as a guiding voice for her people. In 1832 she wrote that if free blacks turned their attention more assiduously to moral worth, prejudice gradually would diminish and white America would be compelled to say: "Unloose those fetters! Though black their skins as shades of night, their hearts are pure, their souls are white."[17]

Throughout the essays she published in the *Liberator*, Stewart

methodically listed the specific forms of moral behavior her people should adopt. In concert with middle-class values, primary
among them was frugality through the judicial use of financial
resources. In her initial essay, Stewart urged readers to stop wast-
ing their money on "nonsense" and to use their financial resources
to establish their own churches, schools, and businesses.[18]

In later essays, it became clear that one form of "nonsense,"
in Stewart's mind, was consuming alcohol. She urged free black
men to form their own temperance societies, suggesting that
nothing would raise the respectability of blacks more than their
overcoming the evils of alcohol use. Gambling, dancing, and
lying were other objectionable forms of behavior, according to
Stewart.[19]

The second prong of Stewart's strategy for achieving progress for her race was through militancy. Her essays not only
discussed an issue but also called her readers to action. In 1832,
Stewart wrote: "I am of a strong opinion that the day on which
we unite, heart and soul, that day the hissing and reproach
among the nations of the earth against us will cease. Let us
make a mighty effort, and arise." Stewart was a proponent of
political power, and she often spoke with a defiance that rarely
emanated from an African-American woman of the early nineteenth century.[20]

Indeed, Stewart, who frequently expressed pride in being an
American, thought that it was more than merely the right of
Americans of African descent to protest—she considered it their
patriotic duty. Only those men and women who demanded equal
rights, she believed, were true Americans in the tradition of the
patriots who had won independence from Britain half a century
earlier. Stewart wrote: "Did the pilgrims, when they first landed
on these shores, quietly compose themselves, and say, 'The Britons
have all the money and the power, and we must continue their
servants forever'? Did they sluggishly sigh and say, 'Our lot is
hard, the Indians own the soil, and we cannot cultivate it.' No;
they first made powerful efforts to raise themselves. My brethren,
have you made a powerful effort?"[21]

The militant attitude that Stewart espoused is intriguing because it contradicts the philosophy of most persons devoted to
the teachings of the Bible. Not only did Stewart defy the peaceful
and submissive stance of most devout Christians, she also openly

criticized African-American ministers, saying they had helped create the difficulties plaguing the race. If black ministers had properly discharged their duties, she wrote, they would have acknowledged the existence of racism long ago.[22]

Stewart believed that God had called her not only to tell her readers about the racism that divided the country but also to chide them into mustering the courage to demand their rights. She wrote: "O ye sons of Africa, when will your voices be heard in our legislative halls, in defiance of your enemies, contending for equal rights and liberty?"[23]

The pioneering journalist went so far as to specify precise ways in which African Americans could empower themselves. In the 1830s, whether or not slavery should be abolished in the nation's capital had become a volatile political issue between slave and free states. Stewart challenged her black readers to raise their voices by signing a petition to the United States Congress to abolish slavery in the District of Columbia.[24]

The fiery Stewart also issued a powerful threat—the same one that has continued to stalk this country since that time. Stewart wrote: "Many powerful sons and daughters of Africa will shortly arise, and declare that they will have their rights; and if refused, I am afraid they will spread horror and devastation."[25]

Women's rights was another theme that maintained a strong presence in Stewart's essays. Her first article in the *Liberator* established that she intended to use her journalistic forum to promote expansion of the role that African-American women played in society. In that essay, Stewart promoted the concept of women moving beyond domesticity, boldly asking: "How long shall the fair daughters of Africa be compelled to bury their minds and talents beneath a load of iron pots and kettles?"[26]

The question was a rhetorical one, as Stewart immediately suggested two methods by which black women could improve their status. First, she advocated women casting aside the concept of dependence upon men. She told her African-American sisters: "Possess the spirit of independence. Possess the spirit of men, bold and enterprising, fearless and undaunted. Sue for your rights and privileges." Second, the pragmatic Stewart recognized the value of black women entering the influential world of commerce. So she suggested they combat the economic barriers to establishing business enterprises by joining forces to operate business ventures.[27]

Stewart anticipated that her ideas about black women expanding into new spheres would have the support neither of white women nor of men of either race. But she thought the cause, like that of the abolition of slavery, was worthy of martyrdom. The defiant Stewart told African-American women: "You can but die if you make the attempt; and we shall certainly die if you do not."[28]

Like many black women's rights activists, Stewart was ambivalent about the issue of whether the sisterhood crossed racial lines. In her earliest essays, she sometimes advocated imitating white women. When she heard about women in Connecticut using the profits from a community garden to erect a church, for instance, she suggested African-American women follow their example and build a high school for black students. But at other times, particularly in her later essays, Stewart criticized white women. When she asked white women to hire black women to work for them, for example, she resented their refusal, saying that white women were both prejudiced and cowardly.[29]

As her journalistic career neared its end, Stewart came to believe that African-American women would have to rely on themselves to lead the race. She called for them to accept the awesome responsibility, writing: "O woman, woman! Your example is powerful, your influence great; it extends over your husbands and your children, and throughout the circle of your acquaintance. O woman, woman! Upon you I call; for upon your exertions almost entirely depends whether the rising generation shall be any thing more than we have been or not."[30]

Members of Boston's African-American community condemned Stewart. Detractors said it was unseemly for a woman to speak so boldly. In a graphic expression of their disapproval, black men pelted Stewart with verbal insults as well as rotten tomatoes. Because of this sexual discrimination, in 1833 Stewart announced that she was leaving Boston.[31]

The thirty-year-old widow then moved to New York City and furthered her education by joining a female literary society, writing unpublished compositions and presenting declamations. It was also soon after moving to New York that Stewart compiled her writing into her first book. Although she included sev-

eral essays originally published in the *Liberator*, the bulk of the
eighty-four-page volume consisted of prayers and meditations.
Productions of Mrs. Maria Stewart, which was published in Boston in 1835, also contained transcripts of the four public speeches
she had delivered in Boston and several pages of autobiographical
material.[32]

Having strengthened her own education and her literary reputation, Stewart shifted into a forty-year career in education. She
first taught in the public schools of Manhattan and then, after a
decade of classroom teaching, was promoted to assistant to the
school principal for the Williamsburg section of Brooklyn.[33]

Stewart never returned to journalistic writing after leaving
Boston, but she continued to dedicate some of her time and resources to the work of newspapers. During the early 1850s, she
helped raise money to operate the *North Star*, the newspaper
that Frederick Douglass had founded in Rochester, New York, in
1847.[34]

In 1852, Stewart lost her position in the New York public
schools and, hearing that southern people were more religious,
moved to Baltimore and attempted to organize her own private
school. That venture failed, and Stewart became destitute. She
then sought help from a man and woman who were influential
members of Baltimore's black community. The couple offered to
organize a benefit to raise the money for Stewart's rent, if she
allowed them to promote the event by publicly describing her
difficult circumstances. The event was a success, raising three
hundred dollars in profits. The couple then gave Stewart thirty
dollars to pay her rent—and kept the rest for themselves. Stewart
later wrote: "I have never been very shrewd in money matters.
They laughed ready to kill themselves to think what a fool they
had made of me."[35]

Another incident during Stewart's years in Baltimore was
more positive. According to correspondence from Stewart's pas-
tor, the daughter of one of Baltimore's most respectable African-
American families had left home to work in a house of prostitution. The young woman's parents rejected her, but the fearless
Stewart went to the house, confronted the mistress, and retrieved
the young woman, who later became an "honored member of
society."[36]

In 1861, as the Civil War was beginning, Stewart moved to

Washington, D.C., and taught in an African-American school. After the war, Stewart became director of housekeeping services at Freedmen's Hospital, which later became the Howard University Hospital. By 1871, the frugal Stewart had raised two hundred dollars to buy a building near Howard University for the school that, for twenty years, she had dreamed of founding. It was an Episcopal Sunday school for neighborhood children. She recruited faculty from the university to help her teach in the school, which charged tuition but also was open to poor children.[37]

It was not until the final year of her life that Stewart recovered the financial security that had been taken from her half a century earlier. In 1879, she took advantage of new legislation that provided pensions for widows of soldiers and sailors who fought during the War of 1812. Stewart then began receiving a monthly pension of eight dollars. Still feeling called to serve God through the written word, she used the money to publish a second edition of her collected works. *Meditations from the Pen of Mrs. Maria W. Stewart* included her essays from the *Liberator* as well as a supporting letter from Garrison.[38]

Stewart died at Freedmen's Hospital in Washington on December 17, 1879, at the age of seventy-six. Funeral services were held at St. Luke's Episcopal Church, where Stewart had been an active member, and she was buried in the city's Graceland Cemetery. After Stewart's death, a local African-American newspaper devoted thirty inches of its front page to a description of her life and contributions. That article began, "Few, very few, know of the remarkable career of this woman whose life has just drawn to a close," and ended, "Mrs. Stewart was a pioneer. . . ."[39]

2

MARY ANN SHADD CARY
Advocate for Canadian Emigration

At various periods during American history, the unrelenting pressure of discrimination has prompted African-American men and women to contemplate abandoning the United States and relocating to a more hospitable environment. The concept of American blacks returning to Africa was first proposed in 1714, and during the first half of the nineteenth century the American Colonization Society worked toward the colonization of Liberia. Early in the twentieth century, Marcus Garvey revived the concept. Other colonization movements have focused on Mexico, Haiti, and South America. One of the more successful of the efforts was directed toward Canada on the eve of the Civil War, fueled by the 1850 Fugitive Slave Law. Feeling threatened by the new provisions, slaves and free blacks fled to Canada, which had abolished slavery thirty years earlier. They settled in Canada West, now the province of Ontario. By 1860, at least fifteen thousand and possibly as many as seventy-five thousand Americans of African descent had emigrated to Canada.[1]

The Canadian Fugitive Slave Movement was facilitated by African-American newspapers published in Canada West. Editors extolled the benefits of living on free soil and described the opportunities in a country where farm land was plentiful and racial prejudice was minimal. The best of the newspapers was the *Provincial Freeman*, a pro-emigration weekly founded in 1853.[2] The force consistently powering the newspaper was Mary Ann Shadd. Born free into an abolitionist family in Delaware, Shadd migrated to Canada West and founded the *Freeman*, thereby becoming the first African-American woman to edit a newspaper.[3]

Shadd was vigorous and outspoken, although she was not blessed with the gift of eloquence. She wrote with conviction, never equivocation. As one historian stated: "Mary Shadd served meat strong even for the time."[4] Sometimes she was guided by logic, her words forming solid, rational arguments. After black Philadelphians condemned the Dred Scott decision, Shadd wrote: "This is not the time for strong words only; when all realize the yoke so forcibly as now, why not act? Do those who took part in the meeting intend to stay in the U. States? If so, the resolutions amount to nothing."[5] Other times, Shadd was fired by passion and the sheer power of racial indignation. She wrote: "Cease to uphold the United States government, if it will, and while it does, uphold human slavery."[6]

Shadd attempted to build the *Freeman*'s circulation by lecturing to audiences in Canada and the United States. She married in 1856 and published the newspaper until 1857. After her husband's death in 1860, Mary Ann Shadd Cary returned to the United States and recruited African-American soldiers to fight in the Civil War. Cary then moved to Washington, D.C., where she wrote for Frederick Douglass's *New National Era* and other newspapers. She later became the first female law student at Howard University, practiced law, and campaigned for women's rights.

Mary Ann Camberton Shadd was born October 9, 1823, in Wilmington, Delaware. She was the oldest of thirteen children born to Abraham and Harriet Parnell Shadd. The Shadds opened their home to runaway slaves as part of the Underground Railroad, and Abraham Shadd gained national prominence as a founder of the American Anti-Slavery Society and a leader of the

National Convention Movement. Abraham Shadd, who amassed wealth as a shoemaker, became involved with journalism as a subscription agent for the *Liberator*. In 1833 the Shadds left Delaware, which did not allow blacks to attend school, and moved to West Chester, Pennsylvania. For the next six years, Mary Ann studied at Price's Boarding School, which was operated by the Society of Friends.[7]

After completing her education, Mary Ann returned to Wilmington and, at age sixteen, founded a school for local blacks. During the next decade, she also taught in New York City and Norristown, Pennsylvania. It was during this period that Shadd gained her first publication experience. In 1849 she wrote a twelve-page pamphlet titled "Hints to the Colored People of the North." One of Shadd's hints was that blacks should take the initiative to gain their civil rights rather than depending on whites to do it for them.[8]

Passage of the Fugitive Slave Law was a turning point in Shadd's life. She was outraged by the law, which allowed freeborn blacks or escaped slaves to be hunted down and returned to their "owners." So in 1851, Shadd decided to share her teaching skills with the fugitive black Americans relocating to Canada to elude slave hunters. She founded an integrated private school in Windsor, across the river from Detroit. The school initially was funded by parents, but Shadd was soon receiving a salary from the American Missionary Association.[9]

While teaching, Shadd pursued her interest in publishing. She conducted interviews and collected statistics on Canada West and, in 1852, published "A Plea for Emigration, or Notes of Canada West." The forty-page pamphlet criticized organizations such as the Refugee Home Society, which sold farms to black fugitives. Shadd opposed such organizations because they were funded by white philanthropy, arguing that blacks should buy land directly rather than relying on such societies. Shadd used the pamphlet to praise the climate, job opportunities, land prices, and race relations in Canada West, painting a positive portrait of blacks living there.[10]

Shadd's rosy description of life in Canada belied her own circumstances, as her outspoken nature had brought her into conflict with prominent black leaders. Her nemesis became Henry Bibb, a fugitive from slavery who published the newspaper *Voice of the Fugitive.* Bibb favored segregated schools; Shadd insisted that schools be integrated. Bibb considered Canada a temporary haven; Shadd saw Canada as a permanent home. Bibb supervised the Refugee Home Society; Shadd criticized the society for buying property and then reselling it to blacks at a higher price. These differences escalated into a bitter feud between Bibb and Shadd. In 1852, for example, the *Voice of the Fugitive* stated: "Miss Shadd has said and written many things which we think will add nothing to her credit as a lady." [11]

Such harsh statements frustrated Shadd because Bibb's ownership of Canada West's only black newspaper gave him a voice that she was denied. She complained to the head of the American Missionary Association: "I have not a paper of my own and must leave the result with God" and "What a vast amount of mischief a man like H. Bibb can do with an organ of his own to nod, insinuate and 'fling' away the reputation of others . . . who have had no means equally extensive to their control to counteract it." The mischief that most concerned Shadd was that which affected her own livelihood. The dispute between Bibb and Shadd led the American Missionary Society to dismiss Shadd from her teaching position. [12]

With no teaching salary, Shadd became committed to sharing her ideas through her own newspaper. Realizing that a woman would have difficulty building the community support necessary for a newspaper to survive, she enlisted the aid of two well-respected men to become nominal editors. Samuel Ringgold Ward was an eloquent anti-slavery orator with a reputation as the "Black Daniel Webster." Ward also had experience in journalism, having been associated with *Frederick Douglass' Paper* and having founded the *Impartial Citizen* in Syracuse, New York. The Reverend Alexander McArthur was a clergyman in Canada West who had left the area in the early 1850s. Although neither Ward nor McArthur was willing to devote large amounts of time or money to the newspaper, they, like Shadd, were eager to build support for their stands on such issues as emigration, assimilation, and self-sufficiency. [13]

On March 24, 1853, Shadd published a prototype of the *Provincial Freeman.* Ward and McArthur were listed as the editors, even though both men were far removed from Windsor. It was left to Shadd to write and edit the articles and to print the four-page newspaper. Despite these broad responsibilities, Shadd was not accorded a title in the pages of the new publication, being mentioned only in the statement: "Letters must be addressed, Post-paid, to Mary A. Shadd, Windsor, Canada West."[14]

The first of the four pages in the newspaper was filled with homilies, moral admonitions, brief news items, and an in-depth discussion of the pros and cons of the Refugee Home Society. An "Introductory," signed by Ward but sounding very much like Shadd, stated: "The *Provincial Freeman* will be devoted to the elevation of the colored people. . . . The news of the day, the state of the markets, foreign and domestic intelligence, shall each have its place in the columns of the Freeman."[15]

Whatever the editorial content, Shadd knew that the business side of the newspaper had to be developed in order for the editorial voice to be heard. She also knew that, in an era when advertising was not yet a major factor in newspapers, revenue had to come from subscriptions. A statement on page one declared that the *Provincial Freeman* would begin appearing weekly only when the number of cash subscribers provided adequate income.[16]

Shadd then began traveling unaccompanied through the United States and Canada, lecturing on the merits of emigration—and the merits of subscribing to her newspaper. Her lecture circuit took her through Canada West as well as to Michigan, New York, Pennsylvania, Ohio, Indiana, and Illinois. Neither her opinions nor her gender was universally welcomed. At the eleventh Colored National Convention in Philadelphia, she had to win a debate with the male convention leaders before she was allowed to speak publicly. Such incidents strengthened Shadd's resolve, and she became a popular lecturer who shared the speaker's platform with such noted orators as Lucretia Mott, Robert Purvis, and Frances Ellen Watkins.[17]

The first weekly issue of the *Provincial Freeman* was published on March 25, 1854, in Toronto. Ward and McArthur were listed as editor and corresponding editor. Shadd had been elevated to "publishing agent," but her gender had been camouflaged behind the name "M.A. Shadd." Her initials also were at the end of the prospectus, which stated that the *Freeman* was not connected with any political party or religious sect.[18]

The same year that Shadd founded the *Freeman*, Bibb became ill. When he died, the *Voice of the Fugitive* ceased publication and the *Provincial Freeman* became the only African-American newspaper in Canada West.

Foremost among the causes that Shadd valued was Canadian emigration. Every week, the *Freeman*, which circulated to many cities in the United States, included articles exhorting African Americans to leave the country that denied them their rights. Shadd insisted that the best way to resolve the question of slavery was to resettle in a free country such as Canada, although she strongly opposed colonization to Africa. She wrote: "We say to the slave, You have a right to your freedom and to every other privilege connected with it and if you cannot secure these in Virginia or Alabama, by all means make your escape, without delay, to some other locality in God's wide universe, where you will be allowed to enjoy the rights and perform the duties as you bear the stamp and impress of manhood." [19]

Only slightly less prominent than emigration was the theme of self-reliance, one which Shadd already had established through her earlier pamphlet. Shadd vehemently opposed organizations that made decisions for the fugitives, insisting that newly freed blacks had to demonstrate their self-sufficiency. Shadd boldly stated her position in the motto that ran below the flag of the *Freeman* each week: "Self-Reliance is the True Road to Independence."

Shadd despised welfare-oriented organizations partly because she distrusted the motivations of their leaders, many of whom were clergymen. Shadd, who broke with all institutional religions because she felt churches were segregationist, described ministers as "self-righteous," "stupid," and "tyrannical." [20] The plainspoken editor lashed out at the clerical opportunists, writing: "The clergy are not sound at heart—they love the smiles of men in powerful position, of churches abounding in wealth and numbers; they love flattery, they love their bread and butter, and they love ease. They are not going to reform men, not they, it is too much trouble." [21]

Shadd named names. Rather than merely criticizing in abstract terms, she fearlessly practiced the modern-day techniques of investigative journalism. She went to the land claimed to have been purchased by the Refugee Home Society's white leader, the Reverend C.C. Foote and found no blacks living there. Shadd then reported the results of her investigation:

"We have been to the Home, we walked over the lands when

C.C. Foote was drawing tears from the eyes, and dollars from the pockets of New England philanthropists, because of these 'poor sufferers,' when there was not one family settled upon it. Something must be done! And in the right direction and that speedily. Meanwhile, we shall agitate to remove the nuisance!"[22]

Shadd agitated a great deal. In 1854, in an early example of consumer reporting, she listed the unhealthy ingredients used in brewing beer. In 1856, she exposed inequities in Canada's public education policy, revealing that black children who completed the first level of education were barred from continuing into the more advanced level. In 1857, she reported that well-meaning people had donated money to expand a manual labor school but that the school did not even exist. Shadd's muckraking did not go unnoticed. She was verbally chastised, accused of libel, physically threatened, and told that, if she did not cease publishing exposes, she would be killed.[23]

Another of Shadd's controversial themes was expansion of the role of women. She asserted that the "woman's sphere" should be enlarged to include any activity that a woman wanted to pursue. Shadd created a "Woman's Rights" column to promote women's civil rights. A typical column began with the statement: "Some Men, foolishly deny to a Woman the right to speak in public, to practice medicine, or to vote. . . . How it can be more indelicate for a female doctor to attend a sick man than for a male doctor to attend a sick woman is beyond our humble ken. A Woman may be a nurse to both sexes. Oh, yes! and as a nurse or 'granny' she may administer medicine, at 2nd-hand, but to prescribe! Oh! That would be dreadful! All we have to say about this, is—Pshaw!"[24]

Translating her words into action, Shadd employed her twenty-three-year-old sister, Amelia, to help her edit the newspaper in the fall of 1854, dropping Ward's and McArthur's names from the masthead. After six months of receiving letters addressed to "Brother Shadd," the editor also informed readers that she was a woman. She excused readers for assuming she was a man, attributing the error to her habit of using initials, but made it clear that a different form of address was in order. She wrote: "We would simply correct, for the future, our error, by giving, here, the name in full, (Mary A. Shadd) as we do not like the Mr. and Esq., by which we are so often addressed."[25]

Shadd's readers, however, were not prepared to feminize journalism. By 1855, public outrage at women editing the *Freeman* threatened the newspaper's survival. So Shadd wrote an editorial acknowledging the fact that she and her sister being editors of the "unfortunate sex" was working against the newspaper and stating that they "never, in their most ambitious moments, aspired to the drudgery." She also said the causes of abolition and emigration were too important to be jeopardized because the voice promoting them was that of women rather than men. She stated: "The *Freeman* must not be discontinued, because obnoxious persons have it in charge."[26]

Three weeks later, Shadd announced her resignation and the appointment of a male editor, the Reverend William P. Newman. The combative woman did not go silently from her editor's chair, however, as she chastised readers for being "captious" to her. Shadd also had words of encouragement for the generations of African-American women who would follow after her. She boasted: "To colored women, we have a word—we have 'broken the Editorial ice,' whether willingly or not, for your class in America; so go to Editing, as many of you as are willing, and able, and as soon as you may, if you think you are ready."[27]

With the change in editors, the *Freeman* moved to Chatham, where Shadd's parents and siblings had settled two years earlier. Significant among the relatives was Shadd's twenty-four-year-old brother, Isaac, who became the *Freeman*'s publishing agent.

Another personal relationship also was emerging as significant in Mary Ann Shadd's life. She had met Thomas F. Cary, a Toronto barber, soon after arriving in Canada West. As an early supporter of the *Freeman*, he had loaned the founder money to produce early issues and had advertised his hair cutting skills in the newspaper. The Shadd-Cary relationship developed, and on January 23, 1856, thirty-three-year-old Shadd married forty-five-year-old Cary. With her wedding vows, the bride also became stepmother to three children, aged seven to fourteen, from Cary's previous marriage. The new Cary marriage was an unconventional one with Thomas living in Toronto and Mary Ann living in Chatham, nearly two hundred miles away.[28]

Despite relinquishing the position of editor—at least in print—and assuming the new role of wife and stepmother, Mary

Ann Shadd Cary did not leave journalism. She continued to write for the *Freeman*, and, five days after her wedding, she embarked on a lecture tour to Chicago to seek additional subscriptions. In short, she remained the energy behind the newspaper. By May 1856, her name—her maiden name of Shadd rather than her married name of Cary—was back in the masthead.[29]

Cary had become an accomplished speaker, with an increasingly high profile in both black and white communities of Canada and the United States. Even though *Frederick Douglass' Paper* opposed emigration, it praised Cary's charisma. After one of her lectures, the newspaper gushed: "The House was crowded and breathless in its attention to her masterly exposition." The correspondent was particularly taken with Cary's physical presence. He described her "fine physical organization—wholly feminine in appearance and demeanor," "flashing" eyes, and "very saucy look." Clearly bedazzled by Cary, the correspondent stated: "She overcomes any apparent imperfection in her speaking by the earnestness of her manner, and the quality of her thoughts. She is a superior woman; and it is useless to deny it."[30]

Even though Cary increased in personal prestige, the *Freeman*'s financial position worsened. Health problems forced Newman to resign after only six months as editor, and keeping the newspaper alive required the efforts not only of Cary but also of her brother and husband. Isaac Shadd became the printer for the town of Chatham; Thomas Cary moved to Chatham and sold oil lamps from the *Freeman* office. The newspaper's publication schedule became sporadic, and the editors distributed a circular describing the newspaper's desperate financial position and soliciting donations. Abolitionist Lucretia Mott was among those responding with a contribution. Never too proud to demand what was rightly hers, Cary threatened to publish the names of subscribers who were delinquent in their payment.[31]

Despite the help from Cary's husband and brother, she remained the driving force behind the *Freeman*. But by mid-1857, that force was hampered by the physical limitations of pregnancy. Sarah Elizabeth Cary was born in August 1857. The last extant copy of the *Freeman* is dated a month later.[32]

Cary soon found other forums in which to raise her voice. One of her most intriguing involvements began in 1858 when radical abolitionist John Brown came to Chatham to develop plans to establish an armed refuge from which fugitive slaves could mount attacks on slaveholding communities in the United States. Brown stayed with Isaac Shadd and shared his plans with Thomas Cary, Isaac Shadd, and Osborne Anderson, who had worked for the *Freeman*. Mary Ann Shadd Cary's direct involvement with Brown and his plans to take over the arsenal at Harper's Ferry are unclear, but her unpublished notes about Brown include the suggestive statements: "How I knew. What can be proven." Two years after Brown's ill-fated raid, Cary helped Anderson, the only black Canadian who had been with Brown at Harper's Ferry, write and publish a book-length account of the incident.[33]

Cary's personal life was turned upside down in 1860 by two momentous events: the birth of her second child, Linton, followed a few months later by the death of her husband. Having full responsibility for her infant son and four-year-old daughter, Cary was financially destitute, forcing her to place her three stepchildren with family members. Cary then returned to teaching at Chatham while occasionally contributing to the *Weekly Anglo-African* in New York in 1861 and 1862.[34]

The Civil War ushered Cary into a new venture. After President Abraham Lincoln issued a plea for five hundred thousand men to replace the Union soldiers lost at Gettysburg and Vicksburg, Cary was commissioned as an army recruiting officer. She sought, interviewed, and examined black men in Indiana and Connecticut to select the best of the applicants to assemble a regiment of African-American soldiers.[35]

After the war, Cary returned to the United States to help educate newly freed blacks. She received her teaching certificate in 1868 and moved to Washington, D.C., to teach African-American students in the city's public school system. With more than twenty years of classroom teaching experience to her credit, she later was promoted to principal of a city grammar school.[36]

At the same time, Shadd continued to work as a journalist. Frederick Douglass hired her to write and solicit subscriptions for the *New National Era*, the weekly he had founded in the nation's capital. She also wrote occasionally for the *New York Freeman*, *Chicago Conservator*, and *People's Advocate*, a Washington weekly.[37]

In one intriguing article, she argued that journalism was an occupation unusually hospitable to the black woman. Cary wrote: "In this unique department of letters and labor she begs not place, but is confessedly an equal;—an honored member of the guild. By intuitive perception of their proper relations the unification of the sexes has been conceded, and so thoroughly accepted, as to demonstrate conclusively that the terms male and female are correlated."[38]

While praising the black press for its treatment of women, Cary did not believe the institution was achieving its full potential. The blunt-speaking critic described the vast majority of African-American newspapers as "waste-basket literature."[39]

Disillusioned by the press, Cary decided that equal rights might be better achieved through legal means. So she broke another barrier for her gender by embarking, at the age of forty-six, on a career in law. In 1869, she became Howard University's first female law student. After completing her coursework, however, she was not allowed to graduate, apparently in a case of sex discrimination. Not until a decade later, in 1883, was the determined Cary finally awarded her law degree. She then resigned her teaching position and, at sixty years of age, began to practice as an attorney.[40]

While Cary earned her livelihood in education, journalism, and law, she also took advantage of Washington being a center of political activity. She served as a delegate to the Colored Men's Labor Convention there in 1869 and lectured on a variety of topics, including race pride and the importance of education.[41]

Increasingly during Cary's final years, however, the focus of her activism was women's rights. She testified on behalf of women's suffrage before the United States House of Representatives Judiciary Committee, demanding that the word "male" be expunged from the Constitution, and she shared the podium with Elizabeth Cady Stanton and Susan B. Anthony at the National Woman Suffrage Association convention in 1878. A woman determined to transform words into action, Cary boldly challenged the male-dominated system of governance. In 1874, she joined sixty other women who attempted to register to vote in the District of Columbia.[42]

In 1880, Cary founded the Colored Women's Progressive Franchise Association, hoping to use the group to establish a newspaper produced by and for African-American women and to promote women's involvement in commercial enterprises. Although the tangible products of the association are unknown, its purposes show it to have been a precursor of *Woman's Era*, the newspaper which was established for black women in 1890, and the African-American women's club movement that united thousands of women in 1895.[43]

Cary continued to work as a journalist, lawyer, and activist throughout the 1880s and early 1890s, despite bouts with rheumatism and cancer. She lived with her daughter, Sarah Evans, a Washington dressmaker. One of life's harshest tragedies struck the aged woman in 1892 when her thirty-two-year-old son, who had worked as a messenger and cloakroom attendant in the United States Capitol for twenty years, preceded her in death. She died five months later on June 5, 1893, at the age of sixty-nine.[44]

Mary Ann Shadd Cary was not quickly forgotten, receiving the praise of prominent African Americans. W.E.B. DuBois's tribute focused on Cary's support of emigration. He wrote: "She threw herself singlehanded into the great Canadian pilgrimage. . . . She became teacher, editor, and lecturer; tramping afoot through winter snows, pushing without blot or blemish through crowd and turmoil." Frederick Douglass stressed her journalistic achievements: "She displayed industry, financial capacity, and literary ability of a high order. . . . She is a pioneer among colored women, and every colored lady in the country has a right to feel proud of her."[45]

3

GERTRUDE BUSTILL MOSSELL
Guiding Voice for Newly Freed Blacks

The last decades of the nineteenth century marked a crucial period in the evolution of black America. Emancipation had released
four million slaves, but Reconstruction had failed to bring them
equality. Beginning with a mass exodus from Louisiana in 1879,
thousands of newly freed men and women left the South; in the
1880s, a quarter of a million African Americans migrated to the
North and West. Because slaveowners had deprived blacks of the
tools necessary for occupational advancement, the flood of humanity was largely unskilled. Despite these formidable obstacles
and an inhospitable white America, the newly freed women and
men successfully created their own unique culture—socially,
morally, and economically—within white-dominated America,
thereby completing one of the most important periods of transition in African-American history.[1]
   Historians have rightly acknowledged the role that the African-American press played in helping to create this unique culture. It was a period of rapid expansion of black journalism, and
various publications and male editors have been praised for their

proactive role in this process. Absent from such lists, however, have been the names of black *women* journalists who also helped lead their people through this difficult period of growth and change.[2]

Gertrude Bustill Mossell, a member of Philadelphia's black elite, was such a woman. Her journalism career included writing and editing for black as well as white newspapers and magazines, many of them distributed nationally. During the period from the early 1870s until the end of the century, she overcame the forces of racism, sexism, and illiteracy to provide a guiding voice to newly freed African Americans.[3] Largely through her "Our Woman's Department" column, Mossell gave female readers practical advice on running a home and raising children. Often her straightforward words, which included medical advice, were relatively mild. She wrote: "For the disagreeable sensation known as heartburn, which so often accompanies indigestion, a saltspoonful of common salt, dissolved in half a waterglass of water, and drank, is an effective remedy."[4]

At other times, her words carried a bolder message. Mossell advised, for instance, that black workers, who for the first time in their lives were earning wages, had not always found it judicious to place their savings in the hands of "white folks." She wrote: "In some case they (whites) were honest, others often not. No wages were collected, no account kept, and often they (blacks) were given only a small portion of what they had really saved. Get some reliable bank or savings fund to receive your savings."[5]

Through such comments, Mossell crossed the gender line to speak to men as well as women. She encouraged all black readers to agitate for racial reform and to break the employment barriers by expanding into new occupations. In particular, Mossell, a committed feminist, repeatedly called for more black women to enter journalism. In a more negative vein, Mossell also was an elitist who focused her advice toward the upper-class black society of which she was part.

Gertrude E.H. Bustill was born in Philadelphia on July 3, 1855. The Bustills were a prominent family who traced their lineage as free African Americans to the 1700s when Cyrus Bustill, a baker, had supplied food to General George Washington and his troops

during the Revolutionary War. Gertrude was the daughter of
Charles and Emily Robinson Bustill. Gertrude's mother died
when her two daughters were infants.[6] The girls' father, to com-
pensate for the absence of their mother, encouraged them to im-
merse themselves in the Bible and such literary classics as *Para-
dise Lost*, as well as such contemporary reading material as the
Atlantic Monthly. Young Gertrude's formal education was in
Philadelphia's public elementary schools and the Institute for
Colored Youth.[7] During her adulthood, Mossell also completed
courses as part of the Chautauqua program in New York State.[8]

Gertrude was directed toward journalism at the age of sixteen. Asked to deliver the oration for her grammar school graduation ceremonies, she wrote a composition titled "Influence."
Bishop Henry McNeal Turner, editor of the *Christian Recorder*,
published the oration, prompting Gertrude to write poetry and
other essays for the nationally distributed church newspaper.[9]

During the 1870s, Bustill combined careers in education and
journalism. She taught public school in Philadelphia and nearby
Camden, New Jersey, for seven years. At the same time, she
wrote, on a part-time basis, for two African-American newspapers, the *Philadelphia Echo* and *Philadelphia Independent*.

Bustill's dual career was curtailed in 1883 when she married
Dr. Nathan F. Mossell of Lockport, New York. In 1881, he had
become the first African American to graduate from the University of Pennsylvania Medical School and then became Philadelphia's leading African-American physician. In keeping with
the custom of the time, his wife focused her life on caring for her
husband and raising a family. Mossell gave birth to four children,
two of whom died in infancy.[10]

But the limited sphere of home and hearth was too confining
for Mossell. By 1885, she began to incorporate her interest in
journalism into her married life. In that year she became woman's editor of the *New York Freeman*, which meant writing a
weekly column for the leading African-American newspaper in
the country. The *Freeman*, which in 1887 became the *New York
Age*, was published by T. Thomas Fortune, the dean of African-
American journalism, and was distributed throughout the North
and West. Leaving her position at the *New York Age* in 1889,
Mossell became woman's editor of the *Indianapolis World* from

1891 to 1892. During this period, she also served as Philadelphia correspondent for *Woman's Era*, a national newspaper for upper-class black women.[11]

Magazines were another outlet for Mossell's words of guidance. During the 1880s and 1890s, her work appeared in such periodicals as the *Colored American Magazine, Our Women and Children*, the *African Methodist Episcopal Church Review, Alumni Magazine*, and *Ringwood's Afro-American Journal of Fashion*.[12]

But the major forum for Mossell's advice was her weekly newspaper column, "Our Woman's Department," the first woman's column in the history of the African-American press. Mossell, similar to her white counterparts such as Beatrice Fairfax and Dorothy Dix,[13] dispensed advice, some of which was in response to letters from her readers. While Fairfax and Dix focused on romance, however, Mossell dealt largely with matters regarding the home and children. Each of her columns, many of which ran on the front page, began with the personalized editor's note: "The aim of this column will be to promote true womanhood, especially that of the African race. All success progress or need of our women will be given prompt mention." The editor's note invited readers to write directly to Mossell, whose home address ended the note.[14]

Mossell's physical appearance and demeanor were those of a no-nonsense woman—"sincere and direct; a plump, compactly built body, five feet high; a symmetrical head and speaking countenance." In keeping with this image, Mossell advocated a no-frills household. She warned readers not to buy fine furniture and silver because they were expensive and required too much time to maintain. She wrote: "Intelligent women throughout our land must at last come to see that living according to their means is the only right way to build up happy homes, free from the curse of debt."[15]

Pragmatism and frugality were consistent themes in Mossell's household tips, as she attempted to teach newly emancipated black women how to lead a comfortable life while economizing. She told her readers how to keep vegetables fresh, to test if milk had been watered down, and to make use of leftover beef by adding curry powder to it. She urged her readers to pay cash for all purchases rather than buying by installments and to dress in cotton and flannel rather than silk and velvet.[16]

Mossell's voice also was that of common sense with regard to childcare, an anxiety-ridden subject for African-American women of the late nineteenth century. She told readers: "The cold winter is upon us; let us clothe our little ones carefully, with due regard to their health, casting appearances aside as a secondary consideration." Mossell further suggested a pragmatic way to end a child's crying, saying: "Put a cross child to bed, fill the bed with toys and read to it alone a little."[17]

Mossell, having lost two of her own children to early deaths, was particularly concerned about children's health. Citing statistics on the high infant mortality rate among urban black children, she blamed many of the deaths on lung disease, describing how to create and to apply a poultice of Indian meal, lard, and mustard. Mossell adamantly opposed mothers giving their children patent medicines. She recounted cases in which such behavior had led youngsters to becoming lethargic in the classroom. She also objected on moral grounds, writing: "The habit of giving children soothing syrup, brandy, etc., is reprehensible in the extreme, as it causes indigestion and a train of evils from which they may never escape."[18]

Mossell, like other upper-class African-American women, felt an obligation to help shape the moral character of her race. As a woman who had been given an education and other opportunities beyond the reach of most of her sisters, she attempted to instill a sense of morality in her readers.[19]

Young African-American women, Mossell counseled, had to guard their virtue. She wrote: "A woman's safeguard is to keep a man's hands off her. If you need his assistance in walking, take his arm instead of his taking yours. Just tell him in plain English to keep his 'hands off.'" To mothers she lectured: "Keep your girls off the street, except when they have business. Teach them it is unnecessary to go to the Post Office every time they go out. If possible, instill in their very nature that they are safer in their own hands than they are in the hands of any man—preachers not excepted." She scolded mothers for not placing sufficient value on good manners and honesty, and she advised them to force their daughters to dress in modest clothing.[20]

Although Mossell's column included a great deal of material directed toward newly freed blacks, it sometimes carried an elitist tone. Mossell, born into an upper-class family and the wife of a prominent physician, was an aristocratic and wealthy woman. The Mossells lived on Lombard Street, Philadelphia's most prestigious residential boulevard for African Americans, and she and her daughters spent their summers vacationing near Niagara Falls. In keeping with her status among the black elite, Mossell also socialized with other upper-class women, both black and white, in the Northeastern Federation of Woman's Clubs.[21]

There are indications that Mossell's social prominence affected her writing, which sometimes was tinged with an elitist tone. This tendency was in keeping with the attitude of most upper-class African-American women activists as well as the black press of the nineteenth century, which was aimed toward the small class of educated blacks rather than toward the black masses.[22]

Although Mossell was writing during a time when most black Americans were working as field hands and domestics, she devoted one entire column to the difficulties of finding and keeping good servants, eight inches of another column to advice about how a woman should carry her pocket book, and ten inches of another to how a woman should carry her umbrella when attending the opera.[23]

Even though the vast majority of African Americans had not attained a financial level that allowed for holidays of any sort, Mossell cautioned parents to think carefully before allowing their daughters to spend the entire summer vacationing at a seaside resort and provided special recipes for busy women who had just returned from summer vacations.[24]

Nepotism also crept into "Our Woman's Department." For instance, Mossell boasted about a New York lawyer who had successfully defended murder charges against a black client by securing a prison term, instead of the death penalty, for the man. She pointed out that the lawyer was the first African-American graduate of the University of Pennsylvania Law School, but she neglected to mention that he also was her husband's brother. Two months later, Mossell found room in her column to discuss the brick manufacturing business that the same lawyer had founded, saying that he was "the only colored man owning and running a

first class steam press brick making yard in the United States."
She again failed to identify the man as her brother-in-law.[25]

In another column, Mossell encouraged readers to contribute
to a scholarship fund being created at Wilberforce College to
honor a particular alumna. Mossell said of the project: "It would
be a noble deed if it were carried out. The Church in honoring
her would honor true, helpful womanhood throughout our broad
land." Mossell also described the namesake of the proposed scholarship as a "sainted missionary," but she did not mention that the
woman was her husband's aunt, Mary Ella Mossell.[26]

Her class prejudices aside, Mossell was committed to the advancement of civil rights for African Americans, and she urged
her readers—rich as well as poor, male as well as female—to
join her in the crusade to fight racism and the injustices manifested by it. She used her column to report instances of inequality
and to encourage her readers to agitate for racial reform.

In an 1886 column, Mossell described various acts of segregation that she had encountered while traveling. She reported
that when she arrived at a church in western New Jersey, for
instance, a black man told her that the congregation was primarily white and that black members had to sit in a gallery above the
pulpit. But Mossell refused to go to the gallery. Instead, she sat
on the main floor of the sanctuary throughout the service, despite the glares from white church members. Mossell also recounted attending a picnic at an "integrated" church and learning that blacks were relegated, after the event, to washing the
dishes and clearing up the grounds while white picnickers rested.
In another case, she was traveling in Delaware when a police
officer insulted her and people on the street ridiculed her because
of her color. In each case, Mossell protested the mistreatment
and practiced her own, personal style of civil disobedience.[27]

Mossell opposed the accommodationist philosophy of Booker
T. Washington. She told her readers to seek change rather than
accept discriminatory conditions and practices, writing: "Always
the cry of peace, peace, when there is no peace. We live in the
hope of developing a manhood and womanhood that will aim at
a real and not a fictitious peace."[28]

While not promoting violence, Mossell supported agitation
as a means of achieving reform. She praised the anti-lynching
speeches and editorials of Bishop Henry McNeal Turner of the

Christian Recorder and Ida B. Wells of the *Memphis Free Speech* and *New York Age*, writing: "Go on, my good brother and sister, and by the time you get through the white folks up north will get hold of some plain facts that we are very desirous of their knowing." Mossell also criticized segregationists. She wrote: "The Southern element is always with one uppermost thought, 'We will never let the Negro out of what we call his place. Let his numbers, his education, his wealth entitle him to what it will. We will not let him have aught except what we choose to give.'" In other columns, Mossell criticized trade unions and realtors for their discriminatory practices.[29]

The columnist believed that one of the most important means through which African Americans could effect racial reform was politics. The politically savvy Mossell, whose husband was one of the first black Philadelphians to break from the Republican Party, encouraged readers not to cling to a particular party but to vote for any candidate who would give African Americans a fair chance. She kept her readers apprised of political races around the country and endorsed all black candidates.[30]

Mossell's own efforts toward racial reform included becoming the first black to write for the *Philadelphia Times*, a white weekly. After desegregating that editorial staff in 1886,[31] Mossell began publishing articles in the city's two major white dailies, the *Philadelphia Inquirer* and *Philadelphia Press*, as well as the largest-circulation magazine in the country, *Ladies' Home Journal*.[32]

One of Mossell's goals in writing for the mainstream press was to improve how it portrayed African Americans. An example illustrating both her efforts and the obstacles she faced occurred in 1886 when a white Philadelphia newspaper reviewed an African-American production of Gilbert and Sullivan's "Mikado." The white reviewer described physical aspects of the cast, using terms such as "mulatto" and "quadroon." Mossell read the review before it was published and recommended that the editors remove the references to the shades of the actors' skin, saying that the references were insulting. The editors defended the writing as humorous and published the review as written. As Mossell had predicted, African-American readers were offended by the review, and the editors later regretted having published it.[33]

A pervasive theme threaded through Mossell's newspaper writing—in both the black and the white press—was her strong feminist leanings. Although she identified herself through her husband by signing her articles "Mrs. N.F. Mossell" or "N.F. Mossell" rather than Gertrude Mossell, she fought for equal rights for women. Her unequivocal stand in favor of women's suffrage was made clear in her first column in 1885. In that column, she encouraged women to become involved in the suffrage movement, recommended several books on the subject of women's rights, and denounced the myth that women advocating women's suffrage would remain unmarried.[34]

Mossell, a member of the Sojourner Truth Suffrage League, consistently used her voice as a newspaper columnist to promote women's suffrage. She reported, for example, that life was proceeding smoothly and peacefully in African tribes, Iceland, and the state of Wyoming where women were allowed to participate in government. She concluded: "Give women more power in the government offices if the desire is for peace and prosperity." Mossell also campaigned for better working conditions for women, for legislation to punish wife beaters, and for women to be allowed to own property and attend college.[35]

"Our Woman's Department" strongly advocated women expanding into new occupational fields. Using the "we" form that she often adopted in her column, Mossell wrote of the American woman: "We believe in her place being at home and in other places also." Mossell announced to her readers when the first African-American women became ministers and prospectors, and she identified occupations ripe for women, including such obscure fields as floral and industrial design, beekeeping, and canary raising.[36]

Mossell was particularly determined to attract more women to journalism. In 1886, she wrote a series of four columns about the field, urging women to submit articles to both black and white publications. Unlike many white women journalists, Mossell found male editors to be patient and supportive. She counseled: "Our bright, busy girl, who goes into journalism, should take things as they come, with imperturbable good nature, and ignore what is unpleasant at first. Then, by and by, when her masculine confreres come to know her, they will regard her with a feeling of brave comradeship and as a good fellow. They will help instead of hindering her."[37]

She stated, however, that journalism was a challenging field that placed demands on women. Mossell wrote of the female journalist: "She must learn to control her emotions and put pride in her pocket. The woman who succeeds in newspaper work must be prepared to give up most of the social enjoyments so dear to the hearts of most young ladies. It will be better if she gives up all thoughts of matrimony until her success is made."[38]

Mossell cautioned that, regardless of the occupational pursuit undertaken, a working woman should not neglect her role as mother. When describing two new books about outstanding women, Mossell criticized the authors for not praising "mothers of distinction." She also chastised husbands and children for not acknowledging the work of the woman of the house, saying: "A pedometer should be fastened to the tired mother and the household made to read the result."[39]

Mossell's journalistic career was a very successful one, and African-American editors praised her leadership in the field. In 1887, an Ohio newspaper stated: "Mrs. Mossell is a ready writer, a good gatherer of news, has literary judgment and is altogether a clever woman."[40] In 1889, *The Journalist*, a professional magazine, said of Mossell: "On matters pertaining to women and the race, there is no better author among our female writers. Her style is clear, compact and convincing."[41] And in 1891 when I. Garland Penn wrote the first history of African-American journalism, he identified only three editors as "sufficiently eminent" to discuss the mission of the black press. Mossell was one of the three, and Penn wrote of her: "Mrs. Mossell is a telling writer, her thoughts being clear and clean-cut."[42]

Mossell recognized the responsibility of the African-American press in guiding newly emancipated blacks, and she used her national prominence to encourage its advancement. Described as "a shrewd business woman," Mossell urged editors to form a black news syndicate similar to the Associated Press, arguing that such a network would raise the quality of the material in black newspapers while raising the salaries of black journalists. She insisted that African-American newspapers had to revamp their circulation techniques as well. She said that selling newspapers through agents was not sufficient and that newsboys should be placed on street corners in African-American neighborhoods. She boldly told black editors: "See to it that boys are put on the streets Sunday morning, and on Saturday night where colored people market. Call out the name of the paper and what it contains of interest. Hundreds of papers would be sold."[43]

In an 1886 column about the black press, Mossell articulated her own reasons for becoming a journalist. Her motives were not altruistic, as she bluntly stated that she entered journalism in order to make money.[44] In that effort, Mossell succeeded. By 1886, she was earning five hundred dollars a year.[45] This was a remarkably high income for a black woman, as it almost doubled the average income of white women working in Pennsylvania at that time.[46]

Another of her motivations was to hone her literary skills "as a stepping-stone to a higher grade of the same labor."[47] Mossell took that step in 1894 when she published *The Work of the Afro-American Woman*. The 180-page feminist tract described the rise of black women during the nineteenth century. She described African-American women's leadership in the abolition, temperance, and suffrage movements, as well their expansion into journalism, literature, medicine, science, business, and education. Half the book presented black women in historical perspective; the other half presented poetry written by them.[48] Mossell's second book, *Little Dansie's One Day at Sabbath School*, was published in 1902. The children's book told the story of a little black girl who was killed while trying to pull her teacher from the path of an oncoming train.[49]

By the turn of the century, Mossell's journalistic work had dwindled to an occasional article. In 1895, Dr. Mossell had founded Frederick Douglass Memorial Hospital, the first hospital in the North to be staffed entirely by blacks.[50] His wife then had begun devoting her ample resources to helping him gain financial support for the hospital.[51] She had become president of the hospital's social service auxiliary, conducting rummage sales and bicycle races to raise money. She also had secured financial support from industrialists Andrew Carnegie and Henry Phipps, raising some forty thousand dollars for the hospital.[52]

In addition, Mossell had increased her commitment to civil rights and civic organizations. In 1899 she helped organize the Philadelphia branch of the National Afro-American Council, precursor of the National Association for the Advancement of Colored People.[53] She also helped found and served on the board of directors of Philadelphia's branch of the Young Woman's

Christian Association. In 1914, Governor John K. Tanner appointed Mossell a delegate to the National Civic Movement
Convention in Kansas City.[54]

Dr. Mossell died in 1946. A year later, Gertrude Bustill
Mossell became a patient in the hospital that her husband had
founded and that she had sacrificed her journalistic career to
sustain. She died there January 21, 1948. The headline for her
obituary did not even mention her name, reading: "Widow of
Dr. Mossell Succumbs at 92 Years."[55]

IDA B. WELLS-BARNETT
Militant Crusader Against Lynching

After the Civil War abolished slavery and the collapse of Reconstruction returned federal troops to the North, the defeated and demoralized South sought a new device to maintain economic and political control over its former slaves. The choice was lynching. The short-term purpose of hanging black men was to terrify and intimidate African Americans; the long-term purpose was to perpetuate second-class citizenship for them. To rationalize such uncivilized action, the South contrived the black man's mythical lust for the white woman. During the final two decades of the nineteenth century, lynching claimed the lives of between three thousand and ten thousand American men of African descent. Many of the victims were mutilated, castrated, and burned.[1]

Public awareness of lynching, like that of many human rights violations, has been credited largely to newspapers. Aiding in this effort was the *Chicago Tribune*, which, beginning in 1883, published an annual summary of the lynchings that had been reported in its pages during the previous year. The first full-scale

journalistic effort to report and counteract the atrocities, however, did not occur until a decade later when a fiercely militant
African-American woman journalist proposed bold action to
stop the violence. In 1892, Ida B. Wells told the readers of the
African-American newspaper she edited that they should save
their money and abandon a community that lynched innocent
men. A few months later, Wells dared to challenge the myth behind which the lynch mob had hidden, speaking frankly about
the most taboo subject in Victorian America: white women willingly engaging in sexual acts with black men. The sharp-tongued
Wells wrote: "Nobody in this section of the country believes the
old thread-bare lie that negro men rape white women. If Southern white men are not careful they will over-reach themselves
and public sentiment will have a reaction or a conclusion will be
reached which will be very damaging to the moral reputation of
their women."[2]

Wells intended her provocative words to be a defense of the
men of her race, but they also launched the anti-lynching movement in this country and unleashed such outrage among Southern manhood that she was forced into exile in the North. Death
threats kept Wells from the South, but they did not silence her.
Indeed, her banishment imbued Wells with a sense of prophetic
mission. For the next three decades, the "Princess of the Black
Press" aroused all of America to the brutalities previously only
whispered about in the rural South. Wells attacked other injustices as well, becoming a community activist and a national leader in the effort to secure woman's suffrage. Although Wells's volatile nature and refusal to equivocate limited her ability to work
within an organizational framework, her defiance and fortitude
made her the most prominent woman among the civil rights
champions of her era.[3]

Ida Bell Wells was born into slavery on July 16, 1862, in Holly
Springs, Mississippi. She was the oldest of eight children born to
Jim Wells, a carpenter and mason, and Lizzie Wells. Ida's life was
turned upside down in 1878 when a yellow fever epidemic killed
her parents. The sixteen-year-old young woman withdrew from
Shaw University (later Rust College) to care for her younger
brothers and sisters. Piling her hair on top of her head so that she
looked older, Ida secured a teaching job.[4]

The roots of Wells's civil rights activism can be traced to a Tennessee train ride she took in 1884. After purchasing a first-class ticket, Wells was seated in the ladies car until a conductor told her to move to the smoking car. Wells refused. When the conductor tried to remove the petite twenty-two-year-old woman from her seat, she bit his hand. Three men finally dragged Wells from the car, as white passengers stood on their seats and applauded. After the incident, Wells sued the Chesapeake and Ohio Railroad. The circuit court ruled in her favor and awarded her five hundred dollars in damages. Although the Tennessee State Supreme Court reversed the ruling three years later, she had established a reputation as an uncompromising woman who was willing to fight the system, regardless of the odds against her.[5]

Wells entered journalism in 1885 when the *New York Freeman* published her tribute to independence of thought, a concept that would increasingly define her personal credo. She wrote: "It is considered a sign of narrow, bigoted mind to be unable to listen to a diverse argument without intolerance and passion, yet how few among so-called 'leaders,' editors (molders of public opinion) but are guilty of this same fault, are ready to cry 'stop thief' to those who dare to step out of the beaten political track and maintain honest opinions and independent convictions of their own?"[6]

For several years, Wells balanced full-time teaching with part-time newspaper writing, while studying at Fisk University during the summers. She secured a position in the city school system of Memphis, where she also was elected editor of a lyceum club publication. Adopting the pen name "Iola," she wrote articles on race issues and brief sermons on self-improvement for the *Detroit Plaindealer, Indianapolis Freeman, Little Rock Sun, New York Freeman, New York Age,* and the religious publications *Living Way* and *African Methodist Episcopal Church Review.*[7]

Wells's gender enhanced her journalistic reputation. In 1887 she was the only woman to participate in a national convention of African-American editors. She received effusive praise from T. Thomas Fortune, editor of the *New York Age.* After meeting Wells, Fortune described her to his readers as "girlish looking in physique" and "as smart as a steel trap." Fortune also gave Wells a compliment that no American woman—black or white—had ever heard before: "She handles a goose quill with a diamond point as handily as any of us men in newspaper work." She was elected secretary of the National Colored Press Association and was widely referred to as the "Princess of the Black Press."[8]

In 1889 Wells bought one-third interest in the *Memphis Free Speech*, a Baptist weekly. The two male partners became business manager and sales manager, while Wells agitated in the community through her militant editorial voice. It was two years later that the audacious Wells criticized the school system for which she worked. After her article exposed unfair hiring practices in the schools, she was fired from her teaching job. Then Wells became a full-time editor with her livelihood depending on the circulation of the *Free Speech*. She traveled by herself through Mississippi, Tennessee, and Arkansas to secure new subscribers. She ran into a complication when white news dealers, realizing that illiterate African Americans were buying the newspaper to pass on to blacks who would read it aloud to them, began selling copies of white newspapers to those blacks who asked for the *Free Speech*. Wells then printed her newspaper on pink paper so illiterate blacks would not be deceived. In less than a year, the *Free Speech* had become, for the first time, a financially self-sustaining enterprise.[9]

Although no copies of the *Free Speech* have survived, Wells's articles reprinted in other newspapers paint a portrait of a hard-hitting journalist. She was relentless in lambasting the federal government's argument that nothing could be done to protect African Americans in the South, writing: "Where are our 'leaders' when the race is being burnt, shot and hanged? Holding good fat offices and saying not a word." She also had vituperative words for blacks who took advantage of other blacks to gain favor with whites, calling them "good niggers." And in response to blacks being sent to prison for stealing five cents while whites thrived after absconding with thousands of dollars, she counseled the black thief: "Let him steal big."[10]

Militancy was a continuing theme in Wells's writing, and at times the opinions she expressed were nothing short of radical. In 1891, for instance, she praised African Americans in Georgetown, Kentucky, who protested the lynching of a local man by burning the town. Calling their action a "true spark of manhood," she wrote: "So long as we permit ourselves to be trampled upon, so long we will have to endure it. Not until the Negro rises in his might and takes a hand in resenting such cold-blooded murders, if he has to burn up whole towns, will a halt be called in wholesale lynching." [11]

When Wells thought it appropriate, she also had scathing words for her admirers. When Fortune proposed forming the Afro-American League to work toward securing civil rights, Wells chastised him for being long on talk and short on action. Likewise, when he wrote an editorial defending white southerners, Wells openly challenged the veracity of the dean of African-American journalism, writing: "Do you really and candidly believe your assertion that if appealed to in honesty the white people of the South 'could not and would not refuse us justice?' I don't believe it." [12]

Wells's controversial statements combined with her gender made her the target of criticism within the black press. In 1890, the *Indianapolis Freeman* published a cartoon of two dogs barking incessantly. The head of one dog was that of a woman wearing her hair in a bun, as did Wells, and sporting a collar that read: "Iola." The white press, on the other hand, paid little attention to Wells or other black journalists. In 1892, however, a series of events occurred that white America could not ignore. [13]

Three friends of Wells had established a cooperative grocery store in a black section of Memphis. When the men's success jeopardized a white grocer's economic security, he instigated a series of threats that escalated until the three black grocers were shot to death. Wells denounced the crime, saying that Memphis was not a fit place for African Americans to live. She wrote: "There is only one thing left that we can do; save our money and leave a town which will neither protect our lives and property, nor give us a fair trial in the courts, but takes us out and murders us in cold blood." [14] The editorial established Wells's lifelong belief that economic reprisal was the muscle that African Americans could use to force change in white behavior. Heeding the editor's call, some two thousand blacks abandoned Memphis, severely damaging the local economy. [15]

Wells had more to say. Adopting the techniques of modern-day investigative journalism, she devoted three months to examining the details of lynchings. She often was the only black who went to the scene after a hanging. She discovered that most of the crimes were prompted by alleged rapes, and she also determined

that every such case involved a white woman who willingly became physically involved with a black man but later accused the
man of rape. Wells then wrote the most incendiary editorial of
her life—suggesting that some white women were physically attracted to black men.[16]

The suggestion that white women of the Victorian Era might
feel such a desire drove white men to hysteria. One mainstream
newspaper proposed that the "scurrilous" editor be lynched; another called for the editor, whom the newspaper assumed to be a
man, to be branded with a hot iron and castrated. Wells was at a
church convention in Philadelphia when a mob destroyed her
newspaper office and threatened to kill her and cause mass
bloodshed if she returned to the South. From that time forward,
Wells kept a pistol in her desk, writing: "A Winchester rifle
should have a place of honor in every black home."[17]

While Wells's editorial drew hatred from most editors, Fortune admired her courage. Not only did he invite Wells to write
two columns a week for his New York Age, but he also gave the
displaced and penniless woman one-fourth interest in his newspaper, the leading African-American publication in the country,
in exchange for her subscription list for the Free Speech.[18]

After joining the staff of the Age, Wells set out to make
northern readers aware of the realities of lynching. To give credibility to her work, she relied on the statistics published in the
Chicago Tribune's annual summary. To make her writing more
vivid, she provided graphic details based on her own observa-
tions of the scenes of lynchings. Because she could no longer
travel in the South, she sometimes hired private detectives to
gather evidence for her.[19]

Wells's first story in the Age, which consisted of seven columns on the front page, described the events in Memphis and
included her own interpretation of the rape myth. Fortune sold
ten thousand copies of that issue, far more than any other publication in the history of the African-American press.[20]

Wells then reproduced her words as the heart of her first
lengthy work, a twenty-five-page pamphlet titled "Southern Horrors: Lynch Law in All Its Phases." Writing in her pithy journalistic style, Wells used the work to discuss interracial marriage, a
concept that still enrages much of white America today. She
wrote: "There are many white women in the South who would

marry colored men if such an act would not place them at once beyond the pale of society and within the clutches of the law. The miscegenation laws of the South leave the white man free to seduce all the colored girls he can, but it is death to the colored man who yields to the force and advances of a similar attraction in white women."[21]

Wells accepted the task of launching the anti-lynching campaign with a sense of duty. In the preface to the pamphlet, she wrote: "Somebody must show that the Afro-American race is more sinned against than sinning, and it seems to have fallen upon me to do so." Frederick Douglass was among her early supporters, admitting that he had accepted the rape myth until Wells had questioned it. Douglass said of Wells's writing: "There has been no work equal to it in convincing power. I have spoken, but my word is feeble in comparison." Leading African-American women also supported their sister. Two hundred women of the eastern black elite organized a spectacular fundraiser in New York. The name "Iola" was spelled out in electric lights across the dais, miniature versions of the *Free Speech* were used as programs, and five hundred dollars was collected and donated to Wells's emerging crusade.[22]

Wells's emotional speech at the fund-raiser launched her career as an orator. She left the *New York Age* to lecture throughout the Northeast. After hearing her speak, the editor of a British newspaper sponsored Wells on a speaking tour in England. The 1893 tour built British opposition to lynching, including formation of a national anti-segregation society. In addition, numerous articles about the tour appeared in such major white newspapers as the *Atlanta Constitution* and *Washington City Post*. Although the articles criticized Wells, they increased her visibility and communicated her message to white America.[23]

Wells was invited to England for another speaking tour in 1894. During the trip, she presented more than one hundred lectures, was honored at a breakfast with members of Parliament, and wrote a weekly column titled "Ida B. Wells Abroad" for the *Daily Inter-Ocean*, a white newspaper in Chicago.[24]

While American newspapers acknowledged Wells as the founder of the anti-lynching crusade, they did not always do so with praise. The *Indianapolis Freeman* lauded her work, stating: "Before the advent of Miss Wells and the consequent Anti-

Lynching movement, the Negro's case in equity had lingered comparatively unnoticed for years," but the *New York Times* denounced her as a fraud: "She knows nothing about the colored problem in the South. . . . A reputable or respectable negro has never been lynched, and never will be."[25]

Some African Americans also were uneasy with the vehemence of Wells's words. In 1894 a delegation of blacks asked her to soften her attack on the South. Wells refused. She argued that the hypocrisy of southern mores had to be exposed as a plot "to keep the nigger down."[26]

Regardless of whether Wells was praised or criticized, her campaign was reaping results. A month after she returned to the United States, Congressman Henry William Blair of New Hampshire called for investigation of all acts of mob violence. Blair's proposal for federal legislation eventually died in committee, but it helped generate new laws on the state level. Between 1893 and 1897, six states passed anti-lynching measures.[27]

Wells maintained the intensity of her crusade. She devoted a year to lecturing in northern cities from the Atlantic to the Pacific and to organizing local lynching societies. In 1895, she published the first comprehensive history of lynching, a one-hundred-page pamphlet titled "A Red Record: Tabulated Statistics and Alleged Causes of Lynching in the United States, 1892-1893-1894."

By this time, Chicago had become Wells's home. She went to the city in 1893, between her trips abroad, to edit a pamphlet criticizing the World's Columbian Exposition for excluding black participants. She stood outside the Haitian exhibit at the fair and handed out copies of "The Reason Why the Colored American is not in the World's Columbian Exposition." The forty-page booklet included sections written by Ferdinand L. Barnett, founder and editor of the *Chicago Conservator*.[28]

Soon after arriving in Chicago, Wells began submitting articles to Barnett, who had been born a slave but in 1878 had received a law degree from Northwestern University and had founded the *Conservator* as the first black newspaper in Chicago. As Wells and Barnett worked together and realized the compatibility of their activism, they became romantically involved. They married on June 27, 1895, with the bride adopting a hyphenated last name in an early instance of the practice. The next month, Wells-Barnett became editor of the *Conservator* while her husband concentrated on his law practice. Within a year, Barnett was appointed the first African-American assistant state's attorney for Cook County. He had two sons from his first marriage, and, a year after her wedding, Wells-Barnett gave birth to her first child.[29]

Wells-Barnett set out to balance marriage and motherhood with her journalistic work and her commitment to women's rights activism. In 1893, she had founded Chicago's first club for black women, serving as president and namesake of the Ida B. Wells Women's Club. The group established the city's first black kindergarten and desegregated the League of Cook County Clubs.[30]

Wells-Barnett also played a central role in formation of the national African-American women's club movement. John Jacks, the white editor of a Missouri newspaper, tried to destroy Wells's credibility in England by attacking her in a letter to the sponsors of her tours. Those sponsors sent a copy of the letter, which indicted all African-American women as blatantly immoral, to Josephine St. Pierre Ruffin, founder of *Woman's Era* newspaper in Boston. To create a united protest against the allegations, Ruffin called the first national convention of African-American women. The 1895 convention endorsed Wells's work and formed the National Federation of Afro-American Women. A year later, Wells-Barnett, with her four-month-old son in tow, participated in a convention that created the National Association of Colored Women.[31]

But the struggle to maintain both a career and a family became too difficult for Wells-Barnett. With the birth of her second son in 1897, she relinquished her position as editor of the *Conservator*. That decision was part of her effort to scale back her public life while her children were small. From that time until the last of her four children entered school in 1912, Wells-Barnett avoided responsibilities that would have interfered with her role as mother. Her decision to place marriage and motherhood ahead of other work did not set well with some feminists. Susan B. Anthony chastised Wells-Barnett, saying talented women had a special calling. Anthony told her: "I know of no one in all this country better fitted to do the work you had in hand than yourself. Since you have gotten married, agitation seems practically to have ceased."[32]

Despite Wells-Barnett's scaling back, she did not abandon the anti-lynching campaign. In 1898, she led a delegation to the White House to protest the lynching of an African-American postmaster in South Carolina. She asked President William McKinley to punish the offenders and to enact a national anti-lynching law. McKinley told her that the appropriate departments would look into the matter, but nothing came of his promises. That same year, Wells-Barnett lobbied for a federal anti-lynching bill introduced by Illinois Congressman William E. Lorimer. Her efforts meant she worked for the defeat of a weaker bill sponsored by North Carolina Congressman George White, raising the wrath of other black leaders because White was the only African American in Congress.[33] In 1900 Wells-Barnett published another fifty-page anti-lynching pamphlet titled "Mob Rule in New Orleans."

The brutality of individual lynchings sometimes propelled Wells-Barnett out of her retirement to investigate them. One case occurred in 1909 when two Illinois men were hanged. The law required that the sheriff who allowed the mob violence be dismissed, but he immediately petitioned to be reinstated. Wells-Barnett traveled alone to southern Illinois to gather the facts and then to the state capital in Springfield to argue before Governor Charles Deneen. Although she provided the only opposition and was the only black present, Wells-Barnett was so convincing that Deneen refused to reinstate the sheriff. In its coverage of the case, the *Chicago Defender* wrote: "If we only had a few men with the backbone of Mrs. Barnett, lynching would soon come to a halt."[34]

Wells-Barnett also took time to denounce accommodationist Booker T. Washington. She lambasted his argument that the individual black should not study the classics but should opt for an industrial education, writing: "This gospel of work is no new one for the Negro. It is the South's old slavery practice in a new dress. It was the only education the South gave the Negro; for two and a half centuries she had absolute control of his body and soul. The Negro knows that now, as then, the South is strongly opposed to his learning anything but how to work."[35]

While Wells-Barnett vehemently opposed Washington's philosophy of conciliation, she actually worked little better with more progressive leaders. Wells-Barnett was effective as an independent force, but she was impatient with the pace, process, and structure of large organizations. She remained on the left of other black leaders and was so sure of the righteousness of her position that she was incapable of tolerating anyone who disagreed with her. Other racial reformers dubbed her the "Lonely Warrior."[36]

In one newspaper editorial, she scorned T. Thomas Fortune, the Washington supporter who had rescued her from poverty a decade earlier, as "a weak man who seems to grow more so as age tells on him." For a time she supported the militant W.E.B. DuBois, but the alliance ended when DuBois failed to secure a position for her on the committee charged with planning the organization that, in 1909, became the National Association for the Advancement of Colored People. Wells-Barnett eventually served on the association's national board, but she found the leaders too conservative for her taste, writing: "I don't expect a great deal to result from their activity. I shall not bother much with the Chicago branch."[37]

Nor did Wells-Barnett work well with the leadership of the National Association of Colored Women, feeling a number of personal insults from the upper-class women. In 1899 when the association met in Chicago, for example, Wells-Barnett was not invited to appear on the convention program. She later learned that she had been excluded because several Chicago members had threatened not to participate if the intractable Wells-Barnett were present. Though she had played a central role in the creation of the association, Wells-Barnett never attained high office in it and was hissed by delegates when she spoke at the national convention in 1909.[38]

Instead of committing her time to national organizations, Wells-Barnett focused on projects in Chicago. An active church woman, she led the members of her Sunday school class in establishing the Negro Fellowship League. She secured private funds from Victor F. Lawson, owner of the *Chicago Daily News*, that allowed the league to open a settlement house in the city's expanding ghetto in 1910. Modeling the Frederick Douglass Center after that of her friend Jane Addams, Wells-Barnett transformed it into an employment service and residence for destitute black men.[39]

In 1913, Wells-Barnett combined her commitment to the center with a new occupation. After enrolling her youngest child in school, she accepted a position as an adult probation officer for the city of Chicago, becoming the first African American to hold such a position. Probationers reported to her at the center.[40]

It was also in 1913 that Wells-Barnett founded yet another organization. She had joined the Illinois Equal Suffrage Association soon after settling in Chicago but had found black women to be apathetic about women's suffrage. So Wells-Barnett founded the Alpha Suffrage Club, the country's first such organization for African-American women. With Wells-Barnett as president, the club attracted two hundred members and registered thousands of black women to vote in local and state elections.[41]

As one of the first activities of the club, Wells-Barnett traveled to Washington, D.C., to join women in the first national parade for women's suffrage, held the day before President Woodrow Wilson's inauguration. When white women from the South learned that black women intended to march, they threatened to withdraw. As a compromise, parade organizers created a separate contingent for African-American women. Refusing to support the segregated policy, Wells-Barnett stood in the crowd until the parade was underway and then slipped into the first section and marched boldly forward to the end of the parade route. She marched in a second suffrage parade three years later when ten thousand women converged on Chicago to demand that the Republican National Convention include a suffrage plank in the party platform.[42]

Wells-Barnett was active in local and state politics as well. She worked in Chicago's mayoral elections and campaigned for the Republican Party throughout Illinois and Missouri. By 1930, Chicago had the most politically aggressive African-American community in the country. In that year, Wells-Barnett sought election to the Illinois State Senate, running as an independent against Republican Adelbert Roberts, an African-American man. Despite blanketing the city with flyers, the outspoken woman received a mere 8 percent of the vote.[43]

Within a year of her bid for elected office, Ida B. Wells-Barnett contracted uremia, a kidney disease. After a brief illness, she died on March 25, 1931, at the age of sixty-nine.[44]

Although Wells-Barnett eventually would become the only African-American woman journalist widely known to twentieth century historians, her eulogies focused not on her newspaper work but on her opposition to lynching. W.E.B. DuBois wrote: "Ida Wells Barnett was the pioneer of the anti-lynching crusade. She began the awakening of the conscience of the nation."[45]

JOSEPHINE ST. PIERRE RUFFIN
Driving Force in the Women's Club Movement

The black women's club movement that began in the late nineteenth century became a vehicle through which thousands of African-American women were able to expand beyond the limited sphere of domesticity, allowing them to gain a greater sense of independence. The fifty thousand middle- and upper-class women uniting to form the National Association of Colored Women made history by establishing the first national African-American organization, predating both the National Association for the Advancement of Colored People and the Urban League. It also was from the women's club movement that a national communication network evolved, linking together African-American women spread across the country. As thousands of club members discovered the benefits of sharing their activities and their aspirations, they found word-of-mouth communication and personal correspondence to be inadequate. So they created the first publications targeted for distribution specifically to large numbers of their race and gender.[1]

Josephine St. Pierre Ruffin of Boston's black aristocracy used her journalistic skills to further the advancement of the club movement. In 1890, Ruffin founded a national newspaper that was published both by and for African-American women. *Woman's Era* became closely connected to the club movement, leading Ruffin into positions of both local and national leadership. She used her newspaper to document the achievements and showcase the strengths of African-American women. In an editorial printed in an early issue of *Woman's Era*, Ruffin wrote: "The stumbling block in the way of even the most cultured colored woman is the narrowness of her environment . . . . It is to help strengthen this class and a better understanding between all classes that this little venture is sent out on its mission."[2]

Ruffin's journalistic work enhanced the pride and confidence of thousands of her black sisters. Her groundbreaking newspaper gave a sense of self-worth to African-American women, allowing this long-denigrated minority to become a more influential segment of society as the nation entered the twentieth century.

Analysis of material published in *Woman's Era* during its seven-year lifespan speaks to Ruffin's women's rights activism and racial activism, as she encouraged her readers to break out of the traditional women's sphere to become knowledgeable about public affairs issues, especially those of direct relevance to the race. Less admirably, the content of Ruffin's newspaper identifies her as an elitist who allowed both favoritism and nepotism to secure a place in the pages of her newspaper.

Josephine St. Pierre was born August 31, 1842, in Boston. She was the youngest of six children born to Eliza Matilda Menhenick St. Pierre, a white woman who was a native of Cornwall, England, and John St. Pierre, the dark-skinned son of a Frenchman from Martinique. Young Josephine's aristocratic ancestry has been traced to her great-great-grandfather, an African prince who came to Massachusetts early in the eighteenth century and married a young Native American woman. Josephine's father gained wealth and prominence as a Boston clothier.[3]

Josephine encountered racial prejudice early in her life. Her parents enrolled their light-skinned daughter in a private grammar school in Boston, but, six months later when her racial background was discovered, Josephine was forced to leave the school. The St. Pierres refused to send her to the city's segregated public schools, enrolling her, instead, in the integrated schools of nearby Salem. She later graduated from Bowdoin Finishing School in Boston and completed two years of private tutoring in New York.

At age fifteen, Josephine married George Lewis Ruffin, a member of another of Boston's leading African-American families. Disheartened by the Dred Scott decree, the newlyweds went immediately from their wedding to a ship that carried them to Liverpool, England, because they did not want to raise a family in a nation that tolerated slavery. After the outbreak of the Civil War, the Ruffins returned to Boston and purchased a home on fashionable Cambridge Street. During the next few years, Ruffin bore five children, the youngest of whom died in infancy.[4]

In 1869, George Lewis Ruffin became the first African American to graduate from Harvard Law School. He served in the Massachusetts State Legislature from 1870 to 1871 and on Boston Common Council from 1876 to 1877. Ruffin received national attention in 1883 when Governor Benjamin Butler appointed him judge of the municipal court of Charlestown, making Ruffin the first African-American judge in the North.[5]

As the career of George Lewis Ruffin advanced, Josephine St. Pierre Ruffin also emerged as a talented and resourceful individual. During the Civil War, she recruited black soldiers and worked with the Sanitary Commission, precursor of the American Red Cross. Ruffin's first major undertaking occurred when she founded the Kansas Relief Association. The need for the association developed when former slaves who had migrated to the West encountered severe economic difficulties. Ruffin convinced wealthy Bostonians to send clothing and money to the destitute refugees. In 1870, Ruffin demonstrated her concern for women's rights by becoming a charter member of the Massachusetts Suffrage Association.[6]

Her involvement with these various crusades brought Ruffin into contact with influential white leaders. She and abolitionist William Lloyd Garrison, who also lived in Boston, collaborated on the relief work in Kansas. Ruffin and women's suffrage leader Ednah Dow Cheney worked together on women's club projects, and Ruffin had frequent contact with Susan B. Anthony, Eliz-

abeth Cady Stanton, Lucy Stone, and Julia Ward Howe. In addition, she was a close friend of the Booker T. Washingtons, spending winters with them in Tuskegee, Alabama.[7]

It was not until after her husband's sudden death in 1886,
however, that Ruffin made her most important contributions.
She was a forty-four-year-old widow with her children grown.
She also was financially secure and had a national reputation for
her organizational ability and philanthropic endeavors.[8]

Ruffin began her most important journalistic work in 1890,
personally financing the creation and operation, from her home,
of a newspaper for African-American women. Ruffin handled all
editing and publishing responsibilities for *Woman's Era*—editing
copy, laying out pages, selling advertisements, and taking care of
clerical duties. She wrote an editorial page for each issue and an
occasional article, leaving most of the writing to upper-class club
women from around the country whom she had recruited to be
unpaid correspondents.[9]

Many articles were substantive news stories. One, based on
interviews with Boston police and hospital officials, reported
that a sixteen-year-old black girl had been held in slavery for
four years. Another, written by Ruffin, stated that a black woman, Fannie Barrier Williams, had been rejected from membership
in the Woman's Club of Chicago. Ruffin adopted a journalistic
style that allowed her to add editorial comments as she saw fit.
At the end of the article about Williams's rejection, for example,
Ruffin stated: "Club principle made a weak surrender to personal prejudice."[10]

Most news and editorial items were placed under headings
for the correspondents—women from states as distant as California, Texas, and Louisiana. Ruffin boasted that all items in
Woman's Era were written specifically for it, rather than the
newspaper relying on reprints from other publications. Her publication measured nine by twelve inches, and varied from sixteen
to twenty-eight pages. Early issues carried two pages of advertisements; later issues carried ten. Each issue had at least one
photograph; some had as many as fifteen. An annual subscription cost one dollar.[11]

Woman's Era was a feminist publication, with all content
being directed specifically toward the advancement of women.
Ruffin made her strong support of women perfectly clear, saying

of *Woman's Era*: "Being a woman's movement, it is bound to succeed." She reiterated her sentiments through statements about black women, such as: "Our indignation should know no limit. We as women have been too unobtrusive, too little known."[12]

Editorial content included items from black women's clubs all over the country, and, when the National Federation of Afro-American Women was formed in 1895, *Woman's Era* became the federation's official publication. Likewise, when the National Association of Colored Women was established a year later, it, too, chose the newspaper as its official voice.[13]

One specific feminist theme threaded through the newspaper was that a woman should not limit herself to the narrow identity of wife and mother. Ruffin wrote of the African-American woman: "The impossibility of mingling freely with people of culture and learning shuts her out of physical touch with the great world of art, science and letters which is open to all other ambitious women."[14]

Ruffin warned the African-American woman not to become "a mere machine to one's children" and that "advice given to women about their staying at home is wrong altogether." Ruffin's strongest endorsement of an expanded role for the black woman was a frank statement containing a personal pronoun suggesting that the statement may have evolved from her own life experience: "Not all women are intended for mothers. Some of us have not the temperament for family life."[15]

The pioneering editor fostered expansion of the woman's sphere by sprinkling *Woman's Era* with examples of African-American women who had broken new ground, ranging from the first named to the District of Columbia school board to the first to operate a gold mining company. Ruffin stated: "Women should indulge and pursue special bent or cultivate a peculiar power as do the men." She also encouraged her readers to fight for national suffrage, highlighting how Colorado and Kentucky had benefited from giving women the vote.[16]

Ruffin recognized, however, that women could not succeed by excluding men from their endeavors. She wrote: "If women wish to advance any worthy cause by organizing, that cause would be better advanced by the co-operation of men and women than by their separatism."[17]

The cause Ruffin most wanted her readers to advance was

racial reform. She insisted that readers should "think in order that they may not sit like idiots" when race questions were debated. Consequently, *Woman's Era* carried articles about political and economic topics. In the advocacy tradition of the black press, when Ruffin viewed an issue as important to African-American women, she willingly sacrificed journalistic objectivity. Her editorial voice grew particularly strident in its opposition to the legalization of segregation. When the U.S. Supreme Court upheld segregated transportation on trains, Ruffin went so far as to advocate breaking the law. She wrote: "If laws are unjust, they must be continually broken until they are killed or altered. The thing to do is to force the recognition of manhood by any and all means. . . . It is evident that the only way now to get what we want is to take it even if we have to break laws in getting it." [18]

Public affairs coverage in *Woman's Era* was not limited to topics directly related to racial reform. Ruffin covered Hawaiian independence, temperance, legislation to penalize wife beating, and, as the 1896 presidential election approached, the free coinage of silver. [19]

Ruffin wanted the women of her race to be aware of the wide range of issues of the day, not to limit themselves to racial reform issues. She wrote: "It is not our desire to narrow ourselves to race work, however necessary it is that such work should be done and particularly by colored women. It cannot but be admitted that we, as a race, have too frequently limited ourselves to this field with the result of contracting our vision, enfeebling our impulses and weakening our power." [20]

Whatever the subject, Ruffin's editorials could be both confrontational and provocative. That she was a member of the doubly disenfranchised minority group of black women did not preclude her from disagreeing with the white men who dominated the country. When Boston realtors denied wealthy African Americans the right to buy homes in affluent sections of the city, Ruffin demanded that they change their policy, writing: "The position is absurd. No other class of vendors may say who shall and shall not buy their wares." Her elevated tone clearly communicated that realtors were a working class segment of the population who existed for the benefit of the monied class—regardless of color. [21]

Nor did Ruffin shrink from conflicts with members of other

minority groups, regardless of color or gender. She criticized the dean of African-American journalism, T. Thomas Fortune, as a man who sometimes forgot his heritage. And she advised black women to shun the political stance of white women, saying: "The exclusion of colored women and girls from nearly all places of respectable employment is due mostly to the meanness of white women."[22]

In addition to speaking with a strong editorial voice, Ruffin also boasted that *Woman's Era* was a publication of integrity and journalistic principle. She wrote: "Personal feeling has no place in newspaper work. A good newspaper gives facts. . . . A paper which is afraid of everybody's feelings has no call to be published."[23]

Despite Ruffin's lofty words, there is evidence that she and *Woman's Era* both were prejudiced. Like most African-American journalists and newspapers of the late nineteenth century, they were elitist, aiming themselves toward the small class of educated blacks rather than the black masses. Each month the masthead of *Woman's Era* unabashedly stated that it was designed for women of the "refined and educated classes."[24]

Editorial content reflected this elitist attitude. An item about a Boston seamstress, for example, included the passage: "Mrs. Casneau makes and furnishes materials for a walking or visiting dress for $23.00. This hardly needs comment. A stylish, well-made cloth dress at $23.00 is a bargain, as the average woman must know." The "average woman," as Ruffin and *Woman's Era* defined her, was far different from the typical black woman of late nineteenth-century America. Another item stated: "Ray, on Chatham Row, sells a prepared icing which is so good it is called 'Perfect Icing.' What an advantage to have an icing which does not spoil or foment, all prepared for us." If nineteenth-century black women had been asked to list the "advantages" they most wanted, few of their lists would have begun with finding a good cake icing.[25]

The items about the dress and icing also demonstrate that Ruffin did not adhere to the journalistic principle that insists that news columns be detached from advertising, as both the dressmaker and the baker advertised in *Woman's Era*. Another article stated: "Mr. U.A. Ridley is another of the successful merchant tailors of Boston. Mr. Ridley's business is of the quiet order, the patronage being almost entirely confined to a certain exclusive set." Besides carrying an elitist tone, the exceedingly complimentary article described one of *Woman's Era's* most loyal advertisers—and the son-in-law of the publisher.[26]

Comparing *Woman's Era* editorial content and staff members provides further evidence of favoritism and nepotism. The newspaper praised "an attractive little volume" titled *Aunt Lindy*; the novel's author was Victoria Earle Matthews, *Woman's Era* correspondent in New York City. The newspaper described as "commendable" a "daintily bound volume" titled *The Work of the Afro-American Woman*; the book's author was Gertrude Bustill Mossell, *Woman's Era* correspondent in Philadelphia. The newspaper lauded Paul Lawrence Dunbar's poetry; Dunbar's wife, Ruth, was *Woman's Era* correspondent in New Orleans.[27]

As with other African-American newspapers, the biggest problems for *Woman's Era* were financial. Details about the newspaper's circulation and revenue are unknown, but Ruffin's correspondence documents that she struggled with the fiscal aspects of the newspaper. She had sufficient resources to launch her journalistic enterprise, but her savings could not sustain it indefinitely. In 1891, she began to supplement her income by working fulltime as editor-in-chief of the *Boston Courant*, a black weekly. After Ruffin edited both the *Era* and the *Courant* for a year, however, her doctor said her health would not allow her to continue both activities. Ruffin then continued to edit *Woman's Era*, cutting back to writing only an occasional article for the *Courant*.[28]

Ruffin, an astute businesswoman, recognized that the economic viability of *Woman's Era* did not depend solely on the quality of the editorial content. In 1894, she told her readers that her journalistic endeavor would succeed only if it produced sufficient revenue to allow her to double the number of pages per issue and to publish twice a month. She then began introducing techniques aimed at amassing that revenue by increasing both her advertising base and circulation.[29]

To attract more advertising, Ruffin created a classified ad section, promoted advertisers in her news columns, and designed a contest to honor the correspondent who solicited the most advertisements from her home city. In 1896, Ruffin also appealed to advertisers by publishing a special souvenir issue distributed free to anyone attending the national convention of African-American women in Washington that year.[30]

To boost circulation, the publisher offered free sample copies of her newspaper and traveled to other cities to solicit new subscriptions. In her most aggressive circulation-building move, Ruffin attacked the competition. She demanded that her readers cancel their subscriptions to *Ladies' Home Journal* and subscribe to *Woman's Era* instead, pointing out that the *Journal* refused to accept articles written by African-American women. Ruffin wrote bitterly: "Think of this, you colored women whose money and efforts are going to support in luxury the writers of that paper, while you hesitate to give ten cents toward the encouragement of writers of your own race! O, the pity of it!"[31]

But Ruffin's journalistic enterprise faced insurmountable problems. Most significant was a scarcity of black-owned businesses and a reluctance by white-owned businesses to advertise to black readers. The national scope of *Woman's Era* added to the challenge; American newspapers had not yet evolved into national enterprises with national advertisers. Regarding circulation, the number of African-American women sufficiently prosperous to afford to purchase a monthly newspaper was relatively small. Ultimately, *Woman's Era* failed to attract a substantial advertising base outside of Boston, and most local advertisers were small businesspersons—a seamstress, wallpaper hanger, baker—who could only afford small advertisements.

By 1896, *Woman's Era* had become a bimonthly; by the end of the year, in a final act of desperation, Ruffin cut the subscription rate in half. The final issue of *Woman's Era* appeared in January 1897.[32]

It is difficult to gauge the impact of any journalistic enterprise, but the existence of a newspaper created both by and for African-American women obviously increased the self-esteem and sense of empowerment of its writers and readers. One historian has called *Woman's Era* "the most successful publication published exclusively by colored women," and another praised it as "exerting an influence that was widely recognized."[33]

At the same time that Ruffin was pioneering as an African-American woman journalist, she also was making history as a leader in the black women's club movement. In 1894, she founded Woman's Era Club, the first organization of African-American women in Boston and the second organization of its kind in the country, having formed a year after the Colored Women's League was founded in Washington, D.C.[34]

The 100-member Woman's Era Club, which included several white women, was committed to educating female members of the black elite. Its bi-weekly meetings were devoted to discussing topics such as civics, domestic science, literature, and race. In addition, the club provided scholarships to young African-American women and lobbied for improved city services in black residential sections of Boston. In 1900, Booker T. Washington praised the club, saying: "It has taken the initiative in many reforms and helpful movements that have had a wide influence on race development." Ruffin remained president of the club until 1903. The position of "honorary president" then was created for her.[35]

A year after founding the local club, Ruffin called African-American women from across the country to a national meeting, largely to defend Ida B. Wells-Barnett and her anti-lynching crusade against widespread criticism. When women from thirty-six clubs in twelve states gathered in Boston in 1895, it marked the first time that American women of African descent had assembled for a national meeting.[36]

By the end of the three-day convention, the women had created the National Federation of Afro-American Women. A year later, the federation merged with the Colored Women's League to become the National Association of Colored Women, with Ruffin serving as first vice president. Within two decades, the association comprised 1,000 local clubs and 50,000 members.[37]

In 1900, Ruffin attempted to desegregate the all-white General Federation of Women's Clubs. She submitted a request for Woman's Era Club to be admitted to the national federation, not volunteering that most members of the Boston club were of African descent. After the application had been approved, Ruffin left for Milwaukee to attend the federation's annual meeting, planning to receive the club's credentials and thereby desegregate the federation. But Ruffin's racial identity became known when women riding on the train with her noticed that she waved at two black children standing on the train platform.[38]

When she arrived in Milwaukee, Ruffin succeeded in securing her individual credentials because she was an elected representative of the New England Women's Press Association and the Massachusetts State Federation of Women's Clubs, both of which she earlier had desegregated. Her Boston club, however, was not allowed to join the national organization. When officials attempted to remove the pale blue ribbon from Ruffin's chest, she thwarted the effort by demonstrating remarkable physical agility for a fifty-eight-year-old woman. Ruffin's effort to break the color barrier became a major issue at the convention when southern delegates threatened to secede from the federation if a black club were admitted.[39]

Federation president Rebecca Lowe of Atlanta blocked Ruffin by requiring that the club's admission be ratified by the federation's board of directors, a provision not previously required. Lowe said of Ruffin: "It is the 'high-caste' negroes who bring about all the ill-feeling. The ordinary colored woman understands her position thoroughly." Ruffin hired a lawyer and threatened to sue the federation. She also appealed to Booker T. Washington to use his influence with white America to support her desegregation effort. No suit was filed and Washington turned a deaf ear to Ruffin, however, and Woman's Era Club was not admitted.[40]

To some degree, Ruffin accomplished her mission, however, as journalists across the country complimented her, thereby improving the nation's image of African-American women. Milwaukee newspapers described Ruffin as a "cultured lady" and "woman of fine presence," while a Los Angeles magazine characterized her as "a woman of charming manners" and a Pittsburgh newspaper said she was "very lady-like in demeanor." Newspapers were critical, on the other hand, of the white leaders of the federation. The *Chicago Tribune* stated: "The federated white-faced women of the clubs have not had the courage to recognize their sisters of the colored race."[41]

During her final years, Ruffin increased her prominence as an orator by lecturing, most frequently on the importance of moral courage, to audiences in Massachusetts, New Jersey, and several western states. She also helped found the American Mount Coffee School Association, which operated a school for Liberian children, and served as vice president of the association under Edward Everett Hale's presidency.[42]

Her organizational skills and national prominence benefited a number of civic organizations. She helped found the Boston branch of the NAACP and the Association for the Promotion of

Child Training in the South, which supported a school for black children in Atlanta. She served on the executive board of the Massachusetts Federation of Women's Clubs.

Ruffin died of nephritis, a disease of the kidneys, on March 13, 1924, at the age of eighty-one. Her body lay in state in a public building in Boston. Funeral services, at which three priests officiated, were held at Trinity Episcopal Church on Copley Square, and she was buried at Mount Auburn Cemetery in Cambridge.[43]

DELILAH L. BEASLEY
Voice for Accommodation and Conciliation

During the late nineteenth and early twentieth centuries, Booker T. Washington led a movement in black America characterized by pacifism and accommodation toward white America. The prominent educator and orator advocated moderate views and acceptance of the existing sociopolitical order. The philosophy set forth by Washington, the head of Tuskegee Institute, included a conciliatory policy with respect to racial reform, broad acceptance of Jim Crow laws, and emphasis on cooperation and mutuality of interests between whites and blacks. The mainstream press supported Washington, with white newspapers hailing him as the successor to Frederick Douglass.[1]

Delilah L. Beasley adhered to Washington's philosophy and committed her journalistic skills to helping promote his concept of accommodationism through her work in the white press. A devout Roman Catholic, Beasley believed that God had called her to use her skills as a newspaper reporter and columnist to break down the barriers between the races.

Beasley's newspaper career, which spanned fifty years, began in 1883 when she was a mere twelve years old. Three years later, Beasley won her place in journalism history by becoming the first American woman of African descent to write on a regular basis for a mainstream newspaper. Her most significant journalistic legacy came in the early twentieth century with her two decades of work as a part-time reporter and columnist for the *Oakland Tribune*, then the largest daily newspaper in Northern California.[2]

Through her writing, especially her weekly *Tribune* column, "Activities Among Negroes," Beasley expanded the boundaries of mainstream press coverage of her race. Beasley drew upon incidents from across the country to paint a portrait of African Americans that focused on their positive characteristics and accomplishments—facets of the race unfamiliar to most of white America. In 1931, Beasley's column included a summary of her journalistic mission. She wrote of herself: "The writer will continue to work for a 'better racial understanding' by giving to the reading public a knowledge of the efforts, ability and progress of the Negro peoples throughout the world."[3]

Despite severe problems with finances and poor health, Beasley succeeded in crafting a newspaper column that portrayed African Americans as possessing a rich history and anchoring their lives in a strong sense of morality. Instead of attacking racial discrimination directly, she focused on successful interracial activities. Beasley, who never married, achieved national prominence as a spokeswoman for Americans of African descent, an organizer of integrated activities, and the leader of an effort to convince white editors to refrain from using such derogatory terms as "pickaninny" and "nigger." Beasley was, in the accommodationist tradition of Washington, a racial reform activist who sought progress through cooperation rather than dissidence.

Delilah Leontium Beasley was born in Cincinnati, Ohio, on September 9, 1871. She was the oldest of five children in the family of Daniel Beasley, an engineer, and Margaret Harris Beasley, a homemaker. Delilah attended Cincinnati's black public schools. Although details of her early life are not known, being the child of an engineer clearly placed her in an economic position above that of many black Americans.[4]

Delilah began her newspaper career in 1883 by writing for

the *Cleveland Gazette*. She sent the African-American newspaper brief items about church and social activities in Cincinnati. The young woman's journalistic ability so impressed African-American journalist Daniel A. Rudd, who edited the *Ohio State Tribune* and *Catholic Tribune*, that he recruited Delilah to write for his two Cincinnati newspapers as well. Delilah first wrote for a mainstream newspaper in 1886 when, at the age of fifteen, she began sending items to the Sunday edition of the *Cincinnati Enquirer*. Because Beasley's articles were unsigned, it is impossible to identify the items she wrote for any of the Ohio newspapers.[5]

Beasley's nascent career as a journalist was disrupted by the deaths of both of her parents. It is not known in what year her parents died, but it probably was in the early 1880s, when Delilah was still a teenager, as the 1880 census classified both Beasley parents as "bedridden or disabled." After their parents' deaths, the five Beasley children were scattered to various households, and young Delilah was forced to seek immediate full-time employment.[6]

Beasley worked first as a domestic for a white judge in Cincinnati. She then began giving massages in Chicago and completed formal study in hydrotherapy, medical gymnastics, and diagnosis. Beasley moved to New York State and joined the staff of the Buffalo Sanitarium, specializing in giving scalp massages to pregnant women. Advancing in the field, she became the head masseuse at a bath house at a Michigan resort.

At the turn of the century, Beasley developed an intense interest in the history of her race. After beginning research in the Midwest, she came to believe that the most overlooked concentration of African Americans was in California. So, in 1910, Beasley moved to Berkeley to serve as a nurse for a former therapy patient and to begin, in earnest, research on the history of California's black pioneers. She attended history classes at the University of California at Berkeley and examined records of county hospitals and poor farms, early black newspapers, and personal letters in the hands of individuals throughout the state.[7]

Beasley resumed her newspaper career in 1915 by protesting D.W. Griffith's epic motion picture "Birth of a Nation." The film portrayed slaves as happy and carefree, while depicting black freed men as drunken savages. Because 95 percent of Oakland's population was white, Beasley decided to express her objections to the film through the area's largest white newspaper, the *Oakland Tribune*. In her articles, Beasley summarized Booker T. Washington's reaction to the film while also promoting his accommodationist philosophy.[8]

In an article that Beasley wrote a few weeks later for the *Oakland Sunshine*, an African-American newspaper, she articulated her reason for writing for the white rather than the black press: "News of special interest to us as a people ought to be discussed in our own papers among ourselves. But, if a bit of news would have a tendency to better our position in the community, then it should not only be published in our own race papers, but in the papers of the other race as well."[9] In the article, Beasley conceded that she had deleted some details from the *Tribune* article, fearing that they would harm her people. The article clearly described Beasley's journalistic mission to improve how white America perceived the black race.[10]

Beasley next covered the World's Fair that San Francisco hosted in 1915. The Panama-Pacific Exposition, commemorating completion of the Panama Canal, was an $80 million extravaganza that attracted 18 million visitors to the Bay Area. Beasley used her articles about the exposition to enhance the image of African Americans. One story reported that a black man directed the Philippine band, which performed daily at the exposition; another pointed out that white and black youngsters stood side by side to create a human American flag.[11]

Beasley's most triumphant story from the fair reported that the winning entry in a contest to choose a "pet name" for the exposition had been submitted by a ten-year-old African-American girl. Contest judges announced that the name "Jewel City" had won several hours before they learned that the entry had been submitted by a black child. Beasley heralded the girl's victory as a dramatic illustration of the success that African Americans could achieve.[12]

While reporting for the *Tribune*, Beasley continued to research the history of black Californians, publishing two articles in the *Journal of Negro History* in 1918. Despite her nearly two decades of research, however, she failed to secure a publisher for her manuscript. In 1919, she finally borrowed money from *Tribune* general manager Francis B. Loomis to pay to have the book printed, even though the loan kept her in debt for three years.[13]

The Negro Trail Blazers of California was the first history of the state's African-American population. In its three hundred pages, Beasley chronicled the evolution of black Californians from the sixteenth through the twentieth centuries. She stressed the achievements of individual women and men, with more than half the book consisting of biographical sketches of black pioneers.[14]

Reviews of the book were mixed. A University of California history professor wrote that Beasley had served her race well; revered African-American historian Carter G. Woodson, however, criticized Beasley's poor grammar.[15]

Writing effectively was always a challenge for Beasley, and her editors in Ohio routinely had rewritten her articles.[16] Because most of her copy was edited before it was published, the quality of her writing is difficult to assess. One sample of Beasley's unedited newspaper copy has been preserved, however, as part of the Francis B. Loomis Papers, which are held at Stanford University. Beasley sent the article to Loomis for the *Tribune's* travel section. The piece, which was never published, recounted Beasley's experiences while traveling through California to market her book. The unedited writing sample suggests that Beasley had to struggle to create clear, grammatically correct prose. She wrote: "The sun in Fresno was very hot, to that extent my feet swelled and I wore point shoes because they were high and did not tire me. This results in this toe getting sun burned and blistered to make it worse that night when I came in from my canvassing after resting on front porch of the house in which I was stopping I went in the house in the dark to get a drink of water stumbled into a large tufted leather chair and bruised the already blistered toe. By next night the toe had swelled terrible. I went to Bakersfield where I take 24 orders, four of which was cash."[17]

Despite Beasley's writing problems, her column began appearing regularly in the Sunday *Tribune* in September 1923. "Activities Among Negroes" carried a distinctive heading that included "By Delilah L. Beasley" in stylized type. The column, placed in the local news section, typically consisted of six to ten independent news items about church activities, social events, births, and deaths. Items were written in a straightforward fashion, such as: "One hundred Negro children will receive toys and candy this afternoon at the Christmas party to be held in the social hall of St. Patrick's Catholic Church" and "Mrs. G.C. Coleman, during the past ten days, has entertained 24 friends from the East." [18]

Items were not all about local events. Beasley traveled throughout the state, at her own expense, to attend and report on activities. Sometimes she had to resort to a horse-drawn buggy to reach rural sections of the state. She also received black newspapers from throughout the country and gleaned from them details about activities among African Americans in other cities. After a tornado struck St. Louis, Beasley gave her readers details that mainstream newspapers had neglected to report—that half the homes destroyed had been owned by African Americans. She wrote: "The two and three story dwellings were of red pressed brick, well kept small front grounds and in many instances newly painted, and none had been owned over seven years. But today the district has the appearance of a war-torn sector that had suffered bombarding by an air force." [19]

Beasley incorporated praise of the race into her column, seeking to educate her white readers about the positive traits of blacks. After reporting that African Americans were struggling to operate banks in Chattanooga, Tennessee, and Birmingham, Alabama, for example, she praised the persistence of the race, writing: "The negro, either as an individual or a race, does not give up in despair, because of the failure of any adventure, if he thinks it will help his race to advance." [20]

To highlight African Americans who had achieved success, Beasley incorporated dozens of mini-profiles into her column. These positivist sketches demonstrated to white readers that blacks could excel in virtually any occupation. Indeed, she specifically stated (or overstated): "There are no lines of business endeavor in the United States in which there are no negroes." [21]

Far more than half of the role models who emerged from the column were women, whom Beasley unabashedly labeled "women of distinction." Typical was Mary Grases, the first African-American teacher in Oakland public schools. Beasley wrote: "Mrs. Grases has lived a life of service for her race. She has been a member of the choir of Fifteenth Street A.M.E. Church for thirty years. She helped to establish and was for years the financial secretary for the Home for Aged and Infirm Colored Peo-

ple." [22] Beasley also spotlighted the first African-American wom-
en to earn a master's degree in music, to be admitted to the California bar, and to become an airplane pilot. [23]

The pioneering columnist recognized the value of black history in increasing self-esteem, pride, and sense of community
among Americans of African descent. So, despite the fact that
history textbooks ignored the existence of an African-American
heritage, Beasley documented how black institutions and organizations had been founded and had evolved. In describing Fisk
University in Nashville, Tennessee, for example, she recounted
how black students had raised the money to construct the university's first building. Beasley related similar historical details about
African-American missionary societies, sororities, the Frederick
Douglass House, and, of course, Washington's Tuskegee Institute. [24]

"Activities Among Negroes" portrayed the black community
as being built on a foundation of morality and social responsibility. Like Washington, Beasley believed that the strong moral
fiber at the core of black life inevitably would lead to racial
equality. She publicized altruistic activities among black churches
and the commitment of civic-minded African-American citizens
whose activities bettered the conditions of their race. Beasley told
about black Catholics in Milwaukee, Wisconsin, building a cha-
pel and organizing a school for four hundred children. In other
items, she listed Los Angeles churches that had undertaken chari-
ty projects and reported that the women's auxiliary of the National Baptist Church had donated seventeen thousand dollars
for missionary work. [25]

Finances were a continuing problem for Beasley, who lived in
a single rented room and never amassed more than one hundred
dollars in savings. Working full-time as a physical therapist
would have placed her securely in the middle class, but she felt
that her true calling was as a journalist who could help change
white America's perception of her race. Therefore, she devoted
most of her time to newspaper work, giving physical therapy
treatments only when she became destitute. [26]

The *Tribune* paid Beasley only ten dollars a week for her
column, even though she often spent far more than forty hours a
week collecting material for it. From her meager weekly salary,
Beasley committed ten cents to the Community Chest. As an un-

married woman with no parents, she had no relatives to turn to for financial support. Only when poverty prevented Beasley from continuing her mission—such as when she broke her eyeglasses or her typewriter—would she turn to the Loomises for money.[27]

Beasley also was plagued by poor health. She suffered from high blood pressure, heart disease, and chronic hearing problems. The physical demands of reporting exacerbated her health problems. In the summer of 1922, she walked the streets of Fresno so long that her right foot became severely blistered and one toe had to be amputated.[28]

Despite enduring these daunting personal difficulties, Beasley insisted upon maintaining a consistently upbeat tone in her column, taking every opportunity to praise even the slightest sign of progress in race relations. She peppered her column with such statements as: "Oakland is one of the greatest cities in America today in regard to race relations" and "The splendid white citizens here are ever willing to cooperate for a better understanding and the uplift of the colored race."[29]

Because of Beasley's personal involvement in Oakland women's clubs, she took special pride in describing their integrated activities. She pointed out, for example, that 350 white club women had invited 20 black women to a meeting at a fashionable restaurant. She also boasted that when club women had interracial meetings, black women were served at the same tables as their white sisters, rather than being expected to withdraw during the meal.[30]

In the mid-1920s, Beasley accelerated her participation in women's organizations. The National Association of Colored Women became a significant part of her life, as it did in the lives of thousands of other women. After becoming active in the local chapter, Beasley brought the national convention to Oakland in 1925. She eventually rose to the position of national historian and wrote the preface to the association's history in 1933.[31]

Beasley also was a leader of the Alameda County League of Women Voters, serving as vice president for several years. In 1925, she represented the local group at the league's national convention in Richmond, Virginia. While on the East Coast, Beasley also traveled to Washington, D.C., to attend the convention of the International Council of Women, sending columns back to Oakland.[32]

Church work carried Beasley into women's organizations. As an active member of St. Francis de Sales Catholic Church, Beasley decided that her home parish could accomplish more substantial community outreach projects if it joined a larger organization. So Beasley became the first African-American member of the Oakland Council of Church Women. She later founded and chaired the council's Race Relations Committee.[33]

In recognition of Beasley's many contributions to local and national women's organizations, young black women in Oakland formed a club named for her. Members defined their purpose by choosing a word to correspond to each letter in the name D-E-L-I-L-A-H L. B-E-A-S-L-E-Y: Deeds Ever Lasting In Lending A Hand. Let's Be Ever Alert Serving Lovingly Every Year. Members participated in various community service and educational projects.[34]

Her women's club activities increased Beasley's skill and self-confidence as an organizer and public speaker, propelling her into civil rights activism. Hers was a subtle advocacy of racial reform that sought improved conditions for her people not through militancy or direct confrontation but through quiet diplomacy.

First, Beasley orchestrated a series of integrated activities in Oakland. After convincing a local rabbi to invite a black choir to perform at the city's ecumenical Thanksgiving service, she then collected public contributions to donate "Slave Mother," a painting by black artist Eugene Burk, to the Oakland Municipal Art Gallery.[35] Such efforts brought Beasley national recognition. In 1929, the *Crisis*, the NAACP's national magazine, praised her as one of the country's leading integrationists.[36]

Buoyed by this combination of success and recognition, Beasley expanded her racial activism. She was among a group of local African Americans who established a branch of the National Urban League in Oakland, serving as chair of the group's publicity committee. Beasley next proceeded into behind-the-scenes political action. When Representative Joseph Crail of California drafted legislation to prohibit discriminatory hiring in federal public works projects, Beasley sent him a telegram that suggested adding a clause to strengthen the wording. Crail incorporated Beasley's suggestion into his proposed bill. Although the legislation was defeated at the federal level, the state of Indiana later enacted legislation modeled on Crail's bill. When the Indi-

ana bill was adopted, Beasley published the complete text in her
column—duly noting her contribution to it.[37]

During this period, Beasley's oratorical skill advanced as well.
She was in demand as a guest speaker for church and civic organizations. Her most frequent topic was the value of a "friendly
press," followed by contributions of African-American women
and the benefits of women's suffrage.[38]

In 1925, Beasley combined her journalistic and oratorical
work in a nationwide campaign to reduce offensive language in
the nation's mainstream newspapers. The campaign evolved from
an incident that occurred during the convention of the International Council of Women. Black singers had agreed to entertain
for the event but had stipulated that the theater had to be integrated. When, on the day of the performance, the women learned
that the theater would be segregated, they refused to perform.
When Beasley noticed that newspaper correspondents reporting
the incident used the terms "darkey," "nigger," and "pickaninny"
in their articles, she called a press conference and advised the reporters that such terms had a negative effect on African Americans
who were trying to better their race.[39]

After the convention, Beasley traveled through the East and
Midwest, making personal visits to editors to appeal to them to
refrain from using the denigrating terms and to capitalize the
word "Negro."[40]

Beasley's mastery at avoiding conflict was severely challenged when she wrote on the topic of offensive language. To
avoid direct confrontation, she delicately placed her emphasis
not on criticism but on cooperation. In recounting her speech to
a group of Baptists, for example, she wrote: "The writer spoke
on the power of the press in moulding public sentiment, and declared the use of the words darkey, pickaninny and nigger is de-
pressing to colored people. She hoped and prayed the church
people would take the lead in helping to abolish their use from
the daily press."[41] Therefore, even when crusading against terms
that denigrated her people, Beasley would not waver from her
accommodationist views. Hers was a career dedicated to convincing white readers that there need not be conflict between the
races. She was determined not to allow a contentious tone to
deter her from her mission.

As Beasley neared old age, she became the object of public

ridicule. Being an unmarried woman was very unusual at the time. In addition, she wore unfashionably long dresses, spoke quickly in a shrill voice, and, as a career woman, broke the conventions of a woman of the early twentieth century. Beasley increasingly was labeled "eccentric" and "odd."[42]

Beasley died of heart disease on August 18, 1934, at the age of sixty-two. Before the funeral at her parish church began, members of the Delilah L. Beasley Club gave each mourner a card containing a quotation from one of Beasley's last "Activities Among Negroes" columns. It read: "Every life casts its shadow, my life plus others make a power to move the world. I, therefore, pledge my life to the living world of brotherhood and mutual understanding between the races."[43] Community leaders suggested that copies of Beasley's column be compiled into a book, but the suggestion was never acted upon.[44]

Although it is impossible to gauge the impact of Beasley's newspaper work, as it is with the work of most journalists, her obituary indicates that her writing had an important influence on her community. Beasley's obituary stated: "It was through her writings that the racial relations were eased greatly in the cosmopolitan city of Oakland. Her articles on activities among Negroes served as an educational contact and were unsurpassed."[45]

7

MARVEL COOKE
Literary Journalist of the Harlem Renaissance

The Harlem Renaissance was the country's first large-scale expression of African-American pride and interest in black history and culture. The movement was centered in large numbers of African-American artists who lived in the Harlem section of New York City. Coinciding with white America's testing of moral and social restraints during the Roaring Twenties, this important moment in the history of black America witnessed talented African-American artists achieving unprecedented success and productivity. The creative energy of the Harlem Renaissance saw black artists translate racial oppression into artistic form through poetry, fiction, dance, theater, music, and painting. Concomitantly, this creative period saw hundreds of artists contributing to the movement to use their artistry to awaken all of America to the realities of racial injustice—and to agitate against those inequities.[1]

Marvel Jackson arrived in Harlem in 1926, at the height of the Harlem Renaissance. With an English degree from the University of Minnesota and a passion for the written word, the twenty-three-year-old was determined to use her literary talent to change

black America. When she was hired to work on the seminal
African-American publication in the country, Jackson began writing under the guidance of the most revered scholar and militant
leader of the era, W.E.B. DuBois. Her mentor ushered Jackson
into the inner circle of Harlem artists. Jackson, who married Cecil
Cooke in 1929, developed a distinctive literary style that she then
adapted to the world of journalism. Cooke, who became a member of the black intelligentsia, rejected the sensationalistic style
that dominated the black press and, instead, used her writing talent to create eloquent examples of literary journalism. For the
next quarter century, her poignant prose in both the black and the
white press painted vivid and powerful portraits of the working
and living conditions of black America. One of her front-page
exposés began: "I was a slave.

"I was part of the 'paper bag brigade,' waiting patiently for
someone to 'buy' me for an hour or two, or, if I were lucky, for a
day.

"That is The Bronx Slave Market, where Negro women wait,
in rain or shine, in bitter cold or under broiling sun, to be hired
by housewives looking for bargains in human labor.

"Born in the last depression, the Slave Markets are products
of poverty and desperation. They grow as employment falls. Today they are growing."[2]

Cooke made journalism history in 1950 when she became
the first American woman of African descent to report full-time
for a mainstream newspaper. Cooke, who still lives in Harlem
today, was a crusader for racial reform not only through journalism but also through the American labor movement and the
Communist Party.[3]

Marvel Jackson was born April 4, 1903, in Mankato, Minnesota.
The Jacksons were firmly in the middle class. Madison Jackson,
Marvel's father, had become the first black member of the South
Dakota bar, but he could not build a law practice because whites
refused to hire a black attorney. So Jackson became a Pullman
porter and a socialist who supported labor organizer Eugene V.
Debs. Amy Wood Jackson had worked as a cook and teacher on
an Indian reservation in South Dakota until she became a full-time
homemaker and mother to Marvel and three younger daughters.[4]

The Jacksons' financial security did not prevent Marvel from feeling the sting of racial prejudice at an early age. When the family bought a house in an all-white neighborhood, townspeople demonstrated on their front lawn. When Marvel turned seventeen, her best friend, a white girl, ended their friendship because of the color difference. For a summer job during college, Marvel scored so high on a Spanish exam that she automatically was hired as a translator for the War Department, but, when her race was discovered, she was assigned to work as a file clerk.[5]

Young Marvel also learned that African Americans could fight back. The first black child born in Mankato, she desegregated her elementary and high schools. A few years later, Marvel, one of only five African-American women among twenty thousand students at the University of Minnesota, helped found a chapter of Alpha Kappa Alpha sorority to raise the visibility of her race. And when she discovered that she had been denied the translation job because of her color, she protested to Senator Henrik Shipstead of Minnesota and was reassigned to a translator position.[6]

Marvel's literary talent surfaced when, as a child, she began writing poetry. Her talent for literary criticism flowered in college as she studied the literary classics. It was also during college that she became committed to racial reform and became engaged to future civil rights leader Roy Wilkins.[7]

When Jackson graduated from college in 1925, her ambition was to write in an area of the country where there were other civil rights activists—which meant Harlem. Her mother had been courted by DuBois, and when Marvel moved to Harlem in 1926, DuBois hired her as editorial assistant for the *Crisis*, the magazine of the National Association for the Advancement of Colored People. The magazine was not a mouthpiece for the association but the leading literary medium for expressing the African-American experience.[8]

Jackson's writing responsibility at the *Crisis* included a monthly column critiquing any magazine article that was of interest to African Americans. Writing "In the Magazines" was a boost for Jackson because she spoke to a national audience of black intellectuals. More important, writing the column required her to analyze material being published in the country's leading magazines, thereby exposing her to the best in contemporary American literature. Cooke reviewed material from publications such as the *New*

Republic, the *New Yorker*, *Atlantic Monthly*, and the *Nation*, critiquing the work of such literary giants as Langston Hughes, Zora Neale Hurston, H.L. Mencken, and Dorothy Parker.[9]

DuBois, the leading African-American male feminist of the era, also escorted his young protégé into Harlem's artistic community. On the recommendation of her boss, Jackson rented an apartment in the building where he lived. If Harlem was the cultural and intellectual capital of black America, 409 Edgecombe Avenue was the White House. The most desirable address in Harlem, it served as home to such leaders as Thurgood Marshall, William Patterson, and Walter White.[10]

Jackson was soon socializing with the leading artists in African-American cultural history. Her closest friends included poets Langston Hughes, Countee Cullen, and Claude McKay, novelist and playwright Arna Bontemps, novelist Jessie Fauset, poet and editor James Weldon Johnson, publicist George S. Schuyler, and singer, actor, and activist Paul Robeson.[11]

She used her insightful prose style to capture moments from the Harlem social life. When writing a column about Dorothy Parker's work in the *New Yorker*, Jackson included a caustic description showing how whites were invading Harlem society: "Inevitably there is that fair pinched-faced one with the benevolent eyes who is obviously—too obviously—unprejudiced and who attempts to convince her audience that she believes in 'ab-so-lute' equality in some such convincing strain: 'I haven't the slightest feeling about colored people. Why I'm just crazy about some of them. . . . I have this colored laundress. I've had her for years and I'm devoted to her. And I want to tell you I think of her as my friend.'"[12]

DuBois recognized Jackson's ability to observe details and translate them into vivid description. He also saw that the fearless young woman wrote in a bold, straightforward style. In short, DuBois saw that Jackson was suited to journalism. In 1928, he helped her secure a job at the *Amsterdam News*, the city's leading black newspaper. Jackson was hired as secretary to the society editor but later was promoted to reporter.[13]

This also was a period of change in Jackson's personal life. She ended her relationship with Wilkins and began dating Cecil Cooke, a Jamaican who had earned a master's degree from Columbia University. They married in 1929. Cecil Cooke, then the fastest quarter-miler in the world, later worked for the New York City Recreation Department, advancing to the position of recreation director for the Bronx. The Cookes did not have children. Throughout their fifty years of marriage, which ended when Cecil Cooke died in 1978, he provided unwavering support for his wife.[14]

When Marvel Jackson joined the *Amsterdam News*, she had no journalism training except from her work for the *Crisis*, which had a standard of quality higher than did African-American newspapers. Because of that high standard and her own intellect, she was disappointed in the black press. She detested the sensationalistic crime stories that the newspaper published, insisting that they should be replaced with in-depth articles on community issues. She said: "Here's a black paper just following the dictates of society, not making any impression at all, not addressing the problems that faced people in this area. I wasn't happy about it."[15]

Cooke set out to change how the newspaper covered the city. The first woman news reporter in the forty-year history of the *Amsterdam News*, she investigated and reported major problems and then wrote stories in the literary style that she had developed at the *Crisis*. Specifically, Cooke pioneered in the newspaper's coverage of the human condition in black America. Cooke exposed the difficult working conditions of the dancers at the Apollo Theater and explored the questions surrounding euthanasia. She also wrote a five-part investigative series detailing the shocking increase in crime in Harlem.[16]

Because of her involvement in the Harlem Renaissance, Cooke also was committed to increasing the newspaper's coverage of the arts. Cooke believed, as did DuBois and other black intellectuals, that the arts were central to African-American life and culture. She recognized the functional relationship between arts and civil rights, convinced that the arts could play a major role in developing a national black identify and advancing her people's quest for reform.[17]

The most historic artistic event Cooke covered was Marian Anderson's performance in the nation's capital in 1939. When the Daughters of the American Revolution refused to allow the black contralto to sing at Constitution Hall, First Lady Eleanor Roosevelt resigned from the organization. Cooke then traveled to Washington, at her own expense, to provide eyewitness coverage of Anderson's performance at the Lincoln Memorial. Cooke's article combined the poignant details and the historic significance of the event: "Marian Anderson stood in quiet, majestic dignity on the steps of the white marble memorial to the emancipator in beautiful Potomac Park here Sunday afternoon and raised her glorious voice in stirring protest to the un-American attitude of the D.A.R." [18]

Cooke also sought out stories about African-American artists. She wrote profiles of a gospel singer who starred in a Broadway musical and of the first black designer to create sets and costumes for a Broadway production. While writing many positive stories, the forthright reporter never shied away from controversy. She criticized how the much-honored motion picture "Gone With the Wind" portrayed her race, and, when the New York Times panned an Ethel Waters performance, Cooke bristled: "Brooks Atkinson, erudite theatrical critic of the New York Times, can't see beyond his sniffling nose." [19]

Uncompromising in her opposition to injustice, Cooke balked at prejudice wherever she found it. When she went to a Park Avenue apartment building to interview a wealthy white woman but was told that blacks could not enter through the front door, Cooke refused to be ushered to a side entrance. She called the woman and told her that the interview could not take place. The woman then demanded that the building manager allow Cooke to enter through the front door. Only then did Cooke proceed with the interview. [20]

In the 1930s, Cooke organized a writer's group to support creative endeavors. Participants included Richard Wright, the first black writer to publish a Book-of-the-Month-Club selection, and George Murphy, editor of the Afro-American newspapers. [21]

In 1935, Cooke also helped organize a more controversial group, the country's first local newspaper guild at a black newspaper. Heywood Broun of the New York World-Telegram had sounded the call for a newspaper union in a 1933 column. Delegates then formed the American Newspaper Guild. Within five years, the guild had been involved in twenty strikes and had joined the Congress of Industrial Organizations. [22]

After several meetings in Cooke's apartment, the editorial staff of the Amsterdam News decided to form a local. When the newspaper's owner heard about the plans, she fired the entire editorial staff. The employees then picketed the newspaper, becoming the first black workers in American history to participate in a labor action against a black-owned business.[23]

During the lockout, the employees violated city restrictions on the number of picketers allowed to protest and were arrested for disorderly conduct. Some female strikers had been reluctant to join the picket line because it was not considered a ladylike activity, but the adventurous Cooke was always eager for new experiences. She said: "It thrilled me. I never minded getting out there on the picket line, and I enjoyed going to jail." The picketers were paroled within a day of their arrests, and charges later were dismissed.[24]

Ten weeks into the strike, the owner sold the newspaper to two businessmen who ended the lockout by giving the employees a 10 percent pay raise. It was the first time in American history that black workers had won a labor dispute.[25]

The dispute brought Cooke into contact with the Communist Party. Members of the party, which some historians believe had taken control of the American Newspaper Guild, supported the strike. Communist leaders recruited African Americans because they believed the U.S. government's mistreatment of blacks made them prospects for party membership. Blacks, partly because they were flattered by the attention, did not view the Communist Party with the same degree of hostility that white Americans did.[26]

The best-known of the Communists who picketed with the journalists was Benjamin J. Davis, who focused a great deal of attention on Cooke. Most black Communists were poorly educated factory workers; a well-educated member of the upper-class who worked as a journalist was very desirable to the party.[27]

Davis told Cooke that the party was committed to improving black living and working conditions. Cooke, remembering her father's support of socialism, listened. She later said: "The Constitution's fine; the Declaration of Independence is fine. But this country is not living up to the things that it proposes." In 1936, Cooke joined the party. If her publisher had known of her membership, she would have been fired.[28]

Cooke continued to write her own brand of stories for the *Amsterdam News*, but the newspaper remained dominated by photographs of crime victims lying dead on the street or in their caskets. In 1940, Cooke told her editor that she no longer would work for a sensationalistic newspaper.[29]

The defiant journalist was more pleased with the philosophy of the *People's Voice*, the next newspaper for which she worked. Cooke joined the staff in 1942, the same year that Adam Clayton Powell founded the weekly newspaper in which crime news was limited to a single column of brief items.[30]

Cooke became assistant managing editor, helping edit and design the newspaper. When the managing editor resigned, Cooke edited all stories and laid out all pages. Despite the increased responsibilities, Cooke was given neither his title nor an increase in salary because the management of *People's Voice* was not ready to promote a woman to the position of managing editor.[31]

Cooke accepted the sexual discrimination as a tradeoff for being allowed to expand the newspaper's arts coverage. Fredi Washington, a well-known actress, was hired to write about African-American theater. Cooke believed Washington could provide the best coverage of black theater in the country, but the actress was not a strong writer. Cooke, in her glib style, said: "Her copy was miserable. She couldn't write a straight line." So Cooke rewrote Washington's stories. Their combined articles were so good that a mainstream daily tried to recruit Washington, who declined because she knew she could not do a credible job without Cooke's editing. Cooke remained at *People's Voice* until the newspaper went out of business in 1947.[32]

In 1950, Cooke became the only African American and the only woman on the staff of the *Daily Compass*, a leftist New York daily whose star reporter was I.F. Stone. Taking the job also gave Cooke a place in journalism history, as she became the first American woman of African descent to write full-time for a white newspaper.[33]

Cooke's first story re-established her journalistic trademark, begun at the *Amsterdam News*, of writing compelling stories about the black human condition. The series, which Cooke proposed, provided an in-depth look at the Bronx Slave Market. Driven by poverty and desperation, black women stood on street corners and were "bought" for the day by white women who hired the workers to clean their homes. Cooke compared the phenomenon to southern plantation owners buying slaves. The workers were exploited in several ways. The white women paid fifty cents an hour, even though the minimum rate established by the New York Employment Service was twice that amount. Workers had no control over working conditions, and employers routinely turned back the hands of their clocks, shaving an hour or two from the wages they paid.[34]

For a firsthand view of the exploitation, Cooke worked as one of the domestics. She wrote: "I was part of the Bronx Slave Market long enough to experience all the viciousness and indignity of a system which forces women to the streets in search of work.

"Twice I was hired. Both times I went home mad—mad for all the Negro women down through the ages who have been lashed by the stinging whip of economic oppression."[35] Cooke's powerful indictment of the slave market included suggestions of how to reduce the injustices.[36]

The *Daily Compass* promoted the series on its front page and ran a photograph of Cooke washing windows in a white woman's home. In an editorial, the newspaper also pleaded with Mayor William O'Dwyer to end the exploitation. Cooke's exposé prompted reform, as the Domestic Workers Union and the State Employment Service organized training courses for household workers.[37]

Cooke's second blockbuster was on prostitution. "Occupation: Streetwalker" described the personal lives of the women as well as the inner workings of the vice squad, women's court, and women's prison. Cooke made full use of her literary style by focusing on a prostitute named Katie. Cooke wrote: "We were in a noisy, busy bar. A customer had put a pack of nickels in the gaudy juke box and Katie talked off-beat to the compelling rhythm of 'Rag Mop.' Ribbons of smoke swirled ceilingward between us, subtly veiling her features. Her hair wasn't red. It was burnished gold. And the scar on her cheek was scarcely visible. When I first met her, she looked hard and tired. Now she was almost pretty."[38] Cooke concluded the twelve-part series by proposing several reform measures.[39]

A third in-depth series—"From Candy to Heroin"—exposed drug use among African-American children. Cooke described the motivations of teenage drug addicts and the desperation of their parents. She also analyzed various drugs and their effects. The

dramatic series led New York City officials to initiate a program
to combat teenage drug addiction. Cooke remained on the staff
of the *Daily Compass* until it ceased publication in 1952.[40]

A year after Cooke left daily journalism, she became front-
page news herself when Senator Joseph McCarthy subpoenaed
her to testify before the Permanent Subcommittee on Investigations. Cooke had been called because McCarthy was investigat-
ing Doris Powell, whom he accused of being a member of the
Communist Party. Powell had worked at *People's Voice* with
Cooke and later had worked for the United States Army.[41]

Cooke's only ongoing activity with the party had been subscribing to its publications. During the hearing, however, Mc-
Carthy accused her of being a major party leader. He asked her:
"Were you what could be referred to as the Communist Party
whip at that paper?" "Were you known by the other employees
as 'Mrs. Commissar'?" "It has been testified by a number of witnesses that you held a position so high that you gave orders to
the Communist National Committee. Would you tell us whether
that testimony is true?" Cooke refused to answer McCarthy's
questions, citing the Fifth Amendment to the Constitution.[42]

McCarthy never again contacted Cooke, but her appearance
before the subcommittee received a great deal of press coverage.
The *New York Times* published the story on the front page, and
the *New York Daily News*, *Washington Post*, and *Washington
Evening Star* also ran prominent stories.[43]

Cooke remained in the Communist Party and continued her
involvement in the arts. In 1953 she became New York director
of the Council of Arts, Sciences and Professions, a political organization whose members included such well-known artists as Arthur Miller and John Randolph.[44]

In 1969, Communist Party officials asked Cooke to work
with the Angela Davis Defense Committee. For the next two
years, Cooke coordinated committee activities in New York, organizing a rally at Madison Square Garden that attracted sixteen
thousand people and raised $40,000 for Davis's defense.[45]

Cooke's major activity now is volunteering with the National
Council for American-Soviet Friendship. The council operates
exchange programs through which Russian professionals tour
the United States and children from all over the world attend
camp in Russia. She serves as the council's vice chairwoman.[46]

Marvel Cooke continues to live in the same Harlem apartment building where she moved in 1926. The intractable Cooke also remains critical of newspapers in general and African-American newspapers in particular. She said: "I don't trust what the papers are. I read them all the time, but I don't necessarily trust them." [47]

8

CHARLOTTA A. BASS
Radical Precursor of the Black Power Movement

In the years immediately following the assassination of Malcolm X in 1965, the Black Power Movement that he had led was vilified as too radical, too extreme. In retrospect, however, a strong respect for the movement's themes has emerged. One area of scholarly interest has been exploration of the roots of Black Power, with many historians tracing the beginnings of the movement to protests that took place during the first half of the twentieth century.[1]

One dynamic leader of black America during those decades of dissidence was Charlotta A. Bass, editor and publisher of the *California Eagle* from 1912 to 1951. Bass fought for equal rights for the millions of African Americans who moved to the West Coast during the migration of the World War I and II era, pitting them against the hegemonic white establishment. As a vehicle for Bass's demands, the *Eagle* became a lightning rod for protest, and she became a target of hatred and violence. She wrote: "When a person, an organization, even a newspaper gets the courage and fortitude that it is going to require to put this old world in such condition that it will be a fit and happy abode for all the people, they must first be prepared to have their heads cracked, their hopes frustrated, and their financial strength weakened."[2]

Bass suffered verbal and physical abuse, libel suits, unlawful arrests, and death threats, but she remained uncompromising in her war against racism. Consequences be damned, the crusading journalist used her fiercely militant newspaper as a forum for blistering attacks on the motion picture industry, Ku Klux Klan, Southern California Telephone Company, Boulder Dam, restrictive housing covenants, among other discriminatory organizations and practices. She blasted wrongdoers on the pages of her newspaper and mobilized the African-American community of Los Angeles as no one before her had been able to.

In 1952, Bass made history by becoming the first American woman of African descent to seek national office, campaigning for vice president on the Progressive Party ticket. When the anti-Communist fervor caught fire, Bass's radicalism became the subject of investigations by numerous agencies of the federal government—including the FBI, Post Office, CIA, State Department, and War Department.

Charlotta Amanda Spear was born February 14, 1874, in Sumter, South Carolina, the sixth of eleven children born to Hiram and Kate Spear. After graduating from public schools, Charlotta attended Penbroke College for one semester. She then moved to Providence, Rhode Island, to live with an older brother and to work as an "office girl" for the *Providence Watchman*.[3]

In 1910, health problems forced Spear to relocate to the warmer climate of Los Angeles. John Neimore, who had founded the *California Eagle* in 1879, paid her five dollars a week to sell subscriptions. On his deathbed in 1912, Neimore asked Spear to assume the editorship of the *Eagle*, then the state's oldest black newspaper. When the weekly was sold at public auction two months later, Spear bought it for fifty dollars. She then became publisher, editor, reporter, business manager, distributor, printer, and janitor. To strengthen her abilities, Spear completed journalism courses at the University of California and correspondence courses through Columbia University.[4]

In 1913, Spear hired Joseph Bass, a fifty-year-old veteran journalist who had edited the *Topeka Plain Dealer* and had founded the *Montana Plain Dealer*. Spear hired Bass as a reporter, but he soon advanced to editor, with Spear as managing editor. Bass and Spear married in 1914.[5]

The crusade that established the *Eagle*'s activist tradition was that against D.W. Griffith's 1915 motion picture "Birth of a Nation." Because of the film's negative depiction of blacks, Charlotta Bass tried to block its production. Even though Griffith was one of Hollywood's leading producers, Bass refused to be intimidated. She wrote: "As long as the Afro-Americans of this country sit supinely by and raise no voice against the injustice heaped upon them, conditions for them in this country will grow worse."[6] Griffith took the battle to court. When dozens of workers—black as well as white—argued that they should not be denied the high wages that Griffith was willing to pay, Bass lost.[7]

Word that Bass had challenged the motion picture industry spread rapidly through black America, and soon her spirit of resistance was in demand by downtrodden African Americans all over the country. In 1915 she told Texas farmers to rebel against their employer, Herbert C. Hoover; in 1917, she spoke fiery words to workers in Kansas City, Chicago, Boston, and New York City. Bass used her speeches to increase subscriptions, expanding the *Eagle*'s circulation far beyond California.[8]

As Bass traveled around the country, the racial injustices that she witnessed broadened her world view. Her emerging radical philosophy also was shaped by her contact with two of the most influential black leaders of the era. The first was W.E.B. DuBois; Bass attended the 1919 Pan-African Conference, which DuBois led in Paris. The second was Marcus Garvey; Bass served as co-president of the Los Angeles branch of Garvey's United Negro Improvement Association during the 1920s. Bass became increasingly convinced that the catalyst for change lay in American blacks uniting into one powerful force, presaging the black nationalist strategy of Malcolm X.[9]

Discriminatory hiring practices were Bass's first target. In 1919, she reported that the Los Angeles County Board of Supervisors refused to hire African Americans to work at the county hospital. When the story provoked no response, she appealed directly to the supervisors. They accepted Bass's argument and agreed to hire black nurse's aides, with only one stipulation—that Bass first interview the applicants and select the best of them. After a year of placing efficient workers in the jobs, Bass eliminated herself from the process.[10]

The editor's next major battle was during the 1920s against the Ku Klux Klan. She exposed the fact that white supremacists had attempted to burn a black family's house and that the Klan was distributing hate literature in Watts. In retaliation, the letters "KKK" were painted a foot high on the sidewalk in front of the *Eagle* office, and Bass received phone calls throughout the day and night: "Is this that nigger newspaper?" "Is this that nigger woman who owns that dirty rag called the *Eagle?*"[11]

Undeterred, Bass delivered a body blow to the Klan when she obtained and printed a letter signed by G.W. Price, the leader of the Klan in California. The letter outlined a plot to rid Los Angeles of its three most effective black leaders by involving them in a traffic accident and having them unfairly convicted of driving while intoxicated. The letter stated: "We could plant a bottle of booze in the enemy's car."

Price sued Bass for libel, a crime that carried a penalty of one year in prison, and damages of five thousand dollars. Price offered to drop the charges if Bass publicly stated that the letter was a fraud. She would have none of it. Instead, the editor fought the charges in an all-white courtroom. Using the editorial "we," she wrote: "If to jail we must go for publishing without malice such propaganda as we in common with all fair minded citizens believe to be prejudicial to good government, we go with a smile and feel that we are rendering a greater service for the protection of society than our fondest imagination would ever make us believe. We go forward unafraid as we continue our steady march for law and order, fighting every inch of the way all things which retard our progress."[12]

Bass won. The triumphant editor boasted: "Heretofore Price had met all the forces against him and won his battles; it remained for the *Eagle* editor representing the Colored group of our citizenship to lay him low."[13]

After the courts failed the vigilantes, they took the law into their own hands. One night when Bass was alone in the *Eagle* office, eight hooded men appeared on the sidewalk in front of the building, staring at her through the plate-glass window. When they demanded that Bass let them inside the building, the fearless editor went to a desk drawer, pulled out a gun, and aimed it at the would-be intruders. The men beat a hasty retreat.[14]

Bass walked fearlessly into the eye of many hurricanes. Joseph Bass supported his wife but sometimes feared for her safety, as well as his own. When he said: "Mrs. Bass, one of these days you are going to get me killed." She responded: "Mr. Bass, it will be in a good cause."[15]

For Charlotta Bass, there were many causes worthy of jeopardizing her safety. During desegregation efforts at a city high school, she worked her way to the center of the crowd—as students yelled, "No niggers wanted here!"—to talk directly to the leaders. While speaking at an anti-draft rally, she was pelted with rotten apples. As she investigated government prejudice against unemployed workers during the Depression, Bass was arrested for disorderly conduct.[16]

The combative editor considered such harassment a small price to pay for the victories that she continued to amass. By 1930, she had become a driving force in the black labor movement that was sweeping the country. The "Don't Spend Where You Can't Work" campaign originated in Chicago, urging blacks to boycott businesses that refused to employ black workers. Bass brought the controversial campaign to Los Angeles, using it against several local employers.[17]

A textbook example of how the campaign worked involved the Southern California Telephone Company. When the monopoly rejected Bass's request that it employ black workers, she convinced black customers to cancel their telephone service, each attributing the action to the all-white hiring policy. When the cancellations reached one hundred, company officials relented and hired their first African-American worker.[18]

Bass founded and was elected president of the Industrial Council, a Los Angeles organization formed to combat unjust hiring policies. Bass's strategy to fight job discrimination ranged from the logic of journalistic prose to the diplomacy of negotiation to the stridency of activism. For example, her scathing editorials were sufficient to change the policy of the Los Angeles City Fire Department. But when similar editorials failed to convince Boulder Dam officials to hire blacks to help construct the facility, Bass joined company officials at the bargaining table.

And when both editorials and personal appeals failed to change the Los Angeles Railway's ban on black employees, Bass mobilized fifteen hundred angry citizens to march against the company. Regardless of the strategy, the outcome eventually was the same: an end to discriminatory hiring.[19]

Although Bass initially represented black workers, she gradually became a spokeswoman for all industrial workers. She promoted integrated strikes, saying that management traditionally had pitted blacks and whites against each other. During the first interracial strike in American history, she encouraged employees of the American Tobacco Company to remain united, writing: "United we stand, divided we fall is a hackneyed phrase, but it makes sense here. These white and Negro workers are the slaves, the victims, of the industrial bosses. All their off-time from labor has been spent fighting each other instead of fighting the forces that keep them miserable in their poverty."[20]

While fighting Goliaths, the "Soaring *Eagle*" did not ignore the Davids. Representative of the hundreds of victims who brought their personal sorrows to Bass was nineteen-year-old Eva Cooper. She told Bass that her white "master" had brought her from Louisiana to California to work as a domestic but had paid her nothing but an occasional quarter. In eleven years, Cooper had been given $13.75—and numerous beatings. Bass not only reported the abuse on the front page of the *Eagle* but also took the man to court, forcing him to pay Cooper's back wages and a fifty-dollar fine.[21]

Charlotta Bass had a high public profile, but she and Joseph Bass actually worked as a team. She provided the editorial voice; he kept the business solvent. By 1925, the *California Eagle* employed a staff of twelve and published twenty pages a week. The *Eagle*'s circulation of sixty thousand made it the largest African-American newspaper on the West Coast.[22]

The formidable publishing team began to lose momentum in the 1930s, however, when illness forced Joseph Bass to spend much of his time in bed. When he died in 1934, Charlotta Bass, who never had children, incorporated the business in order to bring in the capital to expand her national coverage.[23]

The crusade that moved Bass onto the national stage was restrictive housing covenants. As early as 1900, segregationists had begun signing petitions to prevent nonwhites from living in their neighborhoods. Such covenants multiplied as more African

Americans migrated to Los Angeles. In 1945, Bass formed the Home Owners Protective Association to fight the covenants.[24]

The group's first victory was in the "Sugar Hill" case. Thirty black doctors, lawyers, and entertainers—including actresses Hattie McDaniel, Louise Beavers, and Ethel Waters—had purchased homes in an affluent neighborhood. When white residents passed a covenant to force the wealthy homeowners to move, they turned to Bass. She advised them to unite and hire a lawyer; they won the case.[25]

Buoyed by that success, Bass fought restrictive covenants in middle- and lower-class neighborhoods as well. In 1930, Henry and Anna Laws had bought a plot of land and built a house on it. Twelve years later, two real estate agents suddenly announced that a covenant restricted who could live on the property, and a judge ruled that the Laws family had to abandon their home. They took their case to Bass. Her campaign on their behalf began in the pages of her newspaper where she wrote about the "fascist" real estate agents and reported the judge's decision by stating: "After listening to a plea that would have stirred the sympathetic emotions of Hitler, Judge [Allen W.] Ashburn, unmoved, ordered Henry and Anna Laws to vacate their home."[26]

Upon reading that statement, the judge said that if the Laws family did not vacate the house, he would have them arrested and imprisoned for contempt of court. They took Bass's advice and stayed in their home. The judge placed the couple and their daughter in jail indefinitely. Enraged, Bass organized a picket line around the Laws home, directing her readers to "come to the *Eagle* office. Demonstrate your indignation by signing up for duty on the picket line." She also organized a massive demonstration that drew one thousand protesters. After a week of headlines and demonstrations, the judge released the Laws family from jail. Bass had turned the tide.[27]

Bass and other leaders then pushed the housing covenant issue to the California Supreme Court. Finally, in 1948, the United States Supreme Court ruled such covenants to be unconstitutional. Bass had won her first national victory.[28]

Despite Bass's remarkable record of victories, one institution that even her courage and commitment failed to reform was that of law enforcement. Bass used blunt language to describe what she considered to be police wrongdoings. Typical was an incident in which a white police officer said he had killed a young black veteran in self-defense because the man had threatened him with a knife. Bass interviewed the officers who had investigated the shooting, however, and learned there had been no trace of a knife. So she began her front-page story: "Another in a series of police brutalities, resulting in a near riot, occurred here early Saturday night."[29] In successive weeks, the *Eagle* carried two-inch-high headlines across page one, such as: "'TRIGGER-HAPPY' COP FREED AFTER SLAYING YOUTH" and "POLICE BRUTALITY FLARES UP AGAIN."[30]

Simultaneously, Bass moved into her familiar role of community activist. She organized a mass meeting, with more than one thousand people heeding her call. By the end of the session, Bass had prepared a list of four recommendations that she later took to city officials. Those proposals included the Los Angeles Police Department hiring more black officers and requiring white officers to complete courses in racial sensitivity.[31] Despite the editor's efforts, the recommendations were not enacted, however, and the city's reputation for police brutality grew to national proportion.

The early 1940s also saw the rise of another nemesis that would plague Bass for the rest of her life. During the World War II era, publishers of black newspapers became targets of the federal government. Because the newspapers favored the country increasing the human rights of black Americans rather than becoming involved in an international conflict, the government considered black newspaper publishers a threat to national security. Many federal officials favored indicting publishers, including Bass, for sedition.[32]

The Office of the Secretary of War monitored the African-American press. From 1940 to 1947, the office prepared a biweekly report summarizing the events and issues discussed in the newspapers. The report contained dozens of quotations from Bass's weekly column, "On the Sidewalk."[33]

FBI agents arrived unannounced at the *Eagle* office in March 1942 and interrogated Bass, suggesting that her newspaper was financed by Germany and Japan. From that time forward, agents read each issue of the *Eagle* and attended Bass's public speeches, writing confidential reports directly to J. Edgar Hoover.[34]

The bulk of the 563 pages in Bass's FBI file consist of summaries of *Eagle* articles, as the agents considered all statements in support of increased rights for African Americans to be evidence not that she advocated racial justice but that she advocated Communism over democracy. Typical was the comment: "She follows the Communist Party 'Line,' advocating abolition of poll tax, abolition of 'Jim Crow,' etc." In their reports, the agents routinely called Bass a Communist and the *Eagle* a "Communist Party mouthpiece," even though there is no evidence that Bass ever joined the Communist Party.[35]

The Post Office Department also investigated the *Eagle*. In 1943, postal officials asked the Department of Justice to revoke Bass's second-class mailing permit because her newspaper contained subversive material that was illegal to send through the mail. The memo cited an article by Bass that began: "Disturbances which indicate growing racial tension in the city echoed through downtown streets this week." The article summarized several skirmishes that had been reported to the police. Post Office officials stated: "The reading of these statements will create fear and hatred of the white race."[36]

Bass did not cower. She wrote: "The people I speak to weekly through this column know whether or not the things I say are true. I have presented facts gleaned from the most reliable sources at my command with the hope that the racial segment with which my own destiny is linked, and all minorities, may see the light and join the fight for their own and a lasting freedom."[37]

Justice Department officials agreed with Bass. They called her report legitimate and factual news, and they refused to revoke her mailing permit.[38]

After the case was resolved, Bass continued to defend the Communist philosophy. She wrote sarcastically: "Why should we be so afraid of that word Communism? That weapon [is] used by the monopolists to frighten us into voting for their candidates, who would make laws only for their benefit and perhaps grant us a free dinner Thanksgiving or Christmas."[39]

Simultaneous with the investigations, Bass moved into her most strident political phase by becoming a candidate for public office. The move was a logical one as Bass gradually had become recognized as an able leader. She had been the first African American to serve on a Los Angeles grand jury, had served on the executive board of the Los Angeles branch of the National Association for the Advancement of Colored People, and had launched a battleship.[40]

Politically, Bass and the *Eagle* had been affiliated with the Republican Party, and Bass had served as western regional director for Wendell Wilkie's 1940 presidential campaign. Bass became frustrated, however, by the Republican Party's lack of progress in racial reform.[41]

So, in 1944, Bass ran as the Progressive Party candidate for U.S. Congress from the 14th congressional district, and in 1945 she ran in the nonpartisan race for Los Angeles City Council. Although Bass received considerable grassroots support from Los Angeles churches, she suffered decisive defeats in both elections. In 1948 she served as national co-chairwoman of Women for Wallace when Henry A. Wallace, who had been vice president under Franklin Roosevelt, ran for president on the Progressive Party ticket.[42]

Bass's attempts to win public office prompted a flurry of attacks and accusations against her. In 1945, the Ku Klux Klan threatened to kill her if she did not drop out of the city council race. In 1948, the *New York Daily News* and *Los Angeles Tribune*, a moderate black weekly, identified Bass as a member of the Communist Party. She denied the allegations and demanded that the newspapers retract their statements.[43]

Bass moved ever further to the left. In 1946, she called for American troops to leave China, and, in 1950, she opposed American military involvement in Korea, attended a peace conference in Czechoslovakia, and traveled to the Soviet Union. When Los Angeles FBI agents learned of Bass's travel plans, they alerted New York agents to look for a suspect described as "short, elderly, negro, female, gray hair, fat, wearing glasses, waddling walk." CIA agents followed Bass while she was outside the country. After her trip, she wrote articles for *Soviet Russia Today* and the American Communist Party newspaper, praising the positive racial attitudes among the Soviets.[44]

These activities fueled more accusations that Bass was a Communist. In 1951 the State Department determined that she was so dangerous to national security that she should not be allowed to leave the United States. When an agent demanded her passport, however, Bass refused to relinquish it. Iota Phi Lambda, a service sorority that had awarded Bass honorary membership in 1948, rescinded the honor.[45]

In 1951, Bass sold the *Eagle* and moved to New York City, the national headquarters of the Progressive Party, to devote all of her time and energy to the party. She had become so determined to change American society through politics that she was willing to sacrifice her forty-year investment in journalism.[46]

In 1952, Bass became the Progressive Party candidate for vice president. By this time, Wallace had left the party, which had become widely identified with Communism. Bass and her running mate, California lawyer Vincent Hallinan, crisscrossed the country to put their platform before the American people. Their militant message proved unpopular, however, and the ticket received only one-fifth of 1 percent of the vote.[47]

The strenuous campaign exacerbated Bass's longtime battle with arthritis. On her doctor's orders, she retired to smalltown life in Elsinore, a community near Los Angeles. She purchased a small home and transformed the garage into a community reading room. At seventy years of age, she supported the modern civil rights movement by establishing the reading room as a voter registration site for African Americans.[48]

Although Bass had left both the newspaper and political arenas, she was neither inactive nor silent. She frequently presented speeches to church groups and civic organizations, and a testimonial dinner honored her as the "dean of Negro newspaper women." In 1960 she published her book, *Forty Years: Memoirs from the Pages of a Newspaper*, which focused on the relationship between the *California Eagle* and the Los Angeles community. She joined protests against persecution of blacks in South Africa and continued her vehement denial that she was a member of the Communist Party.[49]

The clearest connection between Charlotta Bass and the Black Power Movement came in the early 1960s. Although Bass and Malcolm X never met, their radical messages shared the fundamental themes of rebuking the social order of white America and calling for black nationalism. Bass's final years were her most vitriolic as she attacked not only America's presence in Southeast Asia but also the country's space program. After three-quarters of a century of fierce efforts to bring about racial justice, she had witnessed only marginal progress. She ended one of her last speeches with a threat that could have as easily been delivered by Malcolm X, though he was fifty years her junior: "Beware, ye nations of the world! The people are speaking out louder and more coherently than ever before in their demand for peace and their share of the fruits of their labor. And in the language of Andrew Jackson, 'By the Eternal' they are going to have them!"[50]

Bass suffered a stroke in 1966 and was placed in a Los Angeles nursing home. FBI agents continued to monitor and report on her activities; as late as 1967, when Bass was ninety-one years old and had been residing in the nursing home for a year, agents still classified her as "potentially dangerous." Charlotta Bass died of a cerebral hemorrhage on April 12, 1969, at the age of ninety-five.[51]

9

ALICE ALLISON DUNNIGAN
Champion of the Decline of Jim Crow

World War II was a watershed event in the history of American women as well as American blacks, as the war effort demanded all human resources—female as well as male, black as well as white. During the war, millions of African Americans left the South in search of jobs, and, after the war, the critical mass of black Americans in northern cities brought a new intensity to the drive for racial equality. Political, labor, and religious groups pressed from the private sector, while President Harry S. Truman led governmental reform by desegregating the military and promising equal employment throughout the federal government. The Supreme Court and federal agencies overseeing housing and employment followed suit. Leading the northern cities was the nation's capital itself. Washington's public parks, playgrounds, and swimming pools opened their facilities to African Americans; hotels, theaters, and restaurants began to desegregate. As the nation entered the second half of the twentieth century, many forces combined to make both the nation and the nation's capital a better place for Americans of African descent to live.[1]

Alice Allison Dunnigan was a woman who did not allow the parade of life to pass her by. Her childhood dream was to experience the world through the ubiquitous life of a newspaper reporter. When the war offered her a chance to escape the poverty and deprivation of rural Kentucky, Dunnigan did not think twice. In 1942, she moved to Washington.

In 1947, the determined Dunnigan broke new ground by becoming the first African-American woman accredited to cover Congress. As the Washington reporter for a national black news service until 1961, Dunnigan chronicled the decline of Jim Crow in the North. She wrote: "Black people of every generation since the days of slavery have had to fight their share of battles for consideration, recognition or respectability, and it is very fortunate that there has been a fearless Black press to record some of these victories. Incidents perhaps never would have been brought to public attention had there not been Black reporters."[2]

Dunnigan was one of those brave and noble reporters. She was neither gifted as a writer nor schooled in the principles of journalism, but the racial and sexual discrimination that Dunnigan had suffered in her own life combined with her indomitable spirit compelled her to become an aggressive, streetwise reporter. Dunnigan successfully used the power of the press to trumpet to all of black America that the gap between the principle and the practice of American democracy was beginning to close.

Alice Allison, the granddaughter of slaves, was born April 27, 1906, in a rural area near Russellville, Kentucky. Her father, Willie Allison, was a sharecropper, and her mother, Lena Pittman Allison, took in laundry. At age four, Alice began walking four miles a day to a one-room schoolhouse.[3]

Alice was drawn to journalism to cope with her parents' insensitivity: her mother told Alice she was so physically unattractive that no man would marry her, and her father said it was a waste for a girl to go to school. So Alice turned to fantasy, dreaming that someday she would enter the exciting world of newspapers. She promised herself: "When I grow up, I'll never again feel ashamed of myself. I'll write for a newspaper and let people know what other people are doing."[4] At the age of thirteen, she began writing one-sentence items about church activities for the *Owensboro Enterprise*, a black newspaper in another Kentucky town.[5]

But as Alice Allison was growing up in the rural South, only two occupations were open to African-American women: teaching black students and cleaning white houses. Alice chose teaching, the option closer to journalism. She graduated at the top of her high school class, and, with a personal loan from a local dentist, paid her first year's tuition at Kentucky Normal and Industrial Institute. Even with a part-time job washing dishes, however, she was able to complete only her freshman year.[6]

Poverty continued to plague Allison when, at age eighteen, she began teaching in a one-room schoolhouse near her hometown. In 1924, she was paid five hundred dollars a year. By 1942, that figure had increased only to eight hundred—still barely half the national average. Because of her low salary, Allison also hired herself out to clean houses, wash clothes, and cook meals for white families. She was paid $1.50 for an entire week's work.[7]

Allison struggled in her personal life as well. Soon after her 1926 marriage to Walter Dickinson, the nineteen-year-old young woman learned that her husband, a dirt farmer, had no respect for education—or educators. The marriage lasted four years. A year later, she married Charles Dunnigan, a childhood playmate, and the next year, in 1932, she gave birth to a son, Robert. Alice Dunnigan then faced one of the most difficult decisions of her life. She wanted to continue to teach, but she also felt the need to remain at home and care for her child. When Robert was four months old, Dunnigan turned him over to her parents so that she could pursue her career. The boy did not live with his mother for the next seventeen years. Dunnigan also faced difficulties in her second marriage, as her husband, a maintenance worker, wanted her to devote her life to housekeeping. Within two years after their wedding, the Dunnigan marriage had deteriorated, and Alice Dunnigan became the victim of mental and physical cruelty. She went her own way in 1940, although the marriage continued on paper for another decade.[8]

Throughout Dunnigan's eighteen years of teaching, she kept her childhood dream alive by writing part-time for African-American newspapers. The *Louisville Defender* published her sketches of prominent black Kentuckians; the *Louisville Leader* published her series on black women. In the summer of 1935, she worked as society editor for the *Leader*.[9]

When World War II began, Dunnigan became the first African

American from Logan County, Kentucky, to complete a federal civil service examination. After successfully passing the exam, she accepted a job in Washington, D.C., transplanting herself from the rural South and the security of her familiar environment to a large northern city.[10]

In Washington, Dunnigan finally tasted life beyond poverty. As a clerk-typist for the War Labor Board, she earned $1,440 a year, twice her teaching salary. After a year of night school at Howard University, she was promoted to the position of economist for the Office of Price Administration. By 1946, Dunnigan's salary had climbed to $2,600, twice that of the average African-American woman in Washington.[11]

Despite Dunnigan's improved financial status, her dream of becoming a newspaper reporter remained unfulfilled. So in 1946, she began writing part-time for the Associated Negro Press. Claude A. Barnett, a reporter for the *Chicago Defender*, had founded the national news service in 1919. From its base in Chicago, ANP provided one hundred black newspapers in the United States and Africa with news of events not reported in the mainstream press. Barnett covered the nation's capital by employing four men part-time. After adding Dunnigan to his stable, he wrote a colleague: "Mrs. Dunnigan is an inveterate meeting attender and likes to go to banquets."[12]

By the end of 1946, Barnett had decided that the Washington beat demanded a full-time correspondent. He approached one of his part-time reporters, offering the man $200 a month. When the man turned him down, Barnett offered the job to another man for $250 a month. When the second man also rejected the offer, Barnett approached Dunnigan, but his personal correspondence that has been preserved documents a startling example of the wage discrimination that has plagued generations of women. Dunnigan accepted Barnett's job offer at a salary of only $100 a month.[13]

Barnett also was chauvinistic in his attitude toward women's abilities. He later told Dunnigan: "I was not confident that a girl could do the type of job we needed in Washington." Dunnigan refused to ignore the prejudice of such a statement, telling her new boss: "Should a Negro apply for a job with a white concern and was told that he could not be employed because a man of color could not do the type of work they wanted, there would be a tremendous howl coming from the press. When, on the other hand, one of our own group says he is skeptical about hiring a woman because she may not be able to fill the needs, that is alright [sic]. Same principal [sic]. Segregation is segregation, a minority is a minority." [14]

Ironically, such spunky protests convinced Barnett to hire Dunnigan. He told her: "You have the ambition, the courage, the nerve to make a great name for yourself." Another time, Barnett told her: "I am convinced you will make of yourself an exceptional news woman by sheer grit and determination." [15]

Dunnigan's tenacity was next tested by the Congressional Press Galleries. In January 1947, Dunnigan's childhood dream of becoming a reporter finally had come true. Her first assignment was to cover the ousting of Senator Theodore Bilbo, a racist from Mississippi, for conduct unbecoming to his office. But when Dunnigan arrived at the Capitol, she was told that the gallery was for white reporters only. [16]

A day she would wait; a lifetime she would not. The next morning, she applied to the Standing Committee of Correspondents for press credentials. Her request coincided with Louis Lautier's campaign to integrate the galleries. Lautier was Washington correspondent for the *Atlanta Daily World*, the only black daily in the country. When the Standing Committee rejected Lautier's application, he appealed to the Senate Committee on Rules and Administration, which conducted a hearing on the issue. At the end of the hearing, the Rules Committee overruled the Standing Committee and accredited Lautier. The senators also said other reporters from the African-American press should be given access to the galleries. [17]

On June 17, 1947, Dunnigan became the first African-American woman in history accredited to cover the United States Congress. The persistent Dunnigan promptly secured similar credentials to cover the White House, Supreme Court, and State Department. After receiving her full accreditation, Dunnigan, who was not always a modest woman, hired a professional photographer to capture her image on the Capitol steps. She then paid for prints to be sent to all ANP newspapers, even though it cost her more than a week's salary. [18]

Dunnigan made another breakthrough a year later by becoming the first black woman journalist to travel with a president of the United States, joining President Truman for a cross-country train trip during his re-election campaign. Barnett did not support Dunnigan's effort, and he refused to pay the one-thousand-dollar fee charged to all reporters. His prejudice against women played a role in his decision, as he later wrote: "I did not think a woman could do the best job on a jaunt of that kind." Dunnigan was determined, regardless of Barnett's opposition. She cut expenses to the bone and secured a five-hundred-dollar personal loan to pay for the two-week trip. It took her a year to repay the money.[19]

Although the trip put Dunnigan into contact with the country's leading political reporters, it did not imbue her with the ability to write graceful or grammatically correct prose. Throughout Dunnigan's reporting career, Associated Negro Press editors criticized her writing and rewrote much of the copy that she submitted. Frank Marshall Davis, ANP executive editor, told her she used too many words, buried news angles, wrote incomplete sentences, made capitalization errors, used the wrong pronouns, and created words that did not exist. Barnett hired a Howard University professor to tutor Dunnigan with her writing.[20]

Because Dunnigan's articles were edited in the Chicago office before they appeared in ANP newspapers, her published work does not accurately reflect the quality of her writing. One original article written during the trip and preserved in the Claude A. Barnett Papers, however, provides abundant examples of Dunnigan's writing problems. The lead paragraph reads: "A peaceful relationship between the United States government and the Nebraska Indians was cemented Sunday when Ed White Buffalo, chief of the Sioux Indian tribe climbed on the rear platform of the President's special at Grand Islands Neb. and presented Mr. Truman with a peace pipe and a plaque which read 'Peace to All', and was signed 'The Sioux Indians of Nebraska'."[21] In addition to such problems as the excessive length for a news lead, punctuation errors, awkward phrasing, and convoluted meaning, the article's idea that the presentation of a peace pipe "cemented" relations between the government and the Indian people suggests reportorial naïveté.

An incident during the trip became significant in Dunnigan's career. In Cheyenne, Wyoming, transportation had not been provided for the press corps. So when the president left the train, sixty reporters began walking behind his motorcade. Dunnigan, wearing a press badge three inches in diameter, was the only African American and the only woman among the reporters. Soldiers kept the crowd behind ropes at the edge of the street. Suddenly a military policeman stepped forward and grabbed Dunnigan, yelling: "Get back there behind those ropes!" Too startled to speak, Dunnigan continued to walk forward with the other reporters. The soldier then grabbed her and shoved her toward the edge of the street. Again she continued to walk forward. Only when a white male reporter came to Dunnigan's rescue did the officer back away. The incident made national headlines.[22]

Two days later, Dunnigan was in her compartment on the train typing a story, with her bare feet propped up on the opposite seat and her typewriter on her lap. After a tap at the door, in stepped President Truman. Dunnigan tried to stand, but she could not move because the typewriter was across her lap. So there she sat with her bare toes sticking up as she bounced up and down on the seat, making a futile attempt to stand. "I didn't know what to do," Dunnigan said when recounting the moment. "I tugged at my skirt. I couldn't find my shoes. I knew I should be standing up, but I couldn't move. Then President Truman said, very quietly, 'I heard you had a little trouble. Well, if anything else happens, please let me know.'" Dunnigan credited Truman's words of encouragement with enabling her to ask tough questions to sources at the highest levels of government.[23]

Dunnigan's journalistic work provided a continuous stream of articles chronicling instances of desegregation in government as well as business. Hers was a singular role because she was the only Washington reporter of the era writing to a national audience of black Americans. ANP was a national news service with outlets all across the country; other African-American news organizations covering Washington reached only the readers in their respective cities.[24]

So it was Dunnigan, more than any other reporter, who informed black America that Jim Crow was dying. By ensuring widespread awareness of this progress, Dunnigan bolstered the pride and self-esteem of African Americans throughout the country, helping to galvanize them into a united force that would, during the late 1950s and 1960s, demand their civil rights.

Typical of Dunnigan's stories was one that reported how a Washington hotel had become the first in the city to accommodate

African-American guests. The sixty New York state delegates to
Truman's 1949 inauguration had registered in advance but had
not mentioned to the hotel that eighteen of their members were
black. When the delegation arrived, the hotel manager refused to
register the African Americans in the group. The leader of the
delegation then insisted that if black delegates were not allowed to
stay in the hotel, the entire delegation would cancel its reservation.
Fearing a loss of revenue, the hotel allowed everyone to register.
Dunnigan began her news story by citing it as a symbol of the
progress that would be made during Truman's administration.
Dunnigan, a staunch Democrat, wrote: "Civil Rights got a prelim-
inary start in the Truman administration with defeat of jim crow
by the New York delegation at the Roosevelt hotel here." [25]

Dunnigan's story was published in black newspapers from
Ohio to Texas, but the incident was not reported in the mainstream press. As with many incidents that Dunnigan wrote
about, her story was the only one that documented the advancement toward racial equality. If Dunnigan had not recorded such
incidents, they would have gone unnoticed. [26]

Many of the successes that Dunnigan reported did not occur
quickly. In 1949, for example, local civil rights activists initiated
a challenge to segregation in Washington restaurants, basing
their argument on a nineteenth-century statute requiring service
to "all well-behaved" persons. For four years, Dunnigan perse-
vered in following the case from municipal court, to municipal
appeals court, to federal appeals court, to the United States Supreme Court, where it led to desegregation of city restaurants in
1953. [27]

Other desegregation victories Dunnigan reported included
African Americans being allowed to use movie theaters, city-
operated playgrounds, public housing, a summer camp, Washington National Airport, a teacher's college, and the swimming
pool at the Sheraton-Park Hotel. [28]

Dunnigan also made readers around the country aware of
the employment battles that Washington's black community was
winning. She reported when the Washington Urban League succeeded in breaking down segregation barriers in city newspapers,
leading the *Washington Post* to hire its first black reporter. Dunnigan also documented desegregation of the local bar association
and telephone and transit companies. [29]

By the early 1950s, Dunnigan had built a reputation as a hard-hitting journalist. In 1951, she was named "Newsman's Newsman" as the best African-American reporter in Washington, becoming the first woman to win the award.[30]

Dunnigan was pleased with the honor, but she was more pleased that she was helping to change American history by documenting the desegregation of Capitol Hill. She wrote: "I am proud to have seen, and been a part of, the complete racial evolution in this country. I am proud to have witnessed the appointment of the first Black man to the Capitol police force. I was elated to have the privilege of interviewing the first Black pageboy on Capitol Hill. I was proud to have seen Edward Brooke of Massachusetts come to the Senate of the United States in 1966, being the first Black man to grace that hallowed hall since Reconstruction."[31]

At the same time, when the intractable Dunnigan found indications of lingering racism, she did not hesitate to share her discovery with her readers. When the first African-American secretary at the White House said she would "go to the places I'm supposed to go and stay away from places where I'm not supposed to go," Dunnigan wrote a column that included the fiery retort: "All Americans under the Constitution are equal, or no Americans are equal, and to compromise this basic principle by accepting a Negro 'place' in the Nation's capital is a rape of democracy."[32]

Dunnigan's indignation was fueled by her own continuing brushes with racial discrimination. During the early 1950s, she was barred from entering a Washington theater to cover a presentation by President-elect Dwight D. Eisenhower and was forced to sit through congressional hearings during which African Americans were referred to as "niggers." When she covered the funeral of Senator Robert A. Taft, an usher insisted that she sit with the senator's black servants.[33]

So Dunnigan was committed to exposing racial injustices. She wrote Barnett: "I fight constantly against exploitation. I have seen so much human suffering." Dunnigan's stories documenting discrimination, like those citing progress, often were the only ones describing the events. In 1948, for example, she reported that a six-foot cross had been burned in northeast Washington. No coverage of the incident appeared in the city's two major dailies, the *Washington Post* and *Washington Evening Star*. Another Dunnigan story reported that white families had filed suit to evict a black family from a house that they had purchased in a white neighborhood. Again, neither the *Post* nor the *Star* reported the event. Two years later, she documented that a Georgia congressman had called a civil rights leader a "black son-of-a-bitch." The incident had taken place in a congressional hearing that was open to the public, but mainstream Washington newspapers failed to report it.[34]

The last in the long list of barriers that Dunnigan broke was one created by Washington's elite women journalists. In 1947, Elizabeth May Craig asked Dunnigan to become the first African American in the Women's National Press Club. Craig then invited Dunnigan to a dinner party with Senator Margaret Chase Smith and prominent women from the national press corps. Dunnigan hardly uttered a word the entire evening, however, because she was not comfortable conversing with such socially prominent women. After that evening, Craig never again mentioned the possibility of Dunnigan joining the club. Not until 1955 was Dunnigan officially nominated and unanimously approved as the first black member.[35]

Despite Dunnigan's many achievements, working for the black press was demanding while the tangible rewards were few. Even though Dunnigan often worked sixteen hours a day, by 1960 her salary had risen only to $280 a month. So after thirteen years at ANP, she still earned less than the average Washington worker. In addition, she was a one-person operation without secretarial support, and she had to buy her own typewriter, notebooks, pens, envelopes, and stamps. What is more, her paychecks routinely arrived late, and ANP offered no vacations. Dunnigan's responsibilities to help support her son and aged parents exacerbated her financial difficulties, often forcing her to eat nothing but pig ears and turnips for days at a time. As Dunnigan moved into her mid-fifties, she became increasingly concerned about her future as a single woman working for a financially unstable organization that offered no unemployment compensation and no retirement plan.[36]

The solution to Dunnigan's financial problems evolved from the passion that she, like many journalists, developed for politics. She had become convinced that the Democratic Party represented the best hope for integration. She joined President Truman on his 1948 campaign trip partly because she believed that the presence of an African-American woman would help his campaign, and after Truman was elected she applied to work full-time for him. Although Truman did not hire her, while working for ANP she frequently made speeches on behalf of Democratic candidates and helped the party establish offices in black sections of Washington in 1952, 1956, and 1960. After John F. Kennedy won the presidential nomination in 1960, Dunnigan worked part-time as a press aide for him.[37]

In 1961, three months after his election, President Kennedy appointed Dunnigan to the staff of the Committee on Equal Employment Opportunity, at triple her ANP salary. The committee was charged with ensuring that all Americans had equal access to jobs with the federal government. Dunnigan, as educational consultant for the committee, made speeches and public appearances.

One of her trips took her to Austin, Texas, in 1963 to address a luncheon meeting of the Ralph Bunche Progressive Club. One purpose of the luncheon was to organize a youth division to undertake community service projects. After hearing Dunnigan speak, the young people named their organization the Alice Allison Dunnigan Girls Club.[38]

In 1967, Dunnigan shifted to the staff of the Council on Youth Opportunity. The only African American on the professional staff, she wrote newspaper and magazine articles about model programs for African-American youths. She also joined Lady Bird Johnson on two fact-finding trips—one to Appalachia to determine how the Teachers Corps had affected students, the other across the country to assess the problems of minorities.[39]

When Dunnigan retired from the government in 1970, her major activities became writing her autobiography, *A Black Woman's Experience: From Schoolhouse to White House*, which was published in 1974, and a book about African Americans from her home state, *The Fascinating Story of Black Kentuckians: Their Heritage and Tradition*, which was published in 1979. She also wrote a political column for the *Observer*, an African-American weekly newspaper in Washington. Alice Allison Dunnigan died of an abdominal disease on May 6, 1983, at seventy-seven years of age.[40]

10

ETHEL L. PAYNE
Agent for Change in the Civil Rights Movement

In 1954, the U.S. Supreme Court uttered six words that transformed race relations in this country: "Separate educational facilities are inherently unequal." The unanimous decision in *Brown vs. Board of Education of Topeka* stunned southern whites and spurred black America to challenge the unjust laws that had confined them to second-class citizenship. African Americans galvanized as never before, prompting a series of events across the South that formed the modern civil rights movement. News coverage of the movement has been praised as creating one of the shining moments in the history of the American media because northern reporters went into the South and transformed these events into front-page news all across the country, shoving the realities of southern segregation into the faces of the American people. As one analyst wrote: "It was a brilliant period in the history of the American press."[1]

Ethel L. Payne deserves a share of that praise. A fearless reporter for a leading black newspaper, Payne may have covered—

and participated in—more events in the movement than any other journalist. She reported the Montgomery Bus Boycott in 1956 and desegregation efforts at the University of Alabama the same year and at Little Rock Central High School a year later. She demonstrated in Birmingham in 1963, and, when 250,000 activists marched on Washington later that year, Payne was among them as well. In 1965 when 15,000 activists marched from Selma to Montgomery, Alabama, to demand voting rights, Payne was there. During the same period, she traced the legislative, executive, and judicial decisions that revolutionized public policy toward blacks.

Payne, who never married, became Washington bureau chief for the *Chicago Defender* just as civil rights was gaining momentum.[2] Indeed, Payne added to that momentum by challenging President Dwight D. Eisenhower on the administration's lack of initiative on integration—and feeling his wrath because of her boldness. The uncompromising Payne never apologized for irritating Eisenhower. She said: "There were very few rebels. The privilege of being a White House correspondent—wasn't that enough? Why couldn't I be quiet and not stir up things? Well, I didn't think that was my purpose. If you have lived through the black experience in this country, you feel that every day you're assaulted by the system. You are either acquiescent, which I think is wrong, or else you just rebel, and you kick against it. I wanted to constantly, constantly, constantly hammer away, raise the questions that needed to be raised."[3]

By 1954, Payne had established herself as a tough reporter and powerful writer. The Capital Press Club named her its "Newsman's Newsman," the Washington reporter who best exemplified high journalistic standards,[4] and the Washington press corps came to know her as the "First Lady of the Black Press." But Payne did not always behave in a manner consistent with many people's concept of a "lady." She said: "I admit it. I was obnoxious, stubborn, absolutely impossible to work with, impervious to all suggestions as to how to behave with civility. When you're a black reporter—man or woman—that's part of your job."[5] Payne's commitment to helping African Americans gain their civil rights coupled with her passion for adventure led her wherever a story was breaking, even if angry crowds of segregationists cursed her and tried to harm her.[6]

Ethel Lois Payne, the granddaughter of slaves, was born in Chicago on August 14, 1911. Her father, William Payne, completed eight years of school and worked as a Pullman porter; her mother, Bessie Austin Payne, completed high school and did not work outside the home. Ethel's interest in writing came from her mother, who led her six children in nightly readings of the Bible and the literary work of Louisa May Alcott and Paul Lawrence Dunbar. Life became more difficult for Ethel at age twelve when her father died from a disease contracted while handling soiled laundry on the trains. The Paynes then were forced to open their home to boarders, and Ethel's mother began teaching high school Latin and cleaning other people's homes.[7]

Payne's childhood dream was to become a civil rights lawyer, but she was denied admission to law school because of her race. She briefly attended two colleges and then worked as a clerk at the Chicago Public Library. She also took her first taste of community activism, joining the Illinois Human Rights Commission to fight against residential property in her neighborhood being developed for commercial use. She said: "I just liked to see people get stirred up over issues, and people to exercise voting rights and all of that. I was beginning to have the seeds of rebellion churning up in me."[8]

A sense of the young woman's strong will is captured in a 1947 incident. Payne noticed police officers arresting men outside a neighborhood tavern and asked an officer what had happened. When the officer responded by cursing at her, Payne told him he had no right to use foul language when speaking to her. The officer then hit her with a billy club and dragged her into a paddywagon. When Payne arrived at the police station and protested the police brutality, the captain immediately offered to release her. Payne would not be placated so easily. She refused to leave the station and threatened to tell reporters about the police brutality unless all twenty-five persons arrested in the incident were released. The police met her demands.[9]

In 1948, the adventurous Payne left behind her home, family, and fiancé to become a hostess for an Army Special Services club in Japan, organizing recreational activities and entertainment for African-American troops.[10]

It was while in Japan that Payne was led into journalism. In 1950, a *Chicago Defender* reporter, Alex Wilson, stopped in Japan on his way to cover the Korean War. When Payne showed Wilson her personal diary, he asked to take it back to Chicago with him. The *Defender* then turned excerpts from the diary into front-page news stories to tell readers about the experiences of black soldiers stationed in Japan.[11]

Payne's description was not pretty. She told how black soldiers were being segregated from white soldiers, despite President Harry S. Truman's executive order banning segregation in the military. She also described how "Chocolate Joes" had fathered hundreds of mixed-race babies who were abandoned by their fathers and ostracized by the Japanese. United States military brass objected to the negative tone of the articles and chastised Payne for disrupting troop morale.[12]

Chicago Defender Editor-in-Chief Louis E. Martin, however, admired Payne's pithy writing style. Payne recalled: "The newspapers were just jumping off the stands. Circulation just boomed." When Martin telephoned Payne in Japan and offered her a job, she returned to Chicago and began writing full-time for the *Defender* in 1951. Payne said: "When the opportunity came for me to go into journalism, I really saw that as an alternative to the practice of law. If I had had the opportunity to go to law school, I would have focused on civil rights and civil liberties. But I found that going into journalism, particularly where you could be independent and voice your own views, that that served the same kind of purpose."[13]

Martin hired Payne to write features, but he soon learned that the aggressive reporter found a hard news angle in any story he gave her. Payne said: "I don't go for what I considered the fluff. I want to dig in on things; I want to dig in on something I feel is really important." When one of her features uncovered a crisis in the adoption of African-American babies, she won the Illinois Press Association award for the best news story in 1952. After that, Martin gave Payne free rein to undertake investigative projects such as the traumas of unwed mothers. After two years in Chicago, Payne became restless. So Martin sent her to Washington to take over the *Defender*'s one-person bureau there. She arrived just in time to cover the Army-McCarthy hearings.[14]

As the modern civil rights movement erupted in the 1950s, Payne began tracking the historic measures taken by the Supreme Court, Congress, and the White House. The continuing battle against discrimination was the major national news story in the black press from the early 1950s through the 1960s, and Payne covered every angle of the story.

She may have had her strongest impact by doggedly covering legislative and judicial battles on Capitol Hill and then presenting the results—or lack of results—in her blunt, straightforward style. A month before the *Brown vs. Board of Education* decision, she wrote: "Progressive legislation either directly or indirectly pertaining to civil rights is really getting the run around in Congress these days. Unless some drastic action is taken to goad the lawmakers into action, they are slated for the graveyard." [15]

Even after the historic decision banning segregation in public schools, Payne was still skeptical. While most reporters were euphoric, praising the revolutionary action of the Supreme Court, Payne pointed out that the justices had given no timetable for compliance with the ruling. She wrote: "The Supreme Court Tuesday came up with a 'poor compromise' in its order for implementation of its decision outlawing racial segregation in the public schools. The high court ordered the cases sent back to the federal district courts for administration of integration. In their unanimous decision, the nine justices failed to set a deadline for integration." [16]

While Payne continued to report decisions banning segregation in higher education and housing, she also continued to be vigilant in telling her readers when public officials were not moving as quickly as she would have liked.[17] When covering civil rights decisions, Payne refused to be a "detached" observer. About the role of African-American reporters during the modern civil rights movement she said: "We could not stand aside and be so-called objective witnesses. I could not divorce myself from the heart of the problem, because I was part of the problem. So I had to learn how to give the essence of the story and to somehow or other transmit my own views into that total picture." [18]

One arena in which Payne clearly expressed her views was the White House press conference. By publicly asking questions of President Eisenhower, whom historians have not given high marks regarding civil rights efforts, Payne received national attention. Payne asked her first question of Eisenhower when she learned that the Howard University choir had been barred from performing at a celebration in Washington. The president said he was not familiar with the incident. Both black and mainstream newspapers made much of the fact that a black woman reporter had confronted the leader of the free world. The *Defender* ran a story and photograph of Payne on the front page; the *Washington Evening Star* credited Payne with turning the incident into a civil rights issue.[19]

Payne continued to challenge Eisenhower's civil rights policy by asking him questions about immigration quotas, segregation in interstate travel, and discrimination in federal housing.[20]

But it was Payne's question in July 1954, two months after the *Brown vs. Board of Education* decision, that received the strongest reaction, from both the president and the news media. Payne asked Eisenhower when he planned to ban segregation in interstate travel; Eisenhower barked back that he refused to support any special interest. Payne had irritated the president. Front-page stories in the *Washington Post* and *Washington Evening Star* characterized Eisenhower as being "annoyed" by the question, and the *Star* described him as responding in "clipped words."[21]

After the press conference, *Post* political correspondent Ed Folliard, dean of the White House press corps, said other reporters should have asked the question that Payne had asked. Payne believed the incident may have helped move civil rights onto the national agenda. She said: "From that time on, civil rights was moved to the front burner. Suddenly, civil rights began to be the big issue."[22]

After the incident, Eisenhower boycotted Payne by not recognizing her during press conferences. During the five months between the time she asked her first question and the time Eisenhower became angry with her, he recognized her seven times; in the seventy-nine months after the incident, he called on her only twice.[23]

Payne speculated that Eisenhower's displeasure with her also led White House Press Secretary James Hagerty to call her into his office and accuse her of violating the rules of the White House Correspondents Association. Hagerty told her he had documentation that she was working part-time for the Congress of Industrial Organizations and that such work violated an association rule against correspondents engaging in political activity. Payne said the association required only that a correspondent be working full-time for a news organization, which she was doing because she had only worked part-time for the CIO and no longer was working for the organization at all.[24]

The incident became public when syndicated columnist Drew Pearson reported, in the *Washington Post* and other newspapers, that Hagerty was harassing Payne by threatening to revoke her White House press credentials. Pearson stated that Hagerty had investigated Payne's income tax returns. At the next press conference, Hagerty denied that he had used Payne's income tax returns against her.[25]

Payne did not confine her civil rights activities to Washington. Although her job was to cover only news from the nation's capital, she also became her people's ubiquitous eyewitness to the events that exploded throughout the South in the 1950s. She later recalled: "I've had a box seat on history, and I've been able to chronicle some of the major events that have made a change in society, made a change in the law. My writings may have helped to influence some of that change."[26]

In 1956 after hearing that a seamstress named Rosa Parks had been arrested in Montgomery, Alabama, Payne called Martin, told him that it was a major story and that she was the reporter who should cover it. For the next three months, Payne's byline dominated the front page of the *Defender* as she reported the Montgomery Bus Boycott, which showed the country, for the first time in history, that the African-American population could galvanize into a united force. As fifty thousand blacks became one, Payne quickly recognized that the event was the beginning of a revolution. She wrote: "Mrs. Parks' act of rebellion touched off one of the most amazing reactions in the turbulent history of racial relations in the South. The young, the old, the middle-aged, the lame and the halt, housewives, maids and cooks, bellhops, janitors and laborers, school teachers, doctors and lawyers—they were all taking to the road; for this is not only a fight for courteous and equitable treatment, this is the first organized and disciplined revolt against a cruel and inhuman custom."[27]

Payne also perceived the central role that a twenty-seven-year-old minister from Atlanta was to play in the revolution. Her coverage included an exclusive interview and a full-page profile of the Reverend Martin Luther King, Jr.[28]

Before returning to Washington, Payne traveled through the South, staying in private homes because hotels refused to register African Americans, to write a series titled "The South at the Crossroads." The series, which the *Defender* promoted with a front-page photograph of Payne, provided in-depth analysis of the American South at this crucial moment in its history.[29]

Payne continued to traverse the South. Also in 1956, she covered efforts to integrate the University of Alabama. The next year she reported the violence that erupted in Little Rock, Arkansas, when nine African-American students attempted to enroll in the city's largest public high school. In 1963, Payne returned to the Deep South to cover demonstrations in Birmingham. She made and carried her own sign in the protest and then traveled north to participate in and report on the historic March on Washington in which a quarter of a million Americans displayed their support of civil rights. In 1965 she went into the South again to join men and women from across the country in the voting rights march from Selma to Montgomery.[30]

To cover these events, Payne worked far more than her required forty hours. She routinely worked six days a week, often until 2 or 3 A.M., with no mention of overtime pay. She also faced the hatred of segregationists. To report on the Little Rock desegregation story, Payne stayed in the apartment of a white college professor—until rocks came hurling through her bedroom window and the professor was evicted. Recalling the crowd that surrounded her and other marchers as they left Selma, Payne said: "You could just feel the hatred. It was just like an enveloping cloak around you. I'll never forget the faces, the contorted faces of housewives, standing out and screaming like they were just lunatics from the asylum: 'Nigger! Nigger! Nigger!'"[31]

President Lyndon B. Johnson recognized that Payne was more than a mere chronicler of events. When he signed the Civil Rights Act of 1964 and the Voting Rights Act of 1965, he asked leaders of the modern civil rights movement to join him in the Oval Office for the historic occasions. Among those leaders was one woman: Ethel Payne. Two of the many mementos that Payne displayed in her home were pens Johnson used for those signings.[32]

After the major events of the movement had ended by the mid-1960s, the "First Lady of the Black Press" shifted her attention to international affairs, becoming the first African-American woman to focus on international news coverage. During her long career, Payne reported from more than thirty countries on six continents.[33]

In 1966, Payne traveled to Vietnam to cover African-American troops fighting in the war. She said: "I recognized the danger of it, the risk of it, but it was a gamble and adventure, and it appealed to me." During her three months in Vietnam, Payne went into the field, investigated American military supplies being sold on the black market, and saw firsthand the effects of the chemical agent orange by witnessing the death of a Vietnamese woman.[34]

Payne's next international assignment came in 1969 when she spent six weeks covering the Nigerian Civil War. A year later, she joined Secretary of State William P. Rogers for a ten-nation tour of Africa and two years after that traveled to Zaire to attend the First Ordinary Congress of the Popular Revolution Movement. Later in the 1970s, Payne visited the People's Republic of China, reported on the International Women's Year Conference in Mexico City, and accompanied Secretary of State Henry Kissinger on a six-nation tour of Africa.[35]

Payne broke another barrier by shifting to the broadcast media to become the first African-American woman radio and television commentator employed by a national network. Three times a week from 1972 to 1982, Payne shared her views on public affairs issues with listeners and viewers of CBS.

"Spectrum" commentators ranged from conservatives such as Stop the Equal Rights Amendment founder Phyllis Schlafly to liberal *New York Post* columnist Murray Kempton. Payne possessed the breadth of knowledge on current issues as well as the intellectual and analytical depth that such a program demanded. While working full-time for the *Defender*, she taped commentaries for CBS. After a year on radio, the program expanded into television. Payne worked for "Spectrum" until 1978. She then switched to "Matters of Opinion," a public affairs program on Chicago radio station WBBM. She provided commentary for the CBS affiliate until 1982.[36]

Many of Payne's commentaries focused on topics of particular interest to African Americans. She analyzed, for example,

Carter administration policies toward blacks and identified un-
met needs in the struggle for civil rights. She also lambasted racial stereotypes, racist practices by the news media, and prejudicial treatment of women, Jews, and gays.[37]

A year after Payne became a network commentator, she was
promoted to associate editor of the *Defender* in the Chicago
headquarters, giving her full responsibility for the newspaper's
local news operation. She attempted to improve communication
in the city by organizing a series of town meetings and a citizens'
coalition to work with police to reduce crime. But Payne's venture into newspaper management at the local level was not a
landmark in her career. She said: "I was just like a fish out of
water. Local things just were not my style, not my teabag. I
wanted to get back to Washington." In 1978, Payne ended her
twenty-seven-year career with the *Defender*.[38]

Payne, then approaching seventy years of age, began supporting herself as a syndicated columnist. She carved out her own
niche, establishing a business by syndicating a column to half a
dozen black newspapers from Florida to California. In 1982,
Payne began a year as the first Ethel Payne Professor in Journalism at Fisk University in Nashville, Tennessee. After her one year
in higher education, she returned to Washington and continued
to write her newspaper column, give lectures, and become increasingly involved in church work. She also became a leader in
the campaign to secure the freedom of Nelson Mandela. She
wrote letters, circulated petitions, and was arrested at the South
African Embassy in 1985 during an anti-apartheid demonstration. After Mandela's release, she visited him in South Africa.[39]

Payne died of a heart attack in her home in Washington on
May 28, 1991, at age seventy-nine. The editorial page of the
Washington Post carried a tribute to her. It read: "Her voice was
low, but her questions were piercing, and her reports on the
world were cherished by millions of readers. The proof of professionalism—fairness, straightforward accounts of all sides and
independence of views—was in her writings."[40]

Ethel Payne may not have agreed with the comments about
her reporting being fair or presenting all sides of an issue. During
an oral history interview four years earlier, Payne had said: "I am
biased about anything I see as an injustice." When asked, during

that same interview, how she would like people to remember her, Payne said nothing about fairness. Her reply: "I would like to feel that they saw me as an agent for change. I fought all of my life to bring about change, to correct the injustices and the inequities in the system."[41]

11

CHARLAYNE HUNTER-GAULT
Creator of a Human Face
behind the Contemporary Black Struggle

Events that occurred in the quarter century after the modern civil rights movement of the 1950s and 1960s painfully demonstrated that equality for Americans of African descent remained illusive. The murders of Malcolm X in 1965 and Martin Luther King, Jr., in 1968 contributed to a sense of disillusion that has continued to shroud black America. Teenage pregnancy, broken families, rampant crime, police brutality, inadequate health care, economic hardship, the scourge of drugs, random violence, and gang warfare all have added to the blight that has led many African Americans from disappointment to cynicism to hopelessness to anger to rage. High unemployment and rat-infested slums have made urban centers particularly vulnerable as violence has erupted in more than one hundred cities, leading to riots, looting, vandalism—and a deepening despair.[1]

Charlayne Hunter-Gault has played a dual role in the history of the black struggle during the last thirty years. First she made news; now she reports it. She entered the media spotlight in 1961 when she desegregated the University of Georgia. That experience propelled her into racial activism, at the same time shaping her journalistic philosophy. She has since recalled: "I was fascinated with watching the press watch me. I was germinating simultaneously. The hostility that separated me from the white students, I observed, was caused by ignorance and stereotypes. . . . Early on, I resolved that anything I did (as a journalist) would be through people and their experiences."[2]

As her contribution to reporting from black America, Hunter-Gault has attempted to humanize the stories she has covered, thereby creating a human face behind the contemporary black struggle. She has focused on the individual women and men who each day combat the litany of perils facing them. In her words: "I look for stories that no one else is doing, stories about those who are usually invisible, left out. . . . I try to put flesh on the bones of bare statistics."[3]

While undertaking this mission, Hunter-Gault has built a journalism career spanning both print and broadcast news and encompassing such highly respected organizations as the *New Yorker* magazine, the *New York Times*, and the "MacNeil/Lehrer NewsHour."

Charlayne Hunter was born in Rabbit Stew, the black section of Due West, South Carolina, on February 27, 1942. Her father, Charles S.H. Hunter, Jr., was a Methodist chaplain in the U.S. Army; her mother, Althea Hunter, was an office manager in a real estate firm. After her parents separated, Charlayne and her two younger brothers lived with their mother in Atlanta. Charlayne decided at the age of thirteen that she wanted to be like the redheaded, unstoppable comic strip reporter Brenda Starr. Charlayne took her first step toward that dream by editing the *Green Light*, the newspaper at Atlanta's Henry McNeal Turner High School, where she also was a beauty queen.[4]

Hunter's next step changed her life. After graduating with honors from high school in 1959, Hunter wanted to pursue a journalism degree. But the only institution in the state that offered a journalism program was the venerable University of Georgia, which did not admit African Americans. With the financial and moral support of Atlanta civil rights activists, Hunter and Hamilton Holmes, a high school friend, filed an integration request with the federal court. While the case proceeded through the courts, Hunter enrolled at Wayne State University in Detroit. When the federal court issued an integration order in January 1961, Hunter and Holmes became the first African-American students in the 175-year history of the University of Georgia. She later said: "To become a historic symbol was not the point of what I did. The point of what I did was to have access to the best education I could get to become a journalist. I was a nineteen-year-old woman who would never pass this way again."[5]

Regardless of her intentions, Charlayne Hunter became national news. When she registered for classes, a crowd of angry students surrounded the car in which she was riding and threatened to overturn it. During her second night on campus, a thousand students gathered outside her dormitory. Some held a bedsheet banner stating: "Nigger, go home!" Others lit firecrackers and hurled bricks through Hunter's dormitory room window, splattering glass on the new school clothes she had been unpacking.[6]

Police tried to disperse the crowd by using tear gas, but events surged out of control. Mobs of angry segregationists roamed the campus and burnt effigies of African Americans. Amid the chaos, the university administration suspended Hunter and Holmes. When their lawyers objected, the two students were readmitted the next day.[7]

Media attention centered on Hunter because she, as a female student, was required to live on campus while Holmes lived off campus. Hunter's image was thrust onto the front page of the *New York Times.* One photo showed a young black woman gazing to the ground as white students jeered and screamed obscenities at her; another showed the same young woman, now in tears, being led from her dormitory by police officers.[8]

Harassment continued throughout Hunter's two years at the University of Georgia. Students living on the dormitory floor above hers pounded on the ceiling throughout the night, preventing her from sleeping. Most students ostracized her; some taunted her. Typical was a female student who walked up to Hunter, tossed a quarter on the floor and sneered, "Here, nigger. Here's a quarter. Go change my sheets."[9]

Throughout the torment, Hunter remained focused, poised,

and persistent. Two months after the height of the disturbances, Hunter was denied access to a university dining room. She fearlessly entered the fray once more, demanding access to the facility. A federal judge granted her request. After another two months passed and United States Attorney General Robert Kennedy came to campus to speak about civil rights, Hunter attended the speech, again propelling her to the front page of the *New York Times*.[10]

Hunter survived the trauma by focusing on her embryonic journalism career. She worked weekends for the *Atlanta Inquirer*, a newspaper founded by African-American students who had become frustrated with the lack of coverage in both white and black newspapers. She also became the first woman admitted to the Georgia chapter of the Society of Professional Journalists[11] and obtained a summer internship with the *Louisville* (Kentucky) *Courier Journal*, becoming the first African-American reporter on the staff.[12] Even more important for Hunter's emerging career was her frontline view of how reporters and students treated her, as a participant in the modern civil rights movement, as well as each other. She later said: "If there's anything I carry with me from that time, it's my interest in people. . . . It seems to me that if there were a basic understanding on each side about the humanity of the people, none of us would have been in the situation we were in."[13]

Hunter earned her journalism degree in June 1963 without further controversy, but she returned to the headlines that September when the national press reported that she had secretly married a white student from a well-to-do Georgia family six months earlier. Had university officials known of Hunter's marriage to Walter Stovall while she had still been a student, she would have been dismissed from the university without graduating.[14]

After Hunter secured her degree, she and Stovall moved to Greenwich Village, and she became the first African American on the staff of the *New Yorker*. She was hired as a secretary but advanced, after one year, to a staff writer. For three years, she contributed to the "Talk of the Town" section and wrote poignant short pieces that juxtaposed her childhood experiences in the segregated South against her adult experiences in the North.[15]

Hunter's personal life underwent major changes during this period. Her daughter, Susan, was born in 1963. Hunter and

Stovall divorced in 1968, leaving Hunter a working single mother. Despite her responsibilities as a mother, Hunter did not sacrifice her journalism career. She interrupted her career only for six months immediately after Susan was born. She later reflected on the challenge of being both a mother and a career woman: "It's a mindset. If your mindset is that your career is as important as your role as wife and mother, then you will make it happen—whatever it takes." After Susan was born, Hunter hired someone to care for her daughter.[16]

In 1967, Hunter had been awarded a Russell Sage Fellowship to study the social sciences at Washington University in St. Louis. During that time she also worked for *Trans-Action* magazine, editing stories and traveling to Washington, D.C., to cover the Poor People's Campaign. It was in Hunter's coverage of Resurrection City, which was at the center of the campaign, that she first displayed what was to become the trademark of her journalistic work. She described the tent city not through its politics but through its human inhabitants. She quoted Lila Mae Brooks of Sunflower County, Mississippi, as saying: "'Us who have commodes are used to no sewers.' A tall, thin, spirited woman, Mrs. Brooks talks with little or no prompting. Observing that I was interested, she went on: 'We used to being sick, too. And we used to death. All my children [she has eight] born sickly. . . .' She is 47, and for years has worked in private homes, cotton fields, and churches. . . . I asked Mrs. Brooks how long she planned to stay here. 'I don't know, honey,' she said as she put her sunglasses on. 'They just might have to 'posit my body in Washington.'"[17]

After completing the fellowship, Hunter shifted from print to broadcast news, working as an investigative reporter and anchorwoman for WRC-TV, Channel 4, the NBC television affiliate in the nation's capital. During this phase of her career, she again faced violence. Assigned to cover student demonstrations on the Howard University campus, Hunter was attacked by students who demanded her gas mask. She recalled: "Reporters—especially reporters working for the white media—were the enemy."[18]

In 1968, Hunter returned to print journalism by joining the metropolitan staff of the *New York Times*. She specialized in covering stories in Harlem and founded the *Times*'s one-person bureau in that section of the city. She said: "I was writing about something no one else on staff was—blacks, Harlem, the Bedford-Stuyvesant riots."[19] She provided daily coverage of the rise of the Black Panthers and the Nation of Islam, focusing on the human stories behind the events.

The metropolitan editor of the *Times* praised Hunter's reporting ability. Arthur Gelb said: "She was an exceptionally bright light on our metro staff—a reporter with wit, grace, style and a character of steel." Her additional strengths, as identified by Gelb and other employers, include her insightful understanding of human relationships as well as her "brains, persistence, and hustle."[20]

In 1970 the *New York Times Magazine* sent Hunter back to the University of Georgia to assess how the racial atmosphere had changed since she had helped desegregate the campus seven years earlier. Although university officials boasted of complete integration, African-American students told Hunter that race still divided the institution. She focused on a black graduate student who had just passed the orals for his doctoral degree in African history—but could not wait to leave the segregated university.[21]

By that same year, the most prestigious newspaper in the country had begun to recognize Hunter's ability to paint compelling portraits of African Americans. In 1970, she and Joseph Lelyveld received the *New York Times* Publishers Award for their detailed portrayal of the life and death of Walter Vandermeer, the youngest person in Harlem history known to have died from an overdose of heroin. Walter died two weeks after his twelfth birthday. The front-page story vividly described how the youngster had been shunted among family members and social service agencies until he finally had landed on the street. The disturbing description of Walter read: "His diet was made up of Yankee Doodle cupcakes, Coca-Cola and, when he had the change, fish 'n' chips. It was a life of frightening emptiness and real dangers. The only regular thing about it was a daily struggle for survival.

"'Walter didn't do too bad,' a junkie on the block remarked when he was dead.

"'He didn't do too good,' retorted a black youth, full of bitterness over what heroin has done to Harlem. 'He won't see his 13th birthday.'"[22]

By this time, Hunter's own personal life had stabilized. While living in Washington in 1968, Hunter had met Ronald Gault, a black man who worked for the Department of Justice. They married in 1971, and he now is a managing director of a New York investment banking firm. When their son, Chuma, was born in 1972, Hunter-Gault left work for six months. As a transition between caring for her son and returning to the newsroom, Hunter-Gault taught in the Columbia University Graduate School of Journalism for one semester. The Hunter-Gaults now live in Manhattan.[23]

As an African-American woman juggling a career and a family, Hunter-Gault was uniquely qualified to cover African-American women's struggle to define their role in the women's liberation movement. While the movement was catching fire among white women, Hunter observed that black women tended to be wary of it. She wrote: "The differences are rooted in historical traditions that have placed black women—in terms of work, family life, education and men—in a relationship quite apart from that of white women. . . . Such different perspectives make it all but impossible for some black women to relate to the white 'women's lib' movement."[24]

Hunter-Gault has demonstrated that she is fully capable of reporting the full range of soft as well as hard news. In 1974, she received her second *New York Times* Publishers Award, this time for writing under deadline pressure. She won the award for a front-page story about Mayor Abraham Beame naming the first black deputy mayor in New York City history.[25]

She won her third publishers award in 1976 for outstanding performance on a beat. The award honored her front-page story on the renaming of Harlem's Muslim Mosque for Malcolm X. The story went far beyond who, what, when, and where to provide an insightful analysis of what the renaming said about changes within the African-American culture. Other awards cited her coverage of education and teenage unemployment in Harlem.[26]

It also was Hunter-Gault who, in the mid-1970s, convinced the stylistically conservative *New York Times* to reconsider its use of the term "Negro." The issue evolved after one of Hunter-Gault's articles was edited so that each of her references to "black" was changed to "Negro." In a thirteen-page, carefully reasoned memo, Hunter-Gault told her editors why she and other blacks objected to the term "Negro." In response, the country's newspaper of record adopted a new editorial policy of using the term "black." Hunter-Gault considered the incident of major importance because it told the mainstream news media that they could not hire black reporters and then ignore issues that were an integral part of the lives of those reporters. She said: "It was a fundamental change. It attacked the decision-making policy of the 'white' news media."[27]

During the 1970s when major American newspapers employed only a handful of reporters of African descent, Hunter-Gault was a valuable asset because of her acceptance in and access to the black community. The fearless reporter once rescued Martin Arnold, a *Times* reporter and later an editor for the *New York Times Magazine*, from being beaten. Arnold was covering a Black Power conference when people at the meeting decided he was a spy and threw him out an open window and into a crowd of blacks. Arnold said: "Charlayne was around the corner as they were ready to stomp me. She came bursting around the corner, broke through the line and threw her arms around me, acting like my friend, which she was."[28]

In 1978, Hunter-Gault returned to broadcast journalism by joining the staff of the "MacNeil-Lehrer Report." The half-hour Public Broadcasting Service program was unique because the entire program explored a single topic, thereby providing far more depth than its competitors. Hunter-Gault became the substitute anchor for the national program produced in New York, filling in for Robert MacNeil or Jim Lehrer whenever either anchor was traveling.

Hunter-Gault covered issues related to African-American subjects, such as the fact that desegregation was threatening the livelihood of black colleges and that Congress was considering a busing amendment to achieve integration. Hunter-Gault also examined the effects of unemployment on the black vote, efforts to strengthen fair housing legislation, and the devastating rise in homicides among African-American children.[29]

But Hunter-Gault did not want to be pigeonholed exclusively to African-American news. So she broadened her list of specialties to include health, energy, economics, human rights, women's rights, and international affairs.[30]

While bringing a human dimension to her pieces, Hunter-

Gault also demonstrated that she could, when necessary, ask the tough questions. During a 1979 broadcast, she asked Bishop Abel T. Muzorewa, head of the interim government in the former Rhodesia, whether he was receiving military aid from South Africa, an extremely sensitive question for the leader of a black-majority nation. Muzorewa was so angered by the question that he shot back that it was none of Hunter-Gault's business—a response that clearly answered the question.[31]

During the early 1980s, Hunter-Gault won two National Emmy Awards. The first was for "Zumwalt: Agent Orange." The piece profiled Elmo Zumwalt III, who developed cancer as a result of being contaminated by agent orange in Vietnam. The gripping story explored the human emotions of Zumwalt and his father, Admiral Elmo Zumwalt, Jr., who authorized the defoliant to be sprayed.[32]

Hunter-Gault's propensity for getting to know people on a personal level, as well as blind luck, paved the way for her second national Emmy in 1983. After a casual meeting with an American woman who lived in Grenada, Hunter-Gault developed the acquaintanceship into a friendship. Several years later when U.S. forces invaded Grenada and the American military decided to keep the press at a distance, Hunter-Gault called her friend and immediately had contacts in the little-known Caribbean island. She sent a television crew to the woman's home, which happened to be directly across the road from the hotel that American forces had commandeered for their headquarters.[33]

It also was in 1983 that PBS expanded its nightly news program to a full hour. With that expansion, Hunter-Gault became the national correspondent for the "MacNeil/Lehrer NewsHour," the position she continues to hold today. Unlike the half-hour nightly news programs on the major networks, this one is not held hostage to the ten-second sound bite. The "NewsHour" is known for the depth of its coverage and its ability to explore the texture and nuances of a select number of topics each day. Correspondents often engage experts in lengthy, one-on-one discussions.

Because of its depth, the "NewsHour" is one of the few television programs that the print journalism community respects as a substantive source of information—not entertainment.

The "NewsHour" is committed to fairness and steadfastly avoids crusades. So when Hunter-Gault feels strongly about an issue, she returns to the print media and writes articles for publications that seek a strong author's voice.[34]

One event that propelled her toward such articles was her 1985 visit to South Africa. After the eight-week trip, she wrote a *New Yorker* piece focusing on a white South African cameraman, nicknamed "Dr. Death," who worked with her but later became a victim of the violence. Hunter-Gault wrote: "As painful as it is to contemplate those moments when the blows of the machetes were hacking out his brains and paralyzing his body and ultimately killing him, I have this odd feeling—the perverse, journalistic side of me, I guess—that maybe Dr. Death would not have wanted to die any other way but on the job. . . . Dr. Death will join the long list of the martyrs of South Africa, that country's only truly free citizens."[35]

Such articles allow Hunter-Gault to exchange her reportorial detachment for more passionate expression. An article she wrote for *Vogue* was crafted around mini-profiles of Winnie Mandela and several lesser-known black women. Hunter-Gault told how the police had beaten one particular bar owner. As Hunter-Gault described the woman removing her blouse to reveal the bruises on her breasts, the writer recalled that she was reminded of her own experience with violence a quarter of a century earlier. Hunter-Gault went on to tell readers that she left the room during the interview with the bar owner: "I burst into tears, then silent, uncontrollable sobs. I did not want anyone to see me or to hear me or to know that the armor that had protected me for so long had been pierced."[36]

The South Africa visit resulted in a five-part series for the "NewsHour." "Apartheid's People" explored the effects of apartheid on both black and white South Africans, including a black nun, a white farmer, and a black advertising executive working in a white ad agency. When speaking of the series, Hunter-Gault said: "American TV viewers are now used to seeing the unfolding events and the violence in South Africa on the nightly news, but events ultimately are about people. I think we got at some of the reasons *behind* the events. We talked to people on both sides who, like most of us, normally are not violent. We wanted to see from their perspective how their rage could become so extreme and lead to violent actions."[37]

The series netted Hunter-Gault honors as the journalist of

the year by the National Association of Black Journalists and the most prestigious award of her career and, indeed, the most coveted award in broadcast news: the George Foster Peabody Award for Excellence in Broadcast Journalism.[38]

The award, which often is compared to the Pulitzer Prize in print journalism, is presented by the University of Georgia. To receive the award, Hunter-Gault returned to the institution that had barred her from enrolling twenty-five years earlier. The university also established a lectureship honoring Hunter-Gault, and, in 1988, Hunter-Gault became the first African-American commencement speaker in the university's history.[39]

In 1992, Hunter-Gault published her memoirs about growing up in the segregated South, titling the work *In My Place*.[40] She continues to report the news on one of the most respected programs in broadcast journalism. Her areas of expertise have broadened to a full range of national and international topics, from the banking scandal to the fall of communism to the Persian Gulf War, which she covered from both Saudi Arabia and Iraq. But she also has remained committed to translating into human terms the persistent struggle for Americans of African descent to attain equal rights. Recent pieces have focused on the rise of hate crimes on college campuses, the ambiguities of affirmative action, the sexual harassment battle between Supreme Court nominee Clarence Thomas and law professor Anita Hill, and the underlying reasons for the rage that exploded into the Los Angeles riots.[41]

In short, Charlayne Hunter-Gault continues to emphasize the same themes that have defined her journalistic work since the fiery desegregation battles brought her to national attention thirty years ago. She said: "Being black and a woman and being in the Civil Rights Movement helped me survive. . . . All of those things helped me to forge my armor, because I think you do need a suit of armor, particularly if you're black, if you're a woman, if you're in this kind of business."[42]

A SYNTHESIS

If scholars of African-American history were asked to identify the institutions that have shaped black America, they would agree that the African-American press deserves considerable credit. If the same scholars were asked to name the watershed events in the evolution of black America, they would list the abolition movement, the modern civil rights movement, the African-American migration to the North after emancipation, the Harlem Renaissance, and the rise of Black Power. If such a panel of scholars were further challenged to combine these two categories in an attempt to identify specific black journalists who have played leading roles in shaping the history of black America, their lists still would be similar, including such names as Frederick Douglass, T. Thomas Fortune, and William Monroe Trotter.[1] But if one more factor were added to the equation and the scholars were asked to name the black *women* journalists who have shaped the history of black America, there would no longer be consistency among the lists. Indeed, there would be no lists. For most African-American scholars could name no more than one or two such women.

This book provides such a list. In this final chapter, I have synthesized the material in the individual profiles by responding to three questions:

Why did these women choose to become journalists?

How did they succeed in a competitive and demanding field traditionally dominated by white men?

How have black women journalists differed from other journalists?

Two caveats must be offered before beginning a discussion of the various concepts threaded through the individual biographies. First, this synthesis chapter is consistent with the preceding chapters in that it is written from a journalism history perspective. The glue that holds this book together is the subjects' identities as black women who have worked as journalists. The lives of many of these women previously have been explored in other contexts—such as that of abolitionist or women's club organizer—but this is the first comprehensive work that approaches the eleven women as journalists. The author leaves to other scholars the intriguing task of approaching these same subjects from, for example, an overtly feminist perspective.

Second, I do not presume to suggest that the lives and experiences of a mere eleven individuals tell the definitive history of African-American women journalists during the last 150 years. The journalists profiled in this book share the common denominator of having made significant contributions both to the field of journalism and to the evolution of American history. It would be illogical to assume that these few individuals exhibit all of the dimensions of the hundreds of journalists of their race and gender who have worked for the news media. It *is* logical, however, to suggest that the experiences and works of these journalists represent a rich sampling of the characteristics that have defined the contributions of African-American women journalists.

RACIAL REFORMERS

The prevailing reason these women were drawn to journalism was the profession's potential for helping to bring about racial reform. Since the first black newspaper was founded in 1827, the African-American press has served to sustain the spirit of its readers as they have endured the heavy burden of racial oppression. African-American journalists have chronicled instances of physical and psychological abuse, interpreted policies that have veiled discrimination in housing and employment, and represented the conscience of the black community.

To a woman, the journalists described in these pages used— and Charlayne Hunter-Gault continues to use—their reporting and writing talents to further the ongoing struggle to secure equal rights for Americans of African descent. Last century Ida B. Wells-Barnett and Josephine St. Pierre Ruffin urged continual opposition to racial unjustice, even if that effort meant breaking the law. In this century, Charlotta Bass translated her militancy into action by forcing such giants as Boulder Dam and the Southern California Telephone Company to hire black workers.

In Ethel Payne's youth, she wanted to be a civil rights lawyer; when the doors to law school were slammed in her face, she shifted her sights to journalism. In fact, Payne, like other journalists described in this book but unlike most journalists in general, wore proudly the label of reformer. The year that she died, the intractable Payne barked: "Of *course* I'm an advocate for racial reform before I'm a journalist. I was born with black skin long before I ever sat down at a typewriter."[2]

So these women have balanced their crusade for racial reform with their journalistic professionalism. When Hunter-Gault finishes communicating the issues of the day to three million Public Broadcasting Service viewers and then has difficulty hailing a taxi because Manhattan cab drivers prefer to serve white passengers, the anger burns inside her. She then reminds herself: "I can't let it affect my professional performance. I could get so wrapped up in it, it could consume me. The work I do is too important to let that happen."[3]

Though all of the journalists profiled here have been racial activists, their approaches have varied. Delilah L. Beasley adopted a moderate position, supporting the accommodationist philosophy of Booker T. Washington, and Josephine St. Pierre Ruffin was a close friend of Washington's. Gertrude Bustill Mossell and Ida B. Wells-Barnett, on the other hand, vehemently opposed Washington and his conservative philosophy.

Despite their diversity in approach, the journalistic pioneers whose lives are sketched in this book definitely tended to congregate toward the radical end of the activist continuum. A century and a half ago, Mary Ann Shadd Cary called for anarchy, telling her readers: "Cease to uphold the United States government, if it will, and while it does, uphold human slavery."[4] And this century, Marvel Cooke denounced the democratic form of government, joining the Communist Party and brazenly refusing to back down a single inch—even when pressured by the bullying tactics of Joe McCarthy.

To say that black women journalists have not backed down is not to suggest that they have not paid a high price for their obstinance. Maria Stewart was pelted with rotten tomatoes and driven out of Boston; Ida B. Wells-Barnett was forced into exile in the

North. Mary Ann Shadd Cary and Charlotta Bass were threatened with death. Alice Dunnigan was publicly humiliated on numerous occasions, and Ethel Payne and Charlayne Hunter-Gault
became targets for jeers and curses, bottles and bricks. Neverthe-
less, each woman stood her ground and continued to raise her
voice.

WOMEN'S RIGHTS ACTIVISTS

Sexual prejudice was another form of inequity that led African-
American women first into newspapers and later into the elec-
tronic news media. Though they were operating in a profession
ruled by men, these journalists were intimately familiar with the
suffering that results from sexual discrimination and, therefore,
used journalism to advocate a wider vision for African-American
women.

In 1832, Maria Stewart's first essay in the *Liberator*—the first
piece of journalism written by an American woman of African
descent—insisted that women set aside their dependence on men
and expand beyond the sphere of domesticity to the world of business. Almost a century before American women secured voting
rights, the fiery Stewart demanded: "How long shall the fair
daughters of Africa be compelled to bury their minds and talents
beneath a load of iron pots and kettles?"[5] Stewart believed that
ending the subjugation of women was comparable in importance
to abolishing slavery, vowing her willingness to sacrifice her life
for either cause. The militant journalist also pointed a finger at
her "fairer sisters" for oppressing black women.[6]

Josephine St. Pierre Ruffin chastised white women as well,
saying they prevented black women from expanding into new occupations. But Ruffin's primary goal in founding her nineteenth-
century newspaper was not to criticize white women but to demonstrate that black women, despite racism and sexism, were ac-
complishing far more than white America gave them credit for.
Ruffin filled the pages of *Woman's Era* with an eye-opening collection of profiles and news stories about successful women of her
race. When financial difficulties silenced Ruffin's editorial voice
after seven years, she was neither bitter nor discouraged. Instead,
she congratulated her newspaper—and herself—for helping black

women uplift the race. Ruffin confidently predicted that women would continue to progress, saying: "It is as impossible for women to turn back as for time—they are bound to march on."[7]

Ida B. Wells-Barnett's strong feminist beliefs carried her into leadership in the women's suffrage movement. She founded the country's first suffrage organization specifically for black women, and, when white women from the South refused to allow Wells-Barnett to march beside them in the first national women's suffrage parade in 1913, Wells-Barnett accepted a place in the crowd of onlookers—until the parade was under way and she went to the head of the parade and marched proudly forward.

Charlayne Hunter-Gault's reputation as one of the country's top journalists demonstrates that these women's courageous efforts have paid off. Working for the *New Yorker*, the *New York Times*, and "MacNeil/Lehrer NewsHour," she has triumphed over the sexist attitudes and financial discrimination that have plagued many of the African-American women who came before her. Because she has succeeded in each job, she has demanded proper respect and compensation. She said of her various jobs: "I couldn't have performed them if I hadn't had the ability. . . . I have always been paid the same as most men because I insist on it. I wouldn't be someplace where people didn't treat my contribution as special."[8]

As these women gained ground for themselves, they simultaneously—and sometimes unknowingly—served to empower the women who read or heard their words. Typical was Gertrude Bustill Mossell. She warned each young woman reading her column to guard her virtue by deciding when a man could and could not touch her, writing: "If you need his assistance in walking, take his arm instead of his taking yours. Just tell him in plain English to keep his 'hands off.'"[9] Overtly warning young women about the dangers of men, Mossell was, on another level, suggesting that women should insist upon being responsible for their own well being and, in particular, their own bodies.

INTERPRETERS OF THE NEWS

Contributing to the forces that attracted these strong-willed, independent-minded women to journalism was a tradition much more pronounced in the black press than in the white: interpretive reporting. None of the women described in this book allowed herself to be confined to the limited scope of "objective reporter." Instead, each brought her own perspective to her work. Some wrote editorials, others wrote columns, and still others wrote what could be called interpretive news stories. Whatever the form, each woman wrote from her own unique perspective. At the end of her career, Marvel Cooke recalled an instance during which an editor suggested that he rewrite one of her stories: "I remember getting so angry. I said, 'Nobody, *nobody* rewrites my stuff.' I write the way I want to write. I'm not trying to write for somebody else; I'm writing for myself and expressing things the way I want to." [10]

The desire to express themselves the way they wanted to propelled four of the women to operate their own newspapers. Mary Ann Shadd Cary was the first, founding the *Provincial Freeman* in 1853. Ida B. Wells-Barnett was next, becoming one of the owners of the *Memphis Free Speech* in 1889 and the *New York Age* in 1892. Josephine St. Pierre Ruffin won her ability to interpret the news when she established *Woman's Era* in 1890. Charlotta Bass bought her editorial voice at a sheriff's auction in 1912 when she paid fifty dollars for the *California Eagle*.

The interpretive style of the black press kept Ethel Payne from shifting to mainstream newspapers, a move that she clearly had the talent to make. The "First Lady of the Black Press" said: "I've enjoyed enormous freedom—much more freedom than I would have had I been in the majority media. I don't think I could have existed, because of my own character and personality and everything else. I couldn't express myself the way I do in the black press, say, if I were on the *Washington Post* or the *New York Times*. That's the value of being in the type of press where you can write what you feel is right and just." [11]

Charlayne Hunter-Gault has opted to work for the mainstream news media but has not sacrificed her right to interpret the news. Now a correspondent for one of the most respected broadcast news organizations in the country, she brings the perspective of an African-American woman to her nightly reports. Hunter-Gault said: "Our news program does not take positions, but we'd be sorry persons if we didn't take positions as people. As a journalist, I don't expose what I as a person believe. But I never hide behind what I am—a black, a woman. I expose peo-

ple to as many sides of an issue as I can. And this is consistent
with everything I have been and am." [12]

SPIRITUAL GUIDES

For most of the journalists in this book, to be consistent with
who they are has meant expressing a strong spirituality. The lives
of many of these women, like those of many American women of
African descent, have been firmly anchored in the church, and
they were drawn to journalism by a sense of religious mission.
Spirituality was a particularly important factor in the lives of the
nineteenth-century women.

Maria Stewart established this tradition when she felt a religious calling to blend the power of God's word with the power of
the press to further the cause of the abolition movement. Fired by
the unwavering conviction of religious fervor, this minimally educated domestic attributed the eloquence of her prose style—which
was considerable—to the holy spirit. Stewart, an active member of
the Episcopal Church who ultimately founded her own Episcopal
Sunday school, wrote: "God has fired my soul with a holy zeal for
his cause. It was God alone who inspired my heart to publish." [13]

Religious fervor also was central to Delilah Beasley's decision
to commit her energies to journalism, even though she was not a
gifted writer and her work as a physical therapist was far more
financially lucrative. Beasley felt that God had called her to change
white America's perception of her race. Beasley, a devout Catholic,
responded by dedicating her life to this journalistic mission.

For several of the women, spirituality was not an abstract
concept but a direct influence on their professional lives. Gertrude Bustill Mossell and Ida B. Wells-Barnett began their journalism careers by writing for church newspapers; Delilah Beasley
and Alice Allison Dunnigan gained their first reporting experience by writing about church activities in their hometowns. And
when Charlotta Bass decided to run for elected office, she built
her grassroots support in the black churches of Los Angeles.

The fact that religion and spirituality played an important role
in these women's lives did not, however, guarantee that African-
American women journalists blindly supported organized religion. Mary Ann Shadd Cary lashed out bitterly at the church,

labeling it "the pillar of American slavery." [14] Nor did the journalists' spirituality guarantee that they wholeheartedly supported clergymen. Cary wrote of ministers: "They are not going to reform men, not they, it is too much trouble." [15] Gertrude Bustill Mossell, an active member of the Presbyterian Church, revealed her skeptical attitude toward ministers when she dispensed advice on how mothers should raise their daughters: "Instill in their very nature that they are safer in their own hands than they are in the hands of any man—preachers not excepted." [16]

EDUCATORS

Most of the women whose life stories have unfolded in the pages of this book forged part of their armor in front of a room filled with students. Education historically has been one of the few occupations open to intelligent, career-minded women. So many of these determined individuals used the classroom as a stepping-stone into the newsroom.

For Gertrude Bustill Mossell, the transition from education to journalism was a natural one. After seven years of teaching African-American children, she shifted to writing an advice column in which she taught former slaves how to succeed in an inhospitable North. After Mossell moved from the classroom to the newsroom at this crucial moment in African-American history, many of her statements retained the stern tone of a teacher. In one column, Mossell wrote: "The school of life never closes; there are no vacations." [17]

Not all of the women made their shifts from the classroom to the newsroom entirely by choice. The American Missionary Society did not consider Mary Ann Shadd Cary's propensity toward speaking her mind to be a plus in educating Canada's fugitive slaves. So she was dismissed from her teaching position. Undaunted, Cary entered a field in which that same inclination was valued, becoming the first African-American woman in history to publish her own newspaper. Ida B. Wells-Barnett taught for a dozen years before the Memphis School Board fired her—after the sharp-tongued Wells-Barnett wrote an article criticizing the school system.

When Alice Dunnigan had to choose between teaching black

children and cleaning white houses, she opted for education because it was closer to journalism; Dunnigan taught in Kentucky's
one-room schoolhouses for eighteen years before she found a
way to move to the nation's capital and cover the White House.

For some of the women, it was journalism that served as the
stepping-stone and education that ultimately dominated their
lives. Maria Stewart spent only two years writing for a newspaper but four decades teaching. She later served as a school
principal and eventually founded her own school.

For still others, journalism and education became the positions on either side of a revolving door. Mary Ann Shadd Cary
taught for a dozen years, then founded her own school and
taught for two more years, next earned her livelihood in newspapers for five years, but then returned to more stable employment in education for several decades, while occasionally writing
for newspapers.

BENEFICIARIES OF MALE SUPPORT

Ironically, one factor that helped these black women succeed in
journalism directly involves the most significant obstacle hindering white women working in the same field: men. The male journalists who worked with the women described in this book were
largely supportive of the women's efforts.

More than a century ago, Mary Ann Shadd Cary observed
that the men who edited African-American newspapers were extremely hospitable to the African-American woman, welcoming
her as "an honored member of the guild."[18] Gertrude Bustill
Mossell echoed Cary's statement, citing editors' support of wom-
en journalists as a major incentive for entering the field. In 1886,
Mossell wrote: "When her masculine confreres come to know her
they will regard her with a feeling of brave comradship [sic] and as
a good fellow. They will help instead of hindering her."[19]

Later women also enjoyed supportive relationships with their
male editors. After Ida B. Wells-Barnett's Memphis newspaper
was destroyed and she was banished from the South, T. Thomas
Fortune gave her part ownership in his newspaper. Fortune, then
the dean of black journalism, paid the "Princess of the Black
Press" a compliment that no American woman had ever heard

before: "She handles a goose quill with a diamond point as hand-ily as any of us men in newspaper work."[20] Marvel Cooke's nas-cent career received a huge boost in 1926 when W.E.B. DuBois hired the twenty-three-year-old to write for the *Crisis*, the pre-mier African-American magazine in the country, and ushered her into the social circle of the Harlem Renaissance.

Closely connected to male editors hiring African-American women journalists has been those editors' willingness to assign women to hard news coverage. White women historically have fought—often unsuccessfully—to avoid the "society page ghet-to"; black women have been welcomed onto the front page. Without the encouragement of their male colleagues, African-American women would not have had the impact on the various historical events highlighted in this book.

Ethel Payne, for example, was encouraged to cover the land-mark events that formed the modern civil rights movement, with the *Chicago Defender* editors showcasing her articles on the front page—often accompanying them with photographs of their prize reporter.

The most salient explanation for African-American editors' support is that black women, unlike white women, have never been widely identified with homemaking. Because of economic necessity, African-American women always have worked both in the home and in the field or laundry or factory—the same places that African-American men have worked. Black men always were accustomed to having women in the workplace. So black editors tended not to object to women working in the newsroom. White women, by contrast, have not always maintained a strong pres-ence in the workplace, nineteenth-century white women gener-ally being identified solely with the home. So as white women attempted to move into the newsroom, as well as into other workplaces, white men blocked them, attempting to preserve a male domain.

INDEPENDENT WOMEN

While the presence of African-American men in these women's professional lives have helped pave the way to their success, the absence of men in their personal lives often has done the same. It

traditionally has been a challenge for wives and mothers to succeed in the demanding field of the news media. Most of the
women described in these pages achieved their journalistic successes while living independent, unattached lives that were unen-
cumbered by responsibilities to spouses or children.

Maria Stewart and Josephine St. Pierre Ruffin both entered
journalism soon after they became widows. Others did not marry
at all. With some of the women, such as Delilah Beasley, there is
insufficient evidence to determine if their decisions to remain single were deliberate. But with others, the record is clear. Ethel
Payne left a fiancé waiting on the dock when she moved to Tokyo,
where she launched her journalism career. Payne consciously
chose journalism over marriage: "It wouldn't have been fair to a
husband or a family, because if I was going to continue in that
pursuit of the news and dispensing of the news, it just wouldn't
have fit in."[21]

Some of the women did not marry or have children until after they had succeeded in their journalism careers. Mary Ann
Shadd Cary and Ida B. Wells-Barnett both built their reputations
as militant journalists before marriage, then curtailed their newspaper careers to raise their children. Gertrude Bustill Mossell left
journalism when she married and began raising her two daughters in the early 1880s but returned to the field after two years,
offering telling advice to the woman considering a career in journalism: "It will be better if she gives up all thoughts of matrimony until her success is made. Domestic life and the building of a
career by a woman will not harmonize."[22]

Charlotta Spear did not agree. She bought her own newspaper and then hired a veteran reporter to help her edit it. Two
years later, she married that editor. During the next twenty years,
Charlotta and Joseph Bass transformed the *California Eagle* into
the largest and most hard-hitting African-American newspaper
on the West Coast. When her husband died, Charlotta Bass resumed full responsibilities for the newspaper.

These women's career choices have not been easy ones. Alice
Dunnigan may have had to make the toughest of the decisions.
After giving birth to a son in 1932, during the depths of the
Depression, Dunnigan was torn between caring for her child and
continuing her career. She chose the latter, turning her baby over
to his grandparents to raise. It was not until seventeen years later,

when Dunnigan was firmly established as a Washington journalist, that she brought her son from Kentucky to the nation's capital to live with her again.

FOLLOWERS OF SPORADIC CAREER PATHS

For many of the women described here, marriage and motherhood caused their journalism careers to be brief and/or sporadic—better depicted by a broken line than a solid one. This pattern is consistent with one identified by scholars who have studied the career paths of American working women. Those scholars have observed that women's careers tend to evolve in a stop-and-start pattern, while men's careers are more likely to develop in a continuing line. Interruptions in women's careers often can be attributed to changes in the situations of the men who play important roles in their lives. Another influential factor is economic difficulties, which historically have been more pronounced in the lives of black women than white women.[23]

Delilah Beasley began her journalism career in 1883, but the deaths of her parents later that decade forced her to shift to a more financially lucrative field. The single woman had to wait twenty years before returning to journalism. Though newspaper work was the passion in Beasley's life, she still was able to pursue it only part-time. Her career peaked with her weekly column, which she wrote for only the last eleven years of her life.

Ida B. Wells-Barnett's journalism career also was defined by starts and stops. She wrote part-time for newspapers from 1885 until 1889, shifted to full-time editing for the *Memphis Free Speech* for two years, moved north and wrote for the *New York Age* for a year, left journalism for three years, returned to edit the *Chicago Conservator* for two years, and then made her final exit from journalism, although her public and professional life continued for three more decades.

For many of the journalists described in these pages, the field became little more than a way station. Maria Stewart wrote for the *Liberator* for two years. Josephine St. Pierre Ruffin published *Woman's Era* for only seven. Ida B. Wells-Barnett, the best known African-American woman journalist of the nineteenth century, worked for newspapers full-time for a mere five years.

On the positive side, however, there are indications that the broken line may have been a phenomenon more prevalent in the nineteenth century than in the twentieth. Charlotta Bass's and Ethel Payne's careers both extended without interruption for more than four decades.

For black women considering a journalism career today, the most reassuring profile is that of Charlayne Hunter-Gault, the youngest of the eleven women. Despite marriage and the birth of her first child at twenty-one, a divorce, a period of years as a single mother, remarriage, and the birth of a second child, Hunter-Gault has continued her journalism career for thirty years with only two six-month gaps to give birth to her children.

Appearing on the "MacNeil/Lehrer NewsHour" nightly, Hunter-Gault is now one of the most visible black women in America today. She said: "The civil rights movement was a point of departure. It was the beginning of new possibilities for many people who previously had been excluded. It moved from race to gender to orientation. It opened up everything to people who had been excluded. For the first time, black women began to see new possibilities for themselves.

"My generation started to see things a little differently. We could see that we didn't have to make marriage and children our entire life. I had the choices, the options." [24]

Today's African-American woman journalist also has those choices and those options—thanks in no small part to Hunter-Gault and the other pioneering women described in this book.

NOTES

INTRODUCTION

1. Michael Emery and Edwin Emery, *The Press and America: An Interpretive History of the Mass Media*, 7th ed. (Englewood Cliffs, N.J.: Prentice-Hall, 1992), 228. Emery and Emery mentions half a dozen other African-American women journalists but devotes no more than one line to any of them. See pp. 181, 429-31, 497, 499. Another contemporary history of the American mass media, Jean Folkerts and Dwight Teeter, *Voices of a Nation: A History of the Media in the United States* (New York: Mac-Millan, 1989), mentions no African-American women journalists whatsoever, although it generally is sensitive to the contributions of women and minorities. No black women journalists are mentioned in earlier journalism histories such as James Melvin Lee, *History of American Journalism* (1917; reprint, New York: Garden City Publishing, 1923); Frank Luther Mott, *American Journalism* (1941; reprint, New York: MacMillan, 1960).

2. Roland E. Wolseley, *The Black Press, U.S.A.*, 2nd ed. (Ames: Iowa State Univ. Press, 1990), 40-42, 257-68. In 1992, a new volume on the history of the black press was published. Clint C. Wilson II, *Black Journalists in Paradox: Historical Perspectives and Current Dilemmas* (New York: Greenwood, 1992) confines its material on African-American women journalists to a very few pages (46-48, 74-75, 94). The material on women in two earlier histories of the black press consists of positivist biographies with few specific details. They are I. Garland Penn, *The Afro-American Press and Its Editors* (Springfield, Mass.: Willey, 1891), 366-427, and Martin E. Dann, *The Black Press, 1827-1890: The Quest for National Identity* (New York: Putnam, 1971), 61-67.

3. Kay Mills, *A Place in the News: From the Women's Pages to the Front Page* (1988; reprint, Columbia Univ. Press, 1991), 176. For examples of other calls for more research on the history of African-American women journalists, see Maurine H. Beasley, "Women in Journalism: Contributors to Male Experience or Voices of Feminine Expression?" *American Journalism* 7 (Winter 1990): 54; Maurine Beasley and Sheila Silver, *Women in Media: A Documentary Source Book* (Washington, D.C.: Women's Institute for Freedom of the Press, 1977), viii; Paula Matabane, "Strategies on Studying

Women of Color in Mass Communication," in Pamela J. Creedon, ed., *Women in Mass Communication: Challenging Gender Values* (Newbury Park, Calif.: Sage, 1989), 117-22; Jane Rhodes, "Strategies on Studying Women of Color in Mass Communication," in Creedon, *Women in Mass Communication,* 112-16; Lucy Wilmot Smith, "Woman's Number," *The Journalist* 8 (26 January 1889): 4. The first history of women journalists, Ishbel Ross, *Ladies of the Press* (New York: Harper, 1936), mentioned no African Americans. The next, Marion Marzolf, *Up From the Footnote: A History of Women Journalists* (New York: Hastings House, 1977), devoted seven pages to black women, 25-26, 90-92, 192-93. Other works about women journalists that include information about African-American women include Beasley and Silver, *Women in Media,* 38-46; Jean E. Collins, *She Was There: Stories of Pioneering Women Journalists* (New York: Julian Messner, 1980), 103-19; Alice A. Dunnigan, "Early History of Negro Women in Journalism," *Negro History Bulletin* 28 (May 1965): 178-79, 193, 197; Mills, *Place in the News,* 174-96; Gertrude Bustill Mossell, *The Work of the Afro-American Woman* (1894; reprint, New York: Oxford Univ. Press, 1988), 98-103; Madelon Golden Schilpp and Sharon M. Murphy, *Great Women of the Press* (Carbondale: Southern Illinois Univ. Press, 1983), 121-33; Smith, "Woman's Number," 4-6; J. William Snorgrass, "Pioneer Black Women Journalists from the 1850s to the 1950s," *Western Journal of Black Studies* 6 (Fall 1982): 158.

    4. Angela Y. Davis, *Women, Race and Class* (New York: Random, 1981); Paula Giddings, *When and Where I Enter: The Impact of Black Women on Race and Sex in America* (New York: William Morrow, 1984); Deborah Gray White, *Ar'n't I a Woman? Female Slaves in the Plantation South* (New York: Norton, 1985); Deborah K. King, "Multiple Jeopardy, Multiple Consciousness: The Context of a Black Feminist Ideology," in Micheline R. Malson, Elisabeth Mudimbe-Boyi, Jean F. O'Barr, and Mary Wyer, eds., *Black Women in America: Social Science Perspectives* (Chicago: Univ. of Chicago Press, 1990), 266.

    5. Interview with Ethel L. Payne by Kathleen Currie, Women in Journalism oral history project of the Washington Press Club Foundation, 25 August 1987 through 17 November 1987, Oral History Collection, Columbia University, p. 118.

    6. Charlotta A. Bass, "Fight Against 'The Clansman' Lost by City Council And Many Citizens of both Races," *California Eagle,* 13 February 1915, p. 1.

    7. C. Gerald Fraser, "Charlayne Hunter-Gault: From Front Line to Firing Line," *Essence,* March 1987, p. 110.

    8. Monroe A. Majors, *Noted Negro Women: Their Triumphs and Activities* (Jackson, Tenn.: M.V. Lynk, 1893), 139; Snorgrass, "Pioneer Black Women Journalists," 152.

    9. On the gulf between black women and white women, see Bonnie Thornton Dill, "The Dialectics of Black Womanhood," *Signs* 4 (Spring 1979): 543-45; James A. Geschwender and Rita Carroll-Seguin, "Explod-

ing the Myth of African-American Progress," *Signs* 15 (Winter 1990): 285-86; Giddings, *When and Where*, 64-68, 123-31, 299-311; Charlayne Hunter, "Many Blacks Wary of 'Women's Liberation' Movement," *New York Times*, 17 November 1970, p. 60; Toni Morrison, "What the Black Woman Thinks About Women's Lib," *New York Times Magazine*, 22 August 1971, p. 15; Eleanor Holmes Norton, "For Sadie and Maude," in Robin Morgan, ed., *Sisterhood Is Powerful: An Anthology of Writings from the Women's Liberation Movement* (New York: Vintage, 1970), 400; Natalie J. Sokoloff, "The Economic Position of Women in the Family," in Peter J. Stein, Judith Richman, and Natalie Hannon, eds., *The Family* (Reading, Mass.: Addison-Wesley, 1977).

10. Charlayne Hunter-Gault, "We Overcame Too," *TV Guide*, 17 January 1987, p. 33. On race being a more salient force than gender in the lives of African-American women, see Giddings, *When and Where*, 7, 117, 308-10; Sharon Harley, "For the Good of Family and Race: Gender, Work, and Domestic Roles in the Black Community, 1880-1930," in Malson et al., *Black Women in America*, 161-63; Bell Hooks, *Feminist Theory: From Margin to Center* (Boston: South End, 1984); Gloria Joseph and Jill Lewis, *Common Differences: Conflicts in Black and White Feminist Perspectives* (New York: Avon, 1981); Diane K. Lewis, "A Response to Inequality: Black Women, Racism, and Sexism," *Signs* 3 (Winter 1977): 339-61; Susan A. Mann, "Slavery, Sharecropping, and Sexual Inequality," *Signs* 14 (Summer 1989): 775-76.

11. On African-American women historically having been accepted as coworkers by African-American men, see William A. Blakey, "Everybody Makes the Revolution: Some Thoughts on Racism and Sexism," *Civil Rights Digest* 6 (Spring 1974): 19; Clyde W. Franklin, Jr., and Laurel R. Walum, "Toward a Paradigm of Structural Relations: An Application to Sex and Race in the United States," *Phylon* 33 (Fall 1972): 249; Lewis, "Response to Inequality," 346.

12. On the tradition of black women working outside the home, see Deborah Aldridge, "Black Women in the Economic Marketplace: A Battle Unfinished," *Journal of Social and Behavioral Scientists* 21 (Winter 1975): 48-61; E. Franklin Frazier, *The Negro Family in the United States* (Chicago: Univ. of Chicago Press, 1973), 102; Giddings, *When and Where*, 48, 58-59, 108, 121, 232; Jacqueline Jackson, "Family Organization and Ideology," in Kent Miller and Ralph Dreger, eds., *Comparative Studies of Blacks and Whites in the United States* (New York: Seminar, 1973); Gerda Lerner, ed., *Black Women in White America: A Documentary History* (New York: Random, 1972); Lewis, "Response to Inequality," 339-61; Morrison, "What the Black Woman Thinks," 15; Linda Perkins, "Black Women and Racial 'Uplift' Prior to Emancipation," in Filomena Chioma Steady, ed., *The Black Woman Cross-Culturally* (Cambridge, Mass.: Schenkman, 1981), 317-34; Phyllis A. Wallace, *Black Women in the Labor Force* (Cambridge, Mass.: MIT Press, 1980), 10-11.

13. On education playing a central role in the lives of African- American

women, see Giddings, *When and Where*, 201-5; Sharon Harley, "Beyond the Classroom: Organizational Lives of Black Female Educators in the District of Columbia, 1890-1930," *Journal of Negro Education* 51 (Summer 1982): 254-65; Cynthia Neverdon-Morton, "Self-Help Programs as Educative Activities of Black Women in the South, 1895-1925: Focus on Four Key Areas," *Journal of Negro Education* 51 (Summer 1982): 207-21; Perkins, "Black Women and Racial 'Uplift,'" 317-34; Bettye Collier Thomas, ed., "Special Issue: The Impact of Black Women in Education," *Journal of Negro Education* 51 (Summer 1982).

14. On religion playing a central role in the lives of black women, see Cheryl Townsend Glikes, "'Together and in Harness': Women's Traditions in the Sanctified Church," in Malson et al., *Black Women in America*, 223-44; Teresa Hoover, "Black Women and the Churches: Triple Jeopardy," in Gayraud Wilmore and James Cone, eds., *Black Theology: A Documentary History* (Maryknoll, N.Y.: Orbis, 1979), 377-88; James Tinney, "The Religious Experience of Black Men," in Lawrence E. Gary, ed., *The Black Male* (Beverly Hills, Calif.: Sage, 1981), 269-76; Pearl Williams-Jones, "A Minority Report: Black Pentecostal Women," *Spirit: A Journal of Issues Incident in Black Pentecostalism* 1 (1977): 31-44.

15. There has been little previous effort to synthesize the common experiences of African-American women journalists. The handful of works that have assembled sketches of the lives of this particular category of journalists typically has had either no introduction or a brief introduction devoid of analysis. Examples include Dann, Penn, Snorgrass, and Wolseley. An exception is Gloria Wade-Gayles, "Black Women Journalists in the South, 1880-1905: An Approach to the Study of Black Women's History," *Callaloo* 4 (February-October 1981): 138-52. Wade-Gayles's analysis, however, is limited to black women writing in the South in the nineteenth and early twentieth centuries.

16. Gerda Lerner, *The Majority Finds Its Past: Placing Women in History* (New York: Oxford Univ. Press, 1979), 145-59. For discussion of the stages of conceptualization of women's history applied to journalists, see Catherine Mitchell, "The Place of Biography in the History of News Women," *American Journalism* 7 (Winter 1990): 25-26.

17. Matabane, "Strategies on Studying," 120.

18. Giddings has pointed out that middle-class African-American women activists of the late nineteenth century tended to be elitist. *When and Where*, 98-102.

19. On research about women journalists glorifying those women, see Mitchell, "Place of Biography," 27. For a broad discussion of the conceptual stages of women's history, see Lerner, *Majority Finds Its Past*, 145-59. For examples of scholars calling for more rigorous examination of women journalists, see Mary Ann Yodelis Smith, "Research Retrospectives: Feminism and the Media," *Communication Research* 9 (January 1982): 245-60; Zena Beth McGlashen, "Women Witness the Russian Revolution: Analyzing Ways of Seeing," *Journalism History* 12 (Summer 1985): 54; Susan

Henry, "Changing Media History Through Women's History," in Creedon, *Women in Mass Communication*, 40.

1. MARIA W. STEWART

1. The *Nation*, "The Liberator Released," 4 January 1866, p. 7. For other appraisals of the impact of the *Liberator*, see Emery and Emery, *Press and America*, 121-22; Folkerts and Teeter, *Voices of a Nation*, 189; Oliver Johnson, *William Lloyd Garrison and His Times, or Sketches of the Anti-Slavery Movement in America, and of the Man Who Was Its Founder and Moral Leader* (Boston: B.B. Russell, 1880), 54.

2. Maria W. Stewart, "Lecture Delivered at the Franklin Hall," *Liberator*, 17 November 1832, p. 183. Maria W. Stewart's words first appeared in the *Liberator* 19 March 1831, in the form of a poem, "The Negro's Complaint," p. 46. The rest of her work for the *Liberator* was in the form of essays, the last of which appeared 4 May 1833.

3. Some sources identify Sarah Gibson Jones as the first African-American woman journalist, but Jones began working for the *Cincinnati Colored Citizen* in 1863, thirty years after Stewart's essays appeared in the *Liberator*. See Majors, *Noted Negro Women*, 139; Snorgrass, "Pioneer Black Women Journalists," 152.

4. Stewart provided details about her life in her two books, *Productions of Mrs. Maria Stewart* (Boston: Friends of Freedom and Virtue, 1835), 3-4, 24; *Meditations from the Pen of Mrs. Maria W. Stewart* (Washington, D.C.: 1879), iii, iv, 13-23. This quote is from *Productions*, 3. Another important source of information about Stewart's life is an obituary, "The Late Mrs. Maria W. Stewart," *People's Advocate*, 28 February 1880, p. 1. *People's Advocate* was a black newspaper published in Washington, D.C. Many secondary sources also include profiles of Stewart as a pioneer public speaker and abolitionist. Those profiles, based largely on the details in her books, include William L. Andrews, ed., *Sisters of the Spirit: Three Black Women's Autobiographies of the Nineteenth Century* (Bloomington: Indiana Univ. Press, 1986), 22; Eleanor Flexner, *Century of Struggle: The Woman's Rights Movement in the United States* (Cambridge, Mass.: Harvard Univ. Press, 1959), 44-45, 343; Giddings, *When and Where*, 50, 53; Sue E. Houchins, "Introduction," in Henry Louis Gates, Jr., ed., *Spiritual Narratives* (New York: Oxford Univ. Press, 1988), xxix-xliv; Edward T. James, ed., *Notable American Women, 1607-1950: A Biographical Dictionary*, vol. 3 (Cambridge, Mass.: Belknap Press of Harvard Univ. Press, 1971), 377-78; Lerner, *Black Women in White America*, 83-84; Bert James Loewenberg and Ruth Bogin, eds., *Black Women in Nineteenth-Century American Life: Their Words, Their Thoughts, Their Feelings* (University Park: Pennsylvania State Univ. Press, 1976), 183-200; Lillian O'Connor, *Pioneer Women Orators: Rhetoric in the Ante-Bellum Reform Movement* (New York: Columbia Univ. Press, 1954), 53-55, 142; Dorothy Porter, *Early Negro Writing 1760-1873*

(Boston: Beacon, 1971), 129-40, 460-71; Benjamin Quarles, *Black Abolitionists* (New York: Oxford Univ. Press, 1969), 7, 50, 192; Marilyn Richardson, ed., *Maria W. Stewart: America's First Black Woman Political Writer* (Bloomington: Indiana Univ. Press, 1987), 3; Dorothy Sterling, ed., *We Are Your Sisters: Black Women in the Nineteenth Century* (New York: Norton, 1984), 153-59; Lisa Studier, "Maria W. Stewart," in Jessie Carney Smith, ed., *Notable Black American Women* (Detroit: Gale Research, 1992), 1083-87; Shirley J. Yee, *Black Women Abolitionists: A Study in Activism, 1828-1860* (Knoxville: Univ. of Tennessee Press, 1992); Jean Fagan Yellin, *Women and Sisters: The Antislavery Feminists in American Culture* (New Haven: Yale Univ. Press, 1989), 46-48. See also Rodger Streitmatter, "Maria W. Stewart: The First Female African-American Journalist," *Historical Journal of Massachusetts* 21 (Summer 1993): 44-59.

5. The couple's marriage certificate is at the Registry of Marriages in Boston. It reads: "James W. Stewart & Maria Miller, (people of color) married by the Rev. Thomas Paul, 10 August 1826."

6. James W. Stewart died 16 December 1829. A copy of his death certificate is part of a pension claim that Maria W. Stewart filed in 1879. See Service Pension, War of 1812, Widow's Brief No. 35165, Service Pension, National Archives, Washington, D.C. One comment on that claim form states: "Claimant states that ever since her husband's death she has written her name with 'W' for a middle initial—that it was so written in her husband's will."

7. See Lerner, *Black Women in White America*, 83; Richardson, *Maria W. Stewart*, 7; Sterling, *We Are Your Sisters*, 153.

8. Stewart, *Productions*, 4. On newspaper articles of the early nineteenth century being much like sermons, see Carter R. Bryan, "Negro Journalism in America Before Emancipation," *Journalism Monographs* 12 (September 1969): 3-4.

9. William Lloyd Garrison letter to Maria W. Stewart, 4 April 1879, in Stewart, *Meditations*, 6; James, *Notable American Women*, 377; *Liberator*, "For sale at this office," 8 October 1831, p. 163. Stewart's first public lecture was to the New England Anti-Slavery Society, 21 September 1832, at Franklin Hall in Boston. She also spoke to the Afric-American Female Intelligence Society of Boston in the spring of 1832, but many historians do not consider that speech as historically significant as others because it was to a totally female audience.

10. Stewart, "An Address Delivered Before The Afric-American Female Intelligence Society of Boston," *Liberator*, 28 April 1832, p. 66.

11. Ibid.

12. On the evangelistic movement of the 1830s, see Andrews, *Sisters of the Spirit*, 22; Houchins, "Introduction," xxix-xliv.

13. Stewart, "An Address, Delivered at the African Masonic Hall in Boston," *Liberator*, 4 May 1833, p. 72.

14. Stewart, "An Address, Delivered Before The Afric-American Female Intelligence Society of Boston," *Liberator*, 28 April 1832, p. 66.

15. Stewart, "Lecture Delivered At The Franklin Hall," *Liberator*, 17 November 1832, p. 183.

16. Stewart, "An Address, Delivered at the African Masonic Hall in Boston," *Liberator*, 4 May 1833, p. 72. On the Colonization Movement, see John Hope Franklin and Alfred A. Moss, Jr., *From Slavery to Freedom: A History of Negro Americans* (New York: McGraw-Hill, 1988), 154-57.

17. Stewart, "Lecture Delivered At The Franklin Hall," *Liberator*, 17 November 1832, p. 183. Garrison published only about one-fifth of Stewart's first essay in the *Liberator*; he published the entire essay, under the full title, in pamphlet form. On nineteenth-century African-American women seeing themselves as moral guides, see Giddings, *When and Where*, 99-101.

18. Stewart, "Mrs. Steward's [sic] Essays," *Liberator*, 7 January 1832, p. 2.

19. Stewart, *Liberator*, "An Address, Delivered at the African Masonic Hall in Boston," 4 May 1833, p. 72; "Cause For Encouragement," 14 July 1832, p. 110.

20. Stewart, "Mrs. Steward's [sic] Essays," *Liberator*, 7 January 1832, p. 2.

21. Stewart, "Lecture Delivered At The Franklin Hall," *Liberator*, 17 November 1832, p. 183.

22. Stewart, "An Address Delivered Before The Afric-American Female Intelligence Society of Boston," *Liberator*, 28 April 1832, p. 66.

23. Stewart, "An Address, Delivered at the African Masonic Hall in Boston," *Liberator*, 27 April 1833, p. 68.

24. Stewart, "An Address, Delivered at the African Masonic Hall in Boston," *Liberator*, 4 May 1833, p. 72. On efforts to abolish slavery in the District of Columbia, see William H. Williams, *The Negro in the District of Columbia during Reconstruction* (Howard University Studies in History, no. 5: Washington, D.C., June 1924), 1-6.

25. Stewart, "An Address, Delivered at the African Masonic Hall in Boston," *Liberator*, 4 May 1833, p. 72.

26. Stewart, "Mrs. Steward's [sic] Essays," *Liberator*, 7 January 1832, p. 2.

27. Ibid.

28. Ibid.

29. Stewart, *Liberator*, "Mrs. Steward's [sic] Essays," 7 January 1832, p. 2; "Lecture Delivered At The Franklin Hall," 17 November 1832, p. 183.

30. Stewart, "An Address Delivered Before The Afric-American Female Intelligence Society of Boston," *Liberator*, 28 April 1832, p. 66.

31. Stewart, *Meditations*, 79; Yee, *Black Women Abolitionists*, 115. William C. Nell, a colleague of Garrison's, recalled that Stewart received "opposition even from her Boston circle of friends"; see "Letter from William C. Nell," *Liberator*, 5 March 1852, p. 39.

32. African-American women's literary societies of the era developed the cultural lives of their members while also working for civic improvement and providing social services for members of their race. See Giddings,

When and Where, 49. The entire text of Stewart's book has been reprinted as part of the Schomburg Library of Nineteenth-Century Black Women Writers series. See Gates, *Spiritual Narratives*.

33. Robert J. Swan, "A Synoptic History of Black Public Schools in Brooklyn," in Charlene Claye Van Derzee, *The Black Contribution to the Development of Brooklyn* (Brooklyn: New Music Community Museum of Brooklyn, 1977), 64.

34. Stewart was listed as a member of a committee organized to plan a fair for the benefit of the *North Star*. See *North Star*, "Committee of Arrangements," 12 April 1850, p. 4.

35. Stewart, *Meditations*, 13-14.

36. *People's Advocate*, "The Late Mrs. Maria W. Stewart," 28 February 1880, p. 1.

37. Giddings, *When and Where*, 53; James, *Notable American Women*, 378; Lerner, *Black Women in White America*, 83-84; Richardson, *Maria W. Stewart*, xvi; Yellin, *Women and Sisters*, 190.

38. Stewart, *Meditations*.

39. *Boyd's Directory of the District of Columbia* (1877), p. 713; burial records from St. Luke's Church, Washington, D.C.; *People's Advocate*, "The Late Mrs. Maria Stewart," 28 February 1880, p. 1.

2. MARY ANN SHADD CARY

1. On Canadian emigration, see Franklin and Moss, *From Slavery to Freedom*, 154-57; S.G. Howe, *The Refugees from Slavery in Canada West* (Boston: Wright and Potter, 1964); Marion McDougall, *Fugitive Slaves* (New York: Bergman, 1967), 57-58; Robin W. Winks, *The Blacks in Canada* (Montreal: McGill-Queen's Univ. Press, 1971).

2. Winks, *Blacks in Canada*, 394.

3. On the role newspapers played in Canadian emigration, see Alexander L. Murray, "The *Provincial Freeman*: A New Source for the History of the Negro in Canada and the United States," *Journal of Negro History* 44 (1959): 123-35; Jane Rhodes, "Fugitives and Freemen: The Role of the Abolitionist Press in the Building of a Black Community in Canada West," a paper presented to the History Division of the Association for Education in Journalism and Mass Communication, August 1989, Washington, D.C.

4. Winks, *Blacks in Canada*, 396.

5. Mary Ann Shadd Cary, "Meetings at Philadelphia," *Provincial Freeman*, 18 April 1857, p. 2.

6. Mary Ann Shadd, "The Emigration Convention," *Provincial Freeman*, 5 July 1856, p. 2.

7. A major source of information about Mary Ann Shadd Cary's life is the Mary Ann Shadd Cary Papers, held at Moorland-Spingarn Research Center, Howard University, Washington, D.C. The papers consist of documents filling fifty-six folders. Information about Cary's life also can be gleaned

from articles in the *Provincial Freeman*. Among the numerous secondary sources containing information about her are Jim Bearden and Linda Jean Butler, *Shadd: The Life and Times of Mary Shadd Cary* (Toronto: NC Press, 1977); Hallie Q. Brown, *Homespun Heroines and Other Women of Distinction* (Xenia, Oh.: Aldine, 1926), 92-96; William Wells Brown, *The Rising Son, or the Antecedents and Advancement of the Colored Race* (1874; reprint, Miami: Mnemosyne, 1969), 539-40; Dann, *Black Press*, 332-33, 347-48; Sylvia G.L. Dannett, *Profiles of Negro Womanhood* (New York: M.W. Lads, 1964), 150-57; Elizabeth Lindsay Davis, *Lifting as They Climb* (Washington: National Association of Colored Women, 1933), 294-95; Giddings, *When and Where*, 59, 69-71, 75, 262; Harold B. Hancock, "Mary Ann Shadd: Negro Editor, Educator, and Lawyer," *Delaware History* 15 (April 1973): 187-94; James, *Notable American Women*, vol. 1, pp. 300-301; Clifton H. Johnson, "Mary Ann Shadd: Crusader for the Freedom of Man," *Crisis*, vol. 78 (April-May 1971): 89-90; Lerner, *Black Women in White America*, 323-25; Majors, *Noted Negro Women*, 112-13; Jason H. Silverman, "Mary Ann Shadd and the Search for Equality," in Leon Litwack and August Meier, eds., *Black Leaders of the Nineteenth Century* (Urbana: Univ. of Illinois Press, 1988), 87-100; Murray, *"Provincial Freemen"*; Jessie Carney Smith, "Mary Ann Shadd," in Smith, *Notable Black American Women*, 998-1003; Sterling, *We Are Your Sisters*, 164-75; Bernell E. Tripp, "Abolitionist, Emigrationist, Feminist: Mary Ann Shadd Cary, First Female Editor of the Black Press," paper presented to the American Journalism Historians Association, October 1992, Lawrence, Kansas; Winks, *Blacks in Canada*; Yee, *Black Women Abolitionists*.

8. "Mary Ann Shadd Cary: The Foremost Colored Canadian Pioneer, in 1850," handwritten manuscript, Cary Papers, folder 1; Martin R. Delany, *The Condition, Elevation, Emigration, and Destiny of the Colored People of the United States* (Philadelphia: 1852), 131.

9. The American Missionary Association, based in New York, was founded in 1846 by radical abolitionists dedicated to spreading the gospel through good works.

10. Shadd, "A Plea for Emigration, or Notes of Canada West" (Detroit: 1852). A copy of the pamphlet is held at the Moorland-Spingarn Research Center, Howard University Library, Washington, D.C.

11. *Voice of the Fugitive*, "Schools in Canada," 15 July 1852, p. 2.

12. Shadd letters to George Whipple, 22 July and 25 December 1852, Cary Papers; Sterling, *We Are Your Sisters*, 168; Bearden and Butler, *Shadd*, 124.

13. Although Shadd was the first African-American woman to edit a newspaper, she had been preceded by a white woman who had edited an anti-slavery newspaper; that editor was Jane Grey Swisshelm, who had established the *Saturday Visiter* in Pittsburgh in 1848. *Frederick Douglass' Paper* was published in Rochester, New York, from 1851 to 1860, and the *Impartial Citizen* was published only briefly. See Carter R. Bryan, "Negro Journalism in America Before Emancipation," *Journalism Monographs* 12 (September 1969): 23-24, 32.

14. *Provincial Freeman*, "Letters must be addressed," 24 March 1853, p. 1.

15. Samuel Ringgold Ward, "Introductory," *Provincial Freeman*, 24 March 1853, p. 1.

16. Ibid.

17. *Pennsylvania Freeman*, "Great Anti-Colonization Meeting in Philadelphia," 29 September, 1853, p. 3; Quarles, *Black Abolitionists*, 178; Lerner, *Black Women in White America*, 83.

18. Shadd, "Prospectus for the *Provincial Freeman*," *Provincial Freeman*, 25 March 1854, p. 3.

19. Ibid.

20. Shadd, "Canadian Churches fellowshiping the Pro-slavery Religious Bodies of the United States," *Provincial Freeman*, 13 December 1856, p. 2; Winks, *Blacks in Canada*, 207.

21. Cary, "Rowdyism by three Trustees," *Provincial Freeman*, 18 April 1857, p. 2.

22. Cary, "Refugees in Canada," *Provincial Freeman*, 14 March 1857, p. 2.

23. Cary, *Provincial Freeman*, "Beer," 6 May 1854, p. 1; "Grammar School," 26 July 1856, p. 2; "Exposed at Last," 2 May 1857, p. 2. *Provincial Freeman*, "To the *Provincial Freeman*," 29 December 1855, p. 2.

24. *Provincial Freeman*, "Woman's Rights," 12 August 1854, p. 2.

25. Shadd, "Prospectus for the Provincial Freeman," *Provincial Freeman*, 28 October 1854, p. 1.

26. *Provincial Freeman*, "To our Readers West," 9 June 1855, p. 2.

27. Shadd, "Adieu," *Provincial Freeman*, 30 June 1855, p. 2.

28. "Report, Statement of affairs in the *Provincial Freeman*," 9 June 1854, Cary Papers, folder 25; Sterling, p. 172.

29. *Provincial Freeman*, "Our Agent Going West," 19 January 1856, p. 1.

30. *Frederick Douglass' Paper*, "From Our Brooklyn Correspondent," 9 November 1855, p. 3.

31. *Provincial Freeman*, "Editorial Changes," 19 January 1856, p. 1; "Circular: Slavery and Humanity," February 1857, Cary Papers, folder 51. Cary, "Pay Us What You Owe," *Provincial Freeman*, 28 February 1857, p. 2.

32. Sarah Elizabeth Cary was born 7 August 1857. The last extant issue of the *Provincial Freeman* is dated 20 September 1857.

33. Victor Ullman, *Look to the North Star, A Life of William King* (Boston: Beacon Press, 1969), 246. "John Brown and his times," handwritten notes, Cary Papers, folder 23. Osborne P. Anderson, *A Voice from Harper's Ferry* (1861; reprint, Atlanta: World View, 1980).

34. Thomas F. Cary died 29 November 1860. For samples of Cary's work in the *Weekly Anglo-African*, see Mary A. Shadd Cary, *Weekly Anglo-African*, "Haytian Emigration," 28 September, 1861, p. 2; "Haytian Emigration in Canada," 19 October 1861, p. 2; "Haytian Emigration," 26 October 1861, p. 2; "Haytian Emigration," 9 November 1861, p. 1; "A

Correction," 28 December 1861, p. 2; "The Mission School at Chatham," 5 April 1862, p. 2.

35. "Authorization to Recruit," 24 February 1864, Cary Papers, folder 30; Benjamin S. Pardee letter to Cary, 3 March 1864, Cary Papers, folder 4.

36. Cary Papers, folders 31, 35.

37. Frederick Douglass letter to Cary, 5 July 1871, Cary Papers, folder 3. For samples of Cary's articles, see the *New National Era*, "Letter from Baltimore," 10 August 1871, p. 1; "Letters to the People—No. 1," 21 March 1872, p. 3; "Letters to the People—No. 2," 11 April 1872, p. 1; *New York Freeman*, "Advancement of Women," 19 November 1887, p. 4.

38. Cary, "The Last Day of the 43 Congress," Cary Papers, folder 16.

39. Cary, "Letter No. 5," Cary Papers, folder 21.

40. Cary Papers, folder 24; *People's Advocate*, "Commencement Week—Wayland and Howard," 2 June 1883, p. 2; Bearden and Butler, *Shadd*, 211; Brown, *Homespun Heroines*, 95-96.

41. Samuel Watson letter to Cary, 16 December 1869, Cary Papers, folder 6; "Mrs. Carey [sic] in Mississippi," *New York Freeman*, 11 April 1885, p. 2.

42. Giddings, *When and Where*, 70; Silverman, "Mary Ann Shadd," 98; Elizabeth Cady Stanton, Susan B. Anthony, and Matilde Joslyn Gage, eds., *History of Woman Suffrage (1876-1885)*, vol 3 (Rochester, N.Y.: 1887), 72; Cary Papers, folder 34.

43. *People's Advocate*, "Local," 21 February 1880, p. 3; "Statement of Purpose, Colored Women's Professional Franchise Association," Cary Papers, folder 46. By the turn of the century, the National Association of Colored Women had formed, uniting thousands of African-American women. See Giddings, *When and Where*, 95-117, 135-42; Gerda Lerner, "Early Community Work of Black Club Women," *Journal of Negro History* 59 (April 1973): 158-67; Charles Harris Wesley, *The History of the National Association of Colored Women's Clubs: A Legacy of Service* (Washington: National Association of Colored Women's Clubs, 1984). Josephine St. Pierre Ruffin established *Woman's Era*, the first newspaper published by and for African-American women, in Boston in 1890.

44. *Washington Evening Star*, "Death of Linton Carey [sic]," 22 December 1892, p. 5; "Died," 5 June 1893, p. 5.

45. Julius Lester, ed., *The Thought and Writings of W.E.B. DuBois: The Seventh Son*, vol. 1 (New York: Random House, 1971), 521; *New National Era*, "Mrs. Mary A.S. Cary," 13 July 1871, p. 2; *Frederick Douglass' Paper*, "Canada," 4 July 1856, p. 2.

3. GERTRUDE BUSTILL MOSSELL

1. On African-American migration to the North after slavery, see Martin Rywell and Charles Harris Wesley, eds., *Afro-American Encyclopedia* (North Miami, Fla.: Educational Book Publishers, 1974), 2930-31; Herbert Aptheker, ed., *A Documentary History of the Negro People in the*

United States, vol. 2, 4th ed. (New York: Citadel Press, 1951), 713; W.E.B. DuBois, "Social Effects of Emancipation," in June Sochen, ed., *The Black Man and the American Dream: Negro Aspirations in America, 1900-1930* (Chicago: Quadrangle, 1971), 79-83; Franklin and Moss, *From Slavery to Freedom*, 227-64.

2. Dann, *Black Press*, 294-375; Wolseley, *Black Press, U.S.A.*, 38-40.

3. In 1890, 57.1 percent of black Americans were illiterate, compared to 7.7 percent of white Americans. See "Negroes in the United States," a special report of the Bureau of the Census (Washington, D.C.: Government Printing Office, 1904).

4. Gertrude Bustill Mossell, "Our Woman's Department," *New York Freeman*, 11 September 1886, p. 2.

5. Mossell, "Our Woman's Department," *New York Freeman*, 2 October 1886, p. 2.

6. Gertrude Bustill Mossell's sister Anna was the mother of actor, singer, and activist Paul Robeson.

7. The Institute for Colored Youth was a Quaker school with a national reputation. Graduates included the first African-American woman to win a degree from a four-year college and the first African-American men to graduate from Harvard or to receive a doctoral degree. See Roger Lane, *William Dorsey's Philadelphia and Ours: On the Past and Future of the Black City in America* (New York: Oxford Univ. Press, 1991), xiii.

8. Mossell, "Our Woman's Department," *Indianapolis World*, 10 September 1892, p. 1. Chautauqua, which began in 1874, offered adult courses in education, religion, public issues, music, and art. Courses were offered in Chautauqua County in New York State. See Theodore Morrison, *Chautauqua* (Chicago: Univ. of Chicago Press, 1974). Biographical information about Mossell is contained in Dannett, *Profiles of Negro Womanhood*, 294-95; Roger Lane, *Roots of Violence in Black Philadelphia, 1860-1900* (Cambridge: Harvard Univ. Press, 1986), 155-57; Lane, *William Dorsey's Philadelphia and Ours*, 183-89; Rayford W. Logan and Michael R. Winston, eds., *Dictionary of American Negro Biography* (New York: Norton, 1982), 457; Majors, *Noted Negro Women*, 129; Frank Lincoln Mather, *Who's Who of the Colored Race*, vol. 1 (Chicago: 1915), 201-2; Marzolf, *Up From the Footnote*, 25; J.L. Nichols and William H. Crogman, eds., *Progress of a Race, or the Remarkable Advancements of the American Negro* (Naperville, Ill.: J.L. Nichols, 1925), 414; G.F. Richings, *Evidences of Progress Among Colored People*, (Philadelphia: George S. Ferguson, 1897), 417-19; Lucy Wilmot Smith, "Woman's Number," *Journalist*, vol. 8, 26 January 1889, p. 4; Rosalyn Terborg-Penn, "Gertrude Bustill Mossell," in Smith, *Notable Black American Women* , 775-77; Ida B. Wells, "Mrs. N.F. Mossell," in L.A. Scruggs, *Women of Distinction: Remarkable in Works and Invincible in Character* (Raleigh, N.C.: 1893), 23-25. See also Anna Bustill Smith, "The Bustill Family," *Journal of Negro History* 10 (October 1925), 638-44.

9. The *Christian Recorder* was a general interest weekly newspaper founded by the African Methodist Episcopal Church in Philadelphia in 1852. It was distributed nationally.

10. Lane, *William Dorsey's Philadelphia and Ours*, 174-75. For details on the life of Nathan F. Mossell, see Logan and Winston, *Dictionary of American Negro Biography*, 457-58; Mather, *Who's Who of the Colored Race*, 202. Florence Mossell married John R. Holmes, and Mazie Mossell married Dr. J.H. Griffin, Jr. See Terborg-Penn, "Gertrude Bustill Mossell," 777.

11. On the *New York Freeman*, *New York Age*, and T. Thomas Fortune, see Wolseley, *Black Press, U.S.A.*, 27-28, 47-48. *Woman's Era*, which was closely connected to the National Association of Colored Women, was published monthly from 1890 to 1897.

12. *Colored American Magazine* was published monthly from 1900 to 1909 in Boston and New York. The Library of Congress in Washington, D.C., has 108 extant issues. See Penelope Bullock, "The Negro Periodical Press in the United States, 1838-1909," (Ph.D. diss., University of Michigan, 1971), 358-59. *Our Women and Children* was published monthly from 1888 to 1890 in Louisville. No issues have survived. See Bullock, 386-87. The *African Methodist Episcopal Church Review* was published quarterly in Philadelphia from 1884 to 1908. Among the libraries holding early issues is the Library of Congress. See Bullock, 351. *Alumni Magazine* was published quarterly by the alumni of Lincoln University from 1884 to 1885 in Philadelphia. Nathan F. Mossell, who graduated from Lincoln University, edited the magazine. Four surviving copies of *Alumni Magazine* are held in the Lincoln University Library in Philadelphia. See Bullock, 355. *Ringwood's Afro-American Journal of Fashion* was published monthly from 1891 to 1895 in Cleveland. No issues are extant. See Bullock, 390.

13. Beatrice Fairfax, whose real name was Maria Manning, began writing an advice column for William Randolph Hearst's newspapers in 1898. Dorothy Dix, whose real name was Elizabeth Meriwether Gilmer, began writing a Sunday advice column for the *New Orleans Daily Picayune* in 1896. In 1901 she began working for William Randolph Hearst's newspapers, writing a column three days a week. She continued to write the column until 1949.

14. This chapter is based largely on thirty-nine of Mossell's columns and articles published in the *New York Freeman* from 1885 to 1887 and held in the Newspapers and Current Periodicals Reading Room of the Library of Congress; eleven columns published in the *Indianapolis World* from 1891 to 1892 and held in the Indiana State Library in Indianapolis; and five articles printed in *Woman's Era* in 1895 and held at the Boston Public Library.

15. Wells, "Mrs. N.F. Mossell," 23; Mossell, "Our Woman's Department," *New York Freeman*, 10 April 1886, p. 2.

16. Historian Paula Giddings observed that thrift was a guiding principle among African-American women activists of the late nineteenth century. See Giddings, *When and Where*, 108. Mossell, "Our Woman's Department," *New York Freeman*, 24 April 1886, p. 2; 9 January 1886, p. 2; 13 March 1886, p. 2; 5 February 1887, p. 2; 16 October 1886, p. 1.

17. Giddings, *When and Where*, 99-101; Mossell, "Our Woman's De-

partment," *New York Freeman*, 26 December 1885, p. 2; 17 April 1886, p. 2; *Indianapolis World*, 13 August 1892, p. 2.

18. Mossell, "Our Woman's Department," *New York Freeman*, 30 January 1886, p. 3; 26 December 1885, p. 2.

19. Giddings observed that African-American women activists of the late nineteenth century believed that their moral standing was a rock upon which the race could lean. See Giddings, *When and Where*, 81, 100.

20. Mossell, "Our Woman's Department," *New York Freeman*, 13 March 1886, p. 2; 13 February 1886, p. 2; 23 January 1886, p. 2; 10 July 1886, p. 1.

21. Mather, *Who's Who of the Colored Race*, 201.

22. On middle-class African-American women activists of the late nineteenth century as elitist, see Giddings, *When and Where*, 98-102. On the African-American press of the late 1800s being elitist, see Lee Finkle, *Forum for Protest: The Black Press During World War II* (Rutherford, N.J.: Fairleigh Dickinson University Press, 1975), 31; Wolseley, *Black Press, U.S.A.*, 25.

23. Mossell, "Our Woman's Department," *New York Freeman*, 2 January 1886, p. 1; 20 February 1886, p. 2; 8 January 1887, p. 4; *Indianapolis World*, 10 September 1892, p. 1.

24. Mossell, "Our Woman's Department," *New York Freeman*, 17 April 1886, p. 2; *Indianapolis World*, 24 September 1892, p. 1; 27 August 1892, p. 1.

25. Mossell, "Our Woman's Department," *Indianapolis World*, 18 June 1892, p. 4; 6 August 1892, p. 2.

26. Mossell, "Our Woman's Department," *New York Freeman*, 28 August 1886, p. 2.

27. Mossell, "Our Woman's Department," *New York Freeman*, 27 March 1886, p. 2.

28. Ibid.

29. Mossell, "Our Woman's Department," *Indianapolis World*, 6 August 1892, p. 2; 18 June 1892, p. 4; *New York Freeman*, 11 December 1886, p. 1.

30. Lane, *William Dorsey's Philadelphia and Ours*, 220-22; Mossell, "Our Woman's Department," *Indianapolis World*, 6 August 1892, p. 2; 11 June 1892, p. 1; 10 September 1892, p.1.

31. Mossell, "Our Woman's Department," *New York Freeman*, 13 November 1886, p. 1.

32. Mossell, "Our Woman's Department," *New York Freeman*, 13 November 1886, p. 1; Monroe A. Majors, *Noted Negro Women* (Chicago: Donohue and Hennebery, 1893), 129-33.

33. Lane, *William Dorsey's Philadelphia and Ours*, 184-85; Mossell, "Our Woman's Department," *New York Freeman*, 6 November 1886, p. 4.

34. Mossell, "Our Woman's Department," *New York Freeman*, 26 December 1885, p. 2.

35. Mossell, "Our Woman's Department," *Indianapolis World*, 9 July

1892, p. 1; *New York Freeman*, 3 July 1886, p. 2; *Indianapolis World*, 18 June 1892, p. 4; *New York Freeman*, 27 February 1886, p. 2; "The Open Court," *Woman's Era*, May 1895, p. 19.

36. Mossell, "Our Woman's Department," *New York Freeman*, 4 December 1886, p. 2; 6 February 1886, p. 4; 27 March 1886, p. 2; 19 June 1886, p. 2; 13 March 1886, p. 2, and 24 April 1886, p. 2; *Indianapolis World*, 9 July 1892, p. 1.

37. Mossell, "Our Woman's Department," *New York Freeman*, 8 May 1886, p. 2. See also Mossell, "Our Woman's Department," *New York Freeman*, 5 June 1886, p. 2; Smith, "Woman's Number," 4.

38. Mossell, "Our Woman's Department," *New York Freeman*, 8 May 1886, p. 2.

39. Mossell, "Our Woman's Department," *Indianapolis World*, 6 August 1892, p. 2; 17 September 1892, p. 1.

40. *Cleveland Gazette*, "Women of the Race," 12 March 1887, p. 1.

41. Smith, "Woman's Number," 4.

42. Penn, *Afro-American Press*, 407.

43. Wells, "Mrs. N.F. Mossell," 23; Penn, *Afro-American Press*, 406-7.

44. Mossell, "Our Woman's Department," *New York Freeman*, 6 November 1886, p. 4.

45. Mossell, "Our Woman's Department," *New York Freeman*, 5 June 1886, p. 2.

46. The average yearly income of a white woman working in Pennsylvania in 1900 was $275. See Twelfth Census of the United States, Special Report on Employees and Wages (Washington, D.C.: United States Census Office, 1903). The Bureau of the Census did not collect data regarding incomes of black women in 1900.

47. Mossell, "Our Woman's Department," *New York Freeman*, 6 November 1886, p. 4.

48. Mossell, *Work of the Afro-American Woman*.

49. Mossell, *Little Dansie's One Day at Sabbath School* (Philadelphia: 1902).

50. Lane, *William Dorsey's Philadelphia and Ours*, 175.

51. See the Leon Gardiner Collection of the American Negro Historical Society, Box 3G, folder 10. The collection is held in the Manuscripts Department of the Historical Society of Pennsylvania, which is located in Philadelphia.

52. Leon Gardiner Collection, Box 3G, folder 10; Mather, *Who's Who of the Colored Race*, 201-2; "Mrs. N.F. Mossell Rites," *Philadelphia Recorder*, 24 January 1948, p. 6; "Men of the Month," *Crisis* 13 (December 1916): 75-76.

53. Mather, *Who's Who of the Colored Race*, 201; Mossell, "The National Afro-American Council," *Colored American Magazine* 3 (August 1901): 298. The Afro-American Council was created in 1898 as a revival of the Afro-American League which T. Thomas Fortune had founded in 1890 and which had become defunct by 1893. Both organizations sought

civil rights for African Americans. The Afro-American Council continued until 1908 and was followed by creation of the NAACP a year later. See Emma Lou Thornbrough, "The National Afro-American League, 1887-1908," *Journal of Southern History* 27 (November 1961): 494-512.

54. Leon Gardiner Collection, Box 3G, folder 10; Mather, *Who's Who of the Colored Race*, 201-2; "Mrs. N.F. Mossell Rites," *Philadelphia Recorder*, 24 January 1948, p. 6; "Men of the Month," *Crisis* 13 (December 1916): 75-76.

55. "Widow of Dr. Mossell Succumbs at 92 Years," *Philadelphia Tribune*, 24 January 1948, p. 1.

4. IDA B. WELLS-BARNETT

1. Donald L. Grant, *The Anti-Lynching Movement, 1883-1932* (San Francisco: R and E Research Associates, 1975), viii-ix; Rayford W. Logan, *The Negro in the United States* (Princeton, N.J.: D. Van Nostrand, 1957), 54; August Meier, *Negro Thought in America, 1880-1915* (Ann Arbor: Univ. of Michigan Press, 1963), 19-21. In 1898, Ida B. Wells-Barnett estimated that ten thousand Americans had been lynched during the previous two decades. See *Cleveland Gazette*, "Mrs. Ida Wells Barnett Calls on President McKinley," 9 April 1898, p. 2.

2. "Memphis Stirred Up," *Nashville Daily American*, 26 May 1892, p. 4.

3. On the role newspapers played in the anti-lynching campaign, see James Elbert Cutler, *Lynch-Law: An Investigation into the History of Lynching in the United States* (New York: Longmans, Green, 1905), 157-58; Carter G. Woodson and Charles H. Wesley, *The Negro in Our History*, 11th ed., (Washington: Associated Publishers, 1966), 547-48. See also *Chicago Tribune*, "The Crime of the Year," 1 January 1883, p. 6.

4. The best source of information about Ida B. Wells-Barnett's life is her autobiography, *Crusade for Justice: The Autobiography of Ida B. Wells* (Chicago: Univ. of Chicago Press, 1970), edited by her daughter, Alfreda M. Duster, and published posthumously. The original manuscript for the autobiography and two of her diaries, dated 1885-1887 and 1930, are held in the Ida B. Wells Papers in the Department of Special Collections, Joseph Regenstein Library, University of Chicago. Some of her original works are in the Archives and Manuscripts Division at the Chicago Historical Society, and some correspondence by Wells-Barnett is in the Frederick Douglass Papers at the Library of Congress. The most comprehensive of the dozens of biographical works about Wells-Barnett is Mildred I. Thompson, *Ida B. Wells-Barnett: An Exploratory Study of an American Black Woman, 1893-1930* (Brooklyn, N.Y.: Carlson, 1990). Others include "'Iola' Wells," *Cleveland Gazette*, 6 July 1889, p. 1; T. Thomas Fortune, "Ida B. Wells, A.M.," in Scruggs, *Women of Distinction*, 32-39; Giddings, *When and Where*, 17-31; Thomas C. Holt, "The Lonely Warrior: Ida B. Wells-Barnett and the Strug-

gle for Black Leadership," in John Hope Franklin and August Meier, eds., *Black Leaders of the Twentieth Century* (Urbana: Univ. of Illinois Press, 1982), 39-61; Lerner, *Black Women in White America*, 196-99; Rayford W. Logan, "Ida Bell Wells-Barnett," in Logan and Winston, *Dictionary of American Negro Biography*, 30-31; Majors, *Noted Negro Women*, 187; Nichols and Crogman, *Progress of a Race*, 332; Lucy Wilmot Smith, "Woman's Number," *Journalist*, vol. 8, 26 January 1889, p. 5; Dorothy Sterling, *Black Foremothers: Three Lives* (New York: Feminist Press, 1979), 60-117; David M. Tucker, "Miss Ida B. Wells and Memphis Lynching," *Phylon* 32 (Summer 1971): 112-22.

5. "A Darky Damsel Obtains a Verdict for Damages Against the Chesapeake and Ohio Railroad—What It Cost To Put a Colored School Teacher in a Smoking Car," *Memphis Daily Appeal*, 25 December 1884, p. 4; unpublished Wells diary, 11 April 1887, Wells Papers; Holt, "Lonely Warrior," 42.

6. Ida B. Wells, "Freedom of Political Action; A Woman's Magnificent Definition of the Political Situation," *New York Freeman*, 7 November 1885, p. 2.

7. See, for example, Wells, "Woman's Mission," *New York Freeman*, 26 December 1885, p. 2; "Our Women," *New York Freeman*, 1 January 1887, p. 2; "'Iola' on Discrimination," *New York Freeman*, 15 January 1887, p. 4; "The Model Woman," *New York Age*, 18 February 1888, p. 3; "The League Is a Lever," *Detroit Plaindealer*, 18 October 1889, p. 2; "Temperance," *African Methodist Episcopal Church Review*, vol. 7 (January 1890), pp. 379-81.

8. "The Press Convention," *New York Freeman*, 20 August 1887, p. 4; T. Thomas Fortune, "Mr. Fortune on the West," *New York Age*, 11 August 1888, p. 1; Roland Wolseley, "Ida B. Wells-Barnett: Princess of the Black Press," *Encore*, 5 April 1976, p. 2.

9. Wells-Barnett, *Crusade for Justice*, 35-37, 41-42.

10. Wells, "A Recompense Will Be Had Someday," *Indianapolis Freeman*, 30 April 1892, p. 7; Wells-Barnett, *Crusade for Justice*, 22.

11. Wells, "A Little Plain Talk," *Memphis Appeal-Avalanche*, 6 September 1891, p. 4.

12. Wells, "The League Is a Lever," *Detroit Plaindealer*, 18 October 1889, p. 2; "Freedom of Political Action," *New York Freeman*, 7 November 1885, p. 2.

13. *Indianapolis Freeman*, "Fortune and His Echo," 19 April 1890, p. 4.

14. Wells-Barnett, *Crusade for Justice*, 52.

15. Ibid., 58-59; Holt, "Lonely Warrior," 42.

16. Wells-Barnett, *Crusade for Justice*, 61-66; Lerner, *Black Women in White America*, 196-97.

17. "Colored Folk Protest," *Memphis Appeal-Avalanche*, 30 June 1892, p. 5; "Memphis Stirred Up," *Nashville Daily American*, 26 May 1892, p. 4; "A New Series of Outrages," *Indianapolis Freeman*, 11 June 1892, p. 4.

18. Giddings, *When and Where*, 91-92; Emma Lou Thornbrough, *T. Thomas Fortune, Militant Journalist* (Chicago: Univ. of Chicago Press, 1972), x; Wells-Barnett, *Crusade for Justice*, 77.

19. Holt, "Lonely Warrior," 47.

20. Wells, "Exiled," *New York Age*, 5 June 1892, p. 1.

21. Wells, "Southern Horrors," 6. Three of Wells-Barnett's pamphlets have been reprinted in Ida B. Wells-Barnett, *On Lynchings: Southern Horrors, A Red Record, Mob Rule in New Orleans* (New York: Arno Press and New York Times, 1969).

22. Wells, "Southern Horrors," 1; Wells-Barnett, *Crusade for Justice*, 72; "Southern Horrors," 3; Frederick Douglass letter dated 25 October 1892; Giddings, *When and Where*, 30.

23. "Our Journalists and Literary Folks," *Indianapolis Freeman*, 8 July 1893, p. 6; Wells-Barnett, *Crusade for Justice*, 85, 89.

24. Wells, "Ida B. Wells Abroad," *Chicago Inter-Ocean*, 25 June 1894, p. 10. See also Wells, "Ida B. Wells Abroad," *Chicago Inter-Ocean*, 9 April 1894, p. 8; 16 April 1894, p. 6; 23 April 1894, p. 10; 28 May 1894, p. 6; 4 June 1894, p. 6; 7 July 1894, p. 6.

25. *Indianapolis Freeman*, "His Opinion No Good," 29 September 1894, p. 4; *New York Times*, "Negroes Loyal to Democracy," 4 September 1894, p. 1.

26. Holt, "Lonely Warrior," 47-48.

27. Lloyd W. Crawford, "Ida B. Wells: Her Anti-Lynching Crusades in Britain and Repercussions from Them in the United States," paper presented to the Association for the Study of Negro Life and History, October 1962, Xenia, Ohio, pp. 17-20, 22-24; Cutler, *Lynch-Law*, 245-46.

28. Wells, "The Reason Why the Colored American Is not in the World's Columbian Exposition" (Chicago: Ida B. Wells, 1893); F.L. Barnett letter to Albion W. Tourgee, 23 February 1893, Albion W. Tourgee Papers, Chautauqua County Historical Society, Westfield, N.Y. A copy of "The Reason Why" is held in the Archives and Manuscripts Department at the Chicago Historical Society.

29. "Two Notable People Are Married," *Chicago Tribune*, 28 June 1895, p. 4; Harold F. Gosnell, *Negro Politicians: The Rise of Negro Politicians in Chicago* (Chicago: Univ. of Chicago Press, 1935), 155, 206; Allan H. Spear, *Black Chicago: The Making of a Negro Ghetto, 1890-1920* (Chicago: Univ. of Chicago Press, 1967), 60-61. No copies of the *Chicago Conservator* for the period in which Wells wrote for it have been preserved.

30. "Hold Last Rites for Ida B. Wells-Barnett," *Chicago Defender*, 4 April 1931, p. 2.

31. Emma L. Fields, "The Women's Club Movement in the United States, 1877-1900" (unpublished master's thesis, Howard University, 1948), 63-64.

32. Although the Barnetts sold the *Conservator*, they continued to influence the newspaper's editorial content because they held the mortgage on it. *Indianapolis Freeman*, "Ida Wells-Barnett, Editor," 13 July 1895, p. 4; Wells-Barnett, *Crusade for Justice*, xxiii, 255. Wells-Barnett's four chil-

dren were Charles Aked, born in 1896; Herman Kohlsaat, born in 1897; Ida B. Wells, Jr., born in 1901; and Alfreda M., born in 1904.

33. "Mrs. Ida Wells Barnett Calls on President McKinley," *Cleveland Gazette*, 9 April 1898, p. 2; Aptheker, *Documentary History*, 798; Holt, "Lonely Warrior," 58.

34. Thompson, "Ida B. Wells-Barnett," 117.

35. Wells-Barnett, "Booker T. Washington and His Critics," *World Today* 6 (Apr. 1904): 518.

36. Holt, "Lonely Warrior," 39.

37. Wells-Barnett letter to Joel E. Spingarn, 21 April 1911, Joel E. Spingarn Papers, Moorland-Spingarn Research Center, Howard University Library, Washington, D.C.; Charles Flint Kellogg, *NAACP: A History of the National Association of Colored People, vol. 1: 1910-1920* (Baltimore: Johns Hopkins Press, 1967), 62-63, 92; Holt, "Lonely Warrior," 39, 50-53.

38. Holt, "Lonely Warrior," 56-57.

39. Jane Addams was a leading American social reformer who led the settlement house movement in the early twentieth century and shared the Nobel Peace Prize in 1931. *Chicago Broad Ax*, "Opening of the Negro Fellowship League," 7 May 1910, p. 1; "48th Emancipation Proclamation Exercise by the Negro Fellowship League," 31 December 1910, p. 2; "Grand Emancipation Celebration by the Negro Fellowship League," 30 December 1911, p. 4; "Crime," *Crisis* 2 (May 1911): 53; Holt, "Lonely Warrior," 54-55.

40. Wells-Barnett letter to Spingarn, 29 July 1913, Spingarn Papers; Gosnell, *Negro Politicians*, 204.

41. Alpha Suffrage Record, 18 March 1914, Wells Papers; Holt, "Lonely Warrior," 52.

42. "The Equal Suffrage Parade was Viewed by Many Thousand People From all Parts of the United States," *Chicago Broad Ax*, 8 March 1913, p. 1; "Illinois Women Feature Parade," *Chicago Daily Tribune*, 4 March 1913, p. 3; Aileen S. Kraditor, *The Ideas of the Woman Suffrage Movement, 1890-1920* (Garden City, N.Y.: Doubleday, Anchor, 1971), 212-13.

43. Gosnell, *Negro Politicians*, 11, 15-16, 19.

44. "Hold Last Rites for Ida B. Wells-Barnett," *Chicago Defender*, 4 April 1931, p. 2.

45. W.E.B. DuBois, "Postscript," *Crisis* 40 (June 1931): 207.

5. JOSEPHINE ST. PIERRE RUFFIN

1. On the significance of the African-American women's club movement, see Angela Y. Davis, *Women, Culture, and Politics* (New York: Random, 1989), 3-15; Willard B. Gatewood, *Aristocrats of Color: The Black Elite, 1880-1920* (Bloomington: Indiana Univ. Press, 1990), 210-46; Giddings, *When and Where*, 95-117, 135-42; Elizabeth Kolmer, "Nineteen Century Woman's Rights Movement: Black and White," *Negro History Bulletin* 35 (December 1972): 178-80; Lerner, *Black Women in White*

America, 433-58; Lerner, "Early Community Work"; Jeanne L. Noble, *Beautiful, Also, Are the Souls of My Black Sisters: A History of the Black Woman in America* (Englewood Cliffs, N.J.: Prentice-Hall, 1978), 129-43; Wesley, *History of the National Association.* On the communication network that evolved from the movement, see Gatewood, *Aristocrats of Color*, 237-46; Giddings, *When and Where*, 98-117; Kolmer, "Nineteenth Century Woman's Rights Movement," 178-80; Wesley, *History of the National Association*, 50-52.

2. Josephine St. Pierre Ruffin, "Editorial," *Woman's Era*, 24 March 1894, p. 8.

3. The St. Pierre family tree is in the Ruffin Family Papers, Amistad Research Center, Tulane University, New Orleans. Summaries of Ruffin's work as a club woman include Floris Barnett Cash, "Josephine St. Pierre Ruffin," in Smith, *Notable Black American Women*, 961-65; Julia Ward Howe, ed., *Representative Women of New England* (Boston: New England Historical Publishing Company, 1904), 335-39; James, *Notable American Women*, vol. 3, pp. 206-8; John William Leonard, ed., *Woman's Who's Who of America: A Biographical Dictionary of Contemporary Women of the United States and Canada* (New York: American Commonwealth, 1915), 706; Lerner, *Black Women in White America*, 440-41; Logan and Winston, *Dictionary of American Negro Biography*, 535-36; Richings, *Evidences of Progress*, 371-72; Scruggs, *Women of Distinction*, 144-48. See also Rodger Streitmatter, "Economic Conditions Surrounding Nineteenth-Century African-American Women Journalists: Two Case Studies," *Journalism History* 18 (1992): 33-40.

4. The Ruffins were married June 30, 1858, in Twelfth Baptist Church in Boston. Their marriage certificate is preserved in the Ruffin Family Papers, Amistad Research Center. The four Ruffin children who lived to adulthood all achieved success. Hubert Ruffin practiced law and served on the Boston Common Council and in the Massachusetts State Legislature. Florida Ruffin Ridley taught in Boston public schools. Stanley Ruffin was an inventor and manager of a Boston manufacturing company. George Lewis Ruffin, Jr., was organist at St. Augustine's Church and a music instructor. See Brown, *Homespun Heroines*, 151.

5. Howe, *Women of New England*, 336; Rayford W. Logan, *The Negro in American Life and Thought* (New York: Dial, 1954), 236; Helen Porter Utterback, "Mrs. Ruffin and the Woman's Era Club of Boston," *Los Angeles Herald Illustrated Magazine*, p. 7. (The undated article is preserved in the Sophia Smith Collection at Smith College, Northampton, Mass. Contents of the article indicate it was written in 1902.)

6. Dannett, *Profiles of Negro Womanhood*, 309; Davis, *Lifting as They Climb*, 237; Sterling, *We Are Your Sisters*, 257.

7. Howe, *Women of New England*, 337; letters written by Ruffin to William Lloyd Garrison, 19 April 1879 and 13 January 1875, Department of Rare Books and Manuscripts, Boston Public Library; Margaret Murray Washington, "Club Work Among Negro Women," in Nichols and Crogman, *Progress of a Race*, 178; letters written by Ruffin to Ednah Dow

Cheney, 19 and 22 May 1890, Department of Rare Books and Manuscripts, Boston Public Library; letter written by Booker T. Washington to Francis Jackson Garrison, 22 February 1904, Booker T. Washington Papers, Library of Congress, Washington, D.C. Ednah Dow Cheney was a Boston reformer and author who helped found the New England Woman's Club and Hospital for Women and Children; her foremost interests were woman's suffrage and abolition. Susan B. Anthony and Elizabeth Cady Stanton organized and led the National Woman's Suffrage Association. Lucy Stone was a prominent leader in abolition and women's suffrage. Julia Ward Howe was an author and reformer committed to abolition, women's suffrage, prison reform, and the cause of peace; Howe lectured as a Unitarian preacher and wrote the poem "Battle Hymn of the Republic."

8. George Lewis Ruffin died of kidney disease. See "Death of George L. Ruffin," *New York Freeman*, 27 November 1886, p. 1; obituaries in folder 26 of the George Lewis Ruffin Papers, Moorland-Spingarn Research Center, Howard University Library, Washington, D.C.

9. Several historians (Brown, *Homespun Heroines*, 152; Bullock, "Negro Periodical Press," 169; Sterling, *We Are Your Sisters*, 441) have stated that *Woman's Era* was founded in March 1894, the date of the earliest extant copy. Ruffin correspondence preserved in the Boston Public Library, however, shows that *Woman's Era* existed in 1890. Two letters that Ruffin wrote to Cheney, 19 and 22 May 1890, carry the printed letterhead: "The Woman's Era." In the May 22 letter, Ruffin specifically mentions the "May *Era*." The fact that *Woman's Era* predated the Woman's Era Club, which Ruffin founded in 1894, is verified by two 1902 magazine articles that state that the club took its name from a newspaper called *Woman's Era*. (See Pauline E. Hopkins, "Famous Women of the Negro Race," *Colored American Magazine* 5 (August 1902): 273; Utterback, "Mrs. Ruffin," 7.) Ruffin initially may have distributed *Woman's Era* only in Boston but then expanded to national distribution in 1894.

10. Ruffin, *Woman's Era*, "The Chicago Woman's Club Reject [sic] Mrs. Williams," December 1894, p. 20; "Women in Business," 24 March 1894, p. 13. *Woman's Era*, "Slavery Case in Boston," September 1894, p. 14.

11. Information about *Woman's Era* is contained in Penelope L. Bullock, *The Afro-American Periodical Press: 1838-1909* (Baton Rouge: Louisiana State Univ. Press, 1981), 396-97. Twenty-two issues of *Woman's Era* are preserved in the Rare Books and Manuscripts Department, Boston Public Library. The July 1896 issue also is preserved in the Moorland-Spingarn Research Center, Howard University Library, Washington, D.C.

12. Ruffin, "Why You Should Subscribe for the Woman's Era," *Woman's Era*, 1 May 1894, p. 15; "New York," *Woman's Era*, July 1895, p 3.

13. *Woman's Era*, "National Association of Colored Women," August-September 1896, p. 2.

14. Ruffin, "Editorial Greeting," *Woman's Era*, 1 May 1894, p. 8.

15. Ruffin, "Editorial," *Woman's Era*, 24 March 1894, p. 4.

16. Ruffin, *Woman's Era*, "Washington," May 1895, p. 3; "Bonita

Gold and Silver Mining Co.," January 1896, p. 17. "What Equal Suffrage has done for Colorado," November 1894, p. 12; "Colored Women and Suffrage," November 1895, p. 11; "Women in Politics," November 1894, p. 12.

17. Ruffin, "Editorial," *Woman's Era*, May 1895, p. 10.

18. Ruffin, "Separate Car Law," *Woman's Era*, February 1896, p. 9.

19. *Woman's Era*, "A Danger and a Duty," August-September 1896, p. 8; *Woman's Era*, "Club Gossip," 24 March 1894, p. 15; *Woman's Era*, "The Drink Traffic Vs. Labor," 1 June 1894, p. 2; Gertrude Bustill Mossell, "The Open Court," *Woman's Era*, May 1895, p. 19.

20. Ruffin, "Editorial," *Woman's Era*, 24 March 1894, p. 4.

21. Ruffin, "Editorial," *Woman's Era*, December 1894, p. 10.

22. Ruffin, *Woman's Era*, "We Decline to Name This Child," November 1895, p. 10; "Women in Politics," November 1894, p. 12.

23. Ruffin, "Editorial," *Woman's Era*, February 1896, p. 10.

24. Finkle, *Forum for Protest*, 31; Wolseley, *Black Press, U.S.A.*, 27. On African-American women activists of the era being elitist, see Giddings, *When and Where*, 98-102; *Woman's Era*, "Advertise in *Woman's Era*," 1 June 1894, p. 9.

25. Ruffin, *Woman's Era*, "Notes and Comments," September 1894, pp. 14, 16.

26. *Woman's Era*, "Mr. U.A. Ridley," July 1896, p. 13. U.A. Ridley was the husband of Florida Ruffin Ridley, Ruffin's daughter.

27. *Woman's Era*, "Literature Department," 1 June 1894, p. 14; Medora Gould, "Literature Notes," *Woman's Era*, December 1894, p. 19; *Woman's Era*, "Danger and Duty," August-September 1896, p. 9.

28. Ruffin letters to Cheney, 24 March 1896 and 25 March 1897, Boston Public Library; statement by Florida Ruffin Ridley, Schomburg Center for Research in Black Culture Clipping File, New York Public Library, "George Lewis Ruffin" entry, p. 4; Mossell, *Work of the Afro-American Woman*, 15; Scruggs, *Women of Distinction*, 147-48; *St. Paul* (Minnesota) *Appeal*, letter from Ruffin, 14 November 1891, p. 3; Ruffin letter to William Lloyd Garrison, 13 January 1875, Boston Public Library. The *Boston Courant* was founded in 1890; the earliest extant copies are dated 1900. On the financial difficulties of the black press, see Armistead Scott Pride, "Negro Newspapers: Yesterday, Today and Tomorrow," *Journalism Quarterly* 28 (Spring 1951): 179-82.

29. Ruffin, "Editorial Notes," *Woman's Era*, 24 March 1894, p. 7; Ruffin, "Notes," *Woman's Era*, August 1894, p. 8.

30. *Woman's Era*, "Wants," April 1895, p. 17; May 1895, p. 9; June 1895, p. 20; November 1895, p. 16. Ruffin, "Statement to Advertisers," *Woman's Era*, June 1896, p. 1.

31. Ruffin, *Woman's Era*, "Notice to Subscribers," April 1895, p. 12; "Social Notes," September 1894, p. 11; "A Loyal Woman," December 1894, p. 19; "Editorial," April 1895, p. 8.

32. *Woman's Era*, "National Association of Colored Women," August-

September 1896, p. 2; *Woman's Era*, "An Open Appeal to Our Women for Organization," January 1897, p. 2; Giddings, *When and Where*, 104.

33. Richard T. Greener typed manuscript, Rare Books and Manuscripts Department, Boston Public Library; Howe, p. 337.

34. Gatewood, *Aristocrats of Color*, 242; Litwack and Meier, *Black Leaders of the Nineteenth Century*, 312.

35. Hopkins, "Famous Women of the Negro Race," 273; Howe, *Women of New England*, 338; Booker T. Washington, *A New Negro for a New Century* (Miami: Mnemosyne, 1900), 390-92.

36. Fields, "Women's Club Movement," 65; Flexner, *Century of Struggle*, 189-91; Lerner, *Black Women in White America*, 441-43; Gerri Major, *Gerri Major's Black Society* (Chicago: Johnson, 1976), 273-74.

37. Giddings, *When and Where*, 93-95; Lerner, *Black Women in White America*, 440-41.

38. Howe, *Women of New England*, 337; *Milwaukee Journal*, "Will Draw Color Line," 4 June 1900, p. 5; *Milwaukee Sentinel*, "Color Question May Come Up in a New Form," 4 June 1900, p. 1.

39. *Milwaukee Sentinel*, "Storm Must Break Over Color Line," 6 June 1900, p. 1; *Milwaukee Sentinel*, "Colored Club Is Barred Out by Directors," 5 June 1900, p. 1; "Mrs. Lowe for Presidency," 7 June 1900, p. 1; Mary I. Wood, *The History of the General Federation of Women's Clubs* (New York: General Federation of Women's Clubs, 1912), pp. 128-31.

40. *Chicago Tribune*, "May Take Color Line To Court," 10 June 1900, p. 5; *Milwaukee Journal*, "Mrs. Lowe Is Named Again," 8 June 1900, p. 1; *Milwaukee Sentinel*, "Breach Was Avoided," 9 June 1900, p. 6. Ruffin's appeals to Washington are detailed in Giddings, *When and Where*, 105.

41. *Milwaukee Journal*, "Mrs. Lowe Is Named Again," 8 June 1900, p. 1; *Milwaukee Journal*, "Will Draw Color Line," 4 June 1900, p. 5; Utterback, "Mrs. Ruffin," 7; *Pittsburgh Dispatch*, "Women's Clubs Cannot Avoid Color Issue," 6 June 1900, p. 7; *Chicago Tribune*, "What the Woman's Federation Did," 10 June 1900, p. 36.

42. Edward Everett Hale was an author and Unitarian minister in Boston and Worcester, as well as chaplain of the United States Senate. A humanitarian, Hale advocated an international court to eliminate war.

43. *Boston Evening Transcript*, "Deaths," 15 March 1924, p. 9; Monroe N. Work, *Negro Year Book, 1925-1926* (Tuskegee Institute, Alabama: Negro Year Book Publishing, 1925), 422.

6. DELILAH L. BEASLEY

1. Logan and Winston, *Dictionary of American Negro Biography*, 633-38; W. Augustus Low and Virgil A. Clift, eds., *Encyclopedia of Black America* (New York: McGraw-Hill, 1981), 85, 839-45; Harry A. Ploski and James Williams, eds., *The Negro Almanac: A Reference Work on the African American*, 5th ed. (New York: Gale Research, 1989), 301.

2. The first black man to work for a mainstream newspaper was T. Thomas Fortune, who joined the editorial staff of the *New York Evening Sun* in the early 1880s. See Penn, *Afro-American Press*, 137.

3. Delilah L. Beasley, "Activities Among Negroes," *Oakland Tribune*, 4 January 1931, p. T-7.

4. Information about the Beasley family is contained in the 1880 United States Census. That data describe the "Beesling Family" as being mulatto and Margaret Beasley's occupation as "keep house." See 1880 United States Census for Cincinnati, Hamilton County, Ohio, Roll 1025, Enumeration District 129, p. 46. The handwritten census data are preserved at the National Archives in Washington, D.C. Other sources of information on Beasley's life include the social service records of the hospital where she died, her obituary, an article written in memorial to her, four books that include brief profiles of her, and two recent works about her activities in Oakland. The social service records are held by Fairmont Hospital in San Leandro, Calif. Beasley's obituary is in the Schomburg Center for Research in Black Culture Clipping File at the New York Public Library. The copy is marked "Los Angeles, August 31, 1934," but the publication in which it appeared is not identified. The obituary did not appear in the *Los Angeles Times, Los Angeles Evening Herald Express*, or *New York Times*. It is likely that the obituary appeared in a Los Angeles newspaper that has not been preserved. The memorial article about Beasley is Lena M. Wysinger, "Activities Among Negroes; In Memoriam—Miss Delilah L. Beasley," *Oakland Tribune*, 14 October 1934, p. B-5. The earliest profile of Beasley was published in the history of the National Association of Colored Women by Davis, *Lifting as They Climb*, 188-95. Other profiles were published much later than the Davis book and appear to be based on that material. Those profiles are Dannett, *Profiles of Negro Womanhood*, 224-25; Richard H. Dillon, *Humbugs and Heroes: A Gallery of California Pioneers* (New York: Doubleday, 1970), 32-36; Robert L. Johns, "Delilah Leontium Beasley," in Smith, *Notable Black American Women*, 72-74; Logan and Winston, *Dictionary of American Negro Biography*, 34-35. Results of recent research on Beasley's involvement in local activities in Oakland are an article and a sixty-page book about her by Lorraine J. Crouchett. The article, "Delilah Beasley, Trail Blazer," *Oakland Heritage Alliance News* 8 (Winter 1988-89): 1-6, and book, *Delilah Leontium Beasley: Oakland's Crusading Journalist* (El Cerrito, Calif.: Downey Place, 1990), concentrate on Beasley's work as a local activist. See also Streitmatter, "Economic Conditions," 33-40.

5. Beasley described her early journalism career on a researcher's registration card she completed at the California State Library in 1920. See Beasley entry in Biographical Card File, California Section, California State Library, Sacramento. The *Gazette*, the first black newspaper in Cleveland, was founded in 1883. For many years, the *Gazette* was the oldest black newspaper in the country. It ceased publication in 1945. See David D. Van Tassel and John J. Grabowski, *Encyclopedia of Cleveland's History* (Bloomington: Indiana Univ. Press, 1987). I have searched for Beasley's work in every edition of the *Cincinnati Enquirer* from 1886 to 1892 but have identified no

items that can be attributed to her. The *Enquirer* was a daily newspaper that had been founded in 1841, and, by the 1880s, had become a major regional newspaper that published sixteen pages each day and covered Ohio, Kentucky, Indiana, and Illinois. The *Enquirer* also covered national news and published weekly columns from correspondents in New York, Philadelphia, and Washington. The *Enquirer* had the reputation of being courageous, liberal, and ultra-progressive, and publisher John R. McLean was known for his insistence upon providing a newspaper for all classes. See Francis L. Dale, *The Cincinnati Enquirer: The Extended Shadows of its Publishers* (New York: Newcomen Society in North America, 1966), 5, 20. The earliest published reference to Beasley was one sentence published in the *Cleveland Gazette* in 1887. Near the end of an eight-inch item carrying a Cincinnati dateline was the statement: "Miss Deliah [sic] Beasley has been spending a portion of the week in Springfield." See *Cleveland Gazette*, "Colored Teachers," 10 September 1887, p. 1.

6. 1880 United States Census; Davis, 188-89.

7. Beasley, *The Negro Trail Blazers of California* (Los Angeles: 1919), preface; Davis, *Lifting as They Climb*, 189-90.

8. Davis, *Lifting as They Climb*, 190; Beasley, "G.A.R. Men Score 'Clansman' Play," *Oakland Tribune*, 7 June 1915, p. 5. The *Oakland Tribune* was founded in 1874 and became known as an innovative and crusading newspaper. By 1914, the *Tribune's* circulation exceeded 25,000. See Harry Martin, "The *Tribune's* 100th Year," *Oakland Tribune*, 1 January 1974, p. 1; Leonard Verbarg, "Century of Accomplishment," *Oakland Tribune*, 21 February 1974, p. K-1. Documentation that the *Tribune* was the largest newspaper in Northern California is contained in a letter to the author from Steven LaVoie, 27 September 1990. LaVoie was assistant librarian at the *Oakland Tribune*. According to the 1920 United States Census, the 204,264 residents of Oakland included 5,489 African Americans (2.7 percent).

9. Beasley, "Colored Race at the Exposition," *Oakland Sunshine*, 26 June 1915, p. 2. The *Oakland Sunshine* began publication in 1914 and ceased publication at the end of 1915. Some copies of the newspaper are available at the Library of Congress.

10. Beasley omitted Washington's recommendation that African Americans organize their opposition to "Birth of a Nation" before it opened in Oakland. He said that once theater owners began advertising the motion picture, ticket sales would be so strong that protesters would not be able to convince theater owners to halt the showing of the profit-making film.

11. *Oakland Tribune*, "President Wilson Flashes Signal Across the Continent," 20 February 1915, p. 1; "Exposition Gates Will Close Today," 4 December 1915, p. 1. Beasley, *Negro Trail Blazers*, 303.

12. Beasley, *Negro Trail Blazers*, 301-2.

13. Beasley, "Slavery in California," *Journal of Negro History* 3 (January 1918): 33-34; Beasley and Monroe N. Work, "California Freedom Papers," *Journal of Negro History* 3 (January 1918): 45-54. Letter written by Beasley to Elizabeth Loomis, 25 June 1922, Francis B. Loomis Papers, De-

partment of Special Collections, Stanford University Libraries, Stanford, Calif. The letter is one of four letters and four post cards written by Beasley to Loomis and preserved in the Loomis Papers. Elizabeth Loomis was the wife of Francis B. Loomis, who worked in the press operation for the presidential campaigns of James G. Blaine in 1884, Benjamin Harrison in 1888, and William McKinley in 1902; served as an American diplomat in France, Venezuela, and Portugal; and, after being appointed First Assistant Secretary of State under John Hay, ascended to interim Secretary of State upon Hay's death. Francis B. Loomis's journalistic credits include working as a reporter for the *New York Tribune* and *Philadelphia Press*, editor of the *Cincinnati Daily Tribune*, and general manager of the *Oakland Tribune*. According to the preface of Beasley's book, Loomis hired her to write for the *Tribune*.

14. Lonnie Isabel, "Bay Area's Own Leaders Offer Hope for the Future," *Oakland Tribune*, 23 January 1989, p. 1; Beasley, *Negro Trail Blazers*.

15. Charles E. Chapman, "Negro Trail Blazers of California," *Grizzley* [sic] *Bear Magazine*, June 1919. The page number on which the review appeared is unknown. *Grizzley Bear Magazine* was the official organ of the Native Sons and Daughters of the Golden West. The review is preserved in the Loomis Papers. See Carter G. Woodson, "Review of Negro Trail Blazers of California," *Journal of Negro History* 5 (January 1920): 128-29. In 1915, Woodson founded the Association for the Study of Afro-American Life and History and, in 1926, founded Negro History Week, which expanded into Black History Month in 1976.

16. Biographical Card File, California State Library.

17. Letter written by Beasley to Elizabeth Loomis, 25 June 1922, Loomis Papers.

18. Beasley, "Activities Among Negroes," *Oakland Tribune*, 18 December 1927, p. A-21; 30 September 1923, p. B-3.

19. Beasley, "Activities Among Negroes," *Oakland Tribune*, 23 October 1927, p. A-15. Among the newspapers Beasley received were the *Boston Guardian, Chicago Defender, Cleveland Gazette, Detroit Independent, Pittsburgh Courier*, and *Seattle Searchlight*.

20. Beasley, "Activities Among Negroes," *Oakland Tribune*, 25 January 1925, p. A-15.

21. Beasley, "Activities Among Negroes," *Oakland Tribune*, 9 December 1923, p. B-10.

22. Beasley, "Activities Among Negroes," *Oakland Tribune*, 2 December 1923, p. B-3.

23. Beasley, "Activities Among Negroes," *Oakland Tribune*, 29 March 1925, p. X-7; 16 September 1923, p. B-4; 11 January 1931, p. O-6.

24. Beasley, "Activities Among Negroes," *Oakland Tribune*, 13 November 1927, p. M-6; 16 October 1927, p. B-2; 20 December 1925, p. B-2; 24 August 1930, p. O-6; 11 January 1925, p. B-3; 4 January 1925, p. B-8; 11 November 1923, p. B-8.

25. Beasley, "Activities Among Negroes," *Oakland Tribune*, 29 March 1925, p. X-7; 12 April 1925, p. B-11.

26. Beasley's social service records at Fairmont Hospital, sheet marked "social service data" and dated 13 March 1934.

27. Ibid. Beasley undated post card and 27 December 1922 letter to Elizabeth Loomis, Loomis Papers.

28. Correspondence by Beasley to Elizabeth Loomis, 25 June and 15 September 1922 letters, undated post card, Loomis Papers.

29. Beasley, "Activities Among Negroes," *Oakland Tribune*, 4 October 1925, p. B-4.

30. Beasley, "Activities Among Negroes," *Oakland Tribune*, 7 August 1932, p. M-4; 22 February 1925, p. T-8.

31. The National Association of Colored Women was a national network of clubs for African-American women. It was organized in 1896 and quickly grew to fifty thousand women in more than one thousand clubs. The association initiated social reforms in education, labor, health, and public utilities in African-American communities. See Giddings, *When and Where*, 93-117, 135-36, 349; Lerner, *Majority Finds Its Past*, 107-8. Beasley, "Activities Among Negroes," *Oakland Tribune*, 14 October 1934, p. B-5.

32. Beasley, "Activities Among Negroes," *Oakland Tribune*, 15 March 1925, p. X-8; 10 May 1925, p. B-2; 24 May 1925, p. B-3.

33. Beasley, "Activities Among Negroes," *Oakland Tribune*, 26 November 1933, p. T-12; 22 October 1933, p. B-2; 5 November 1933, p. T-11.

34. Wysinger, "In Memoriam," p. B-5.

35. Beasley, "Activities Among Negroes," *Oakland Tribune*, 1 December 1929, p. B-4; 20 April 1930, p. A-7.

36. *Crisis* 36 (Oct. 1929): 346. W.E.B. DuBois founded the *Crisis* in 1910. During this period it became the seminal publication in the country recording progress in black America.

37. Beasley, "Activities Among Negroes," *Oakland Tribune*, 7 August 1932, p. M-4; 2 April 1933, p. B-6.

38. Beasley, "Activities Among Negroes," *Oakland Tribune*, 9 July 1933, p. S-6; 15 October 1933, p. B-2; 8 November 1925, p. B-3; 13 December 1925, p. B-12; 15 October 1933, p. B-2.

39. Dannett, *Profiles of Negro Womanhood*, 225; Davis, *Lifting as They Climb*, 191-92; Logan and Winston, *Dictionary of American Negro Biography*, 25.

40. Davis, *Lifting as They Climb*, 191-92. In her crusade against denigrating language, Beasley was not consistent with Washington. During speeches, he frequently amused his white audiences by telling stories about "darkeys." See Logan and Winston, *Dictionary of American Negro Biography*, 634.

41. Beasley, "Activities Among Negroes," *Oakland Tribune*, 28 June 1925, p. A-12.

42. Crouchett, *Delilah Leontium Beasley*, 59.

43. Beasley, "Activities Among Negroes," *Oakland Tribune*, 14 October 1934, p. B-5.

44. Beasley's social service records at Fairmont Hospital, sheet marked "Admissions Record" and dated 23 February 1934; Wysinger.

45. Beasley obituary, Schomburg Clipping File.

7. MARVEL COOKE

1. On the Harlem Renaissance, see Franklin and Moss, *From Slavery to Freedom*, 324-38; Low and Clift, *Encyclopedia of Black America*, 417-19.

2. Marvel Cooke, "I Was a Part of the Bronx Slave Market," *Daily Compass*, 8 January 1950, p. 1.

3. *Chicago Defender*, "N.Y. Daily Gets First Negro Woman," 28 January 1950, p. 10; Timothy V. Johnson, "409—The House at the Top of Sugar Hill," *People's Daily World*, 8 September 1990, p. 8. The first black man to work for a white newspaper was T. Thomas Fortune, who joined the editorial staff of the *New York Evening Sun* in the early 1880s. See Penn, *Afro-American Press*, 137.

4. A major source of information about Marvel Cooke's life is the transcript of an interview with her by Kathleen Currie, Women in Journalism oral history project of the Washington Press Club Foundation, 3 October to 3 November 1989, Oral History Collection, Columbia University. Other sources on Cooke are Mills, *Place in the News*, 66, 176-79, 249-51; Rodger Streitmatter and Barbara Diggs-Brown, "Marvel Cooke: An African-American Woman Journalist Who Agitated for Racial Reform," *Afro-Americans in New York Life and History* 16 (July 1992): 47-68. As a Pullman porter, Madison Jackson had been involved in a pioneer labor movement. The Brotherhood of Sleeping Car Porters was the country's largest black union and the first admitted to the American Federation of Labor. See Daniel S. Davis, *Mr. Black Labor: The Story of A. Philip Randolph* (New York: Dutton, 1972), 78. Eugene V. Debs was a labor organizer and the foremost leader of the socialist movement in the United States. In 1893, Debs organized the American Railway Union. He ran for president of the United States on the Social Democratic ticket in 1900 and the Socialist Party ticket in 1912. In 1918, Debs was sentenced to ten years in prison for sedition. He was pardoned in 1921.

5. Oral history, pp. 5, 7-8, 24-25.

6. Author's interview with Marvel Cooke, 9 January 1991. The interview took place in Cooke's apartment at 409 Edgecombe Avenue in the Harlem section of New York City. Oral history, p. 26. Henrik Shipstead was a United States senator from Minnesota; elected on the Farmer-Labor Party ticket in 1922, Shipstead continued to serve in the Senate until 1947.

7. Oral history, pp. 11, 13, 60. Roy Wilkins, who replaced DuBois as editor of the *Crisis*, later became executive secretary of the NAACP and a leading figure in the modern civil rights movement.

8. Author's interview with Cooke, 9 January 1991; oral history, pp. 8, 26, 68. W.E.B. DuBois was a leading African-American scholar, author, editor, and educator. DuBois advocated Marxian socialism and the elim-

ination of discrimination against blacks. A bold critic of the American social order, he opposed accommodationist views. He founded the *Crisis* in 1910 and eventually wrote more than a dozen books. On the *Crisis*, see Walter C. Daniel, *Black Journals of the United States* (Westport, Conn.: Greenwood, 1982), 139-48.

9. Marvel Jackson, "In the Magazines," *Crisis* 34 (September 1927): 247; 34 (October 1927): 283; 34 (September 1927): 338; 35 (January 1928): 31. For Jackson's comments on the works of major literary figures, see Jackson, "In the Magazines," *Crisis* 35 (April 1928): 123 (Hughes); 35 (June 1928): 211 (Hurston); 34 (December 1927): 338 (Mencken); 34 (December 1927): 338 (Parker). Zora Neale Hurston was an author who became known as "Queen of the Harlem Renaissance." Also an anthropologist, Hurston wrote several volumes of African-American folklore based on her research in the southern United States, Haiti, and the West Indies. Her books included three novels and her autobiography. Langston Hughes was the foremost poet of the Harlem Renaissance. He published his first volume of poetry, *The Weary Blues*, in 1926 and his first volume of short stories, *Ways of White Folks*, in 1934. Hughes published ten volumes of poetry and sixty short stories. His play "Mulatto" had a triumphant Broadway run in 1935-37, and he produced numerous dramas and operas. H.L. Mencken was an incisive and iconoclastic satirist and editor who was most closely identified with the *Baltimore Sun* and the *American Mercury*, a newspaper that he founded and edited. Dorothy Parker was a satirist, drama critic, and book reviewer with a reputation for trenchant and devastating witticisms. Many of her short stories, which often presented variations on the theme of frustration in everyday life, first appeared in the *New Yorker*.

10. Historian Paula Giddings stated that DuBois, upon the death of Frederick Douglass, became the country's leading black male feminist, knowing that black women gaining the right to vote would increase the power of black America. See Giddings, *When and Where*, 121. In 1915, DuBois made his position clear in the concise statement: "Votes for women, means votes for black women." See W.E.B. DuBois, "Votes for Women: A Symposium by Leading Thinkers of Colored America," *Crisis* 10 (August 1915): 176. For discussion of the importance of 409 Edgecombe Avenue, see Johnson, "409." Thurgood Marshall, as legal counsel to the NAACP, successfully argued the 1954 *Brown vs. Board of Education of Topeka* school integration case before the U.S. Supreme Court. He later became the first African American to serve on the Court. William Patterson was the leader of the American Communist Party. Walter White, president of the NAACP, was instrumental in forming the Committee on Fair Employment Practices and served as adviser to presidents Franklin Roosevelt and Harry Truman. He also was a successful writer, completing seven major fiction and nonfiction works.

11. Oral history, pp. 34, 87. Claude McKay was a novelist and poet. His major themes were love, nature, and religion, and his major works included *Harlem Shadows*, *Banjo*, and *A Long Way to Come Home*. George Schuyler was a conservative journalist who wrote a column for the *Pittsburgh Courier*

for a quarter of a century. He also edited *National News* and served as business manager for the *Crisis*. His books included *Racial Intermarriage in the United States*, *Slaves Today*, and *Black No More*. Countee Cullen was the second most important poet of the Harlem Renaissance, behind Hughes. Cullen received a master's degree from Harvard University and studied at the Sorbonne in Paris before writing several volumes of poetry. Arna Bontemps was a central figure in discovering and disseminating African-American literature. He became a leader in the renaissance while teaching at the Harlem Academy. James Weldon Johnson was a poet, lyricist, and editor of the *New York Age*; he also served as an American diplomat in Venezuela and Nicaragua. Paul Robeson triumphed in "Othello" on Broadway. He starred in such plays as "All God's Children Got Wings," "Porgy," "Showboat," and "The Hairy Ape." Robeson's political beliefs led him to make several trips to Russia in the 1930s to speak against the Nazis. After World War II, he campaigned strenuously for black civil rights. The United States government revoked his passport, and he was barred from concert halls. His passport later was reissued.

12. Jackson, "In the Magazines," *Crisis* 34 (December 1927): 338.

13. The *Amsterdam News* was founded in 1909 and continues to be published today. On the *Amsterdam News*, see James Booker, *History of the New York Amsterdam News* (New York: Amsterdam News, 1967).

14. Author's interview with Cooke, 9 January 1991.

15. Oral history, p. 68. See also, pp. 18, 66.

16. Cooke, *Amsterdam News*, "Apollo Girls Are 'Dogged' Around; Work Like Slaves!" 4 March 1939, p. 1; "Should Incurables Have the Right to Die?", 4 January 1936, p. 3. St. Clair Bourne and Cooke, "The Truth About Harlem Crime; Factual Evidence Of A Mounting Problem To The Community," *Amsterdam News*, 4 March 1939, p. 1; 11 March 1939, p. 7; 18 March 1939, p. 11; 25 March 1939, p. 6; 8 April 1939, p. 11.

17. On the functional relationship between the arts and black civil rights, see Harold Cruse, *The Crisis of the Negro Intellectual* (New York: William Morrow, 1967), 43.

18. Cooke, "New Laurels for Marian Anderson," *Amsterdam News*, 5 April 1939, p. 1. See also, Cooke, "Close to 100,000 at Lincoln Memorial Awed by Contralto," *Amsterdam News*, 5 April 1939, p. 5.

19. Cooke, *Amsterdam News*, "Holy Roller Singer Toast of Broadway," 4 March 1939, p. 16; "Designer Watkins On Way To The Top," 25 February 1939, p. 16; "Stand Up And Fight," 18 February 1939, p. 16; "About Face!" 21 January 1939, p. 16. Ethel Waters starred in many Broadway shows in the 1930s, 1940s, and 1950s, including "Blackbirds," "Rhapsody in Black," and "Member of the Wedding." Her film credits included "Tales of Manhattan," "Cabin in the Sky," and "Pinky."

20. Oral history, p. 43.

21. Oral history, p. 45. Richard Wright received a Guggenheim Fellowship that enabled him to complete *Native Son*, which became a Book-of-the-Month-Club selection. Wright's other works included four novels, four nonfiction works, a book of short stories, and his autobiography.

22. Heywood Broun, "It Seems to Me," *New York World-Telegram*, 7 August 1933, p. 13.

23. Oral history, pp. 68-69, 80, 91.

24. Oral history, p. 87. *New York Times*, "Newspaper Is Picketed," 10 October 1935, p. 52; "Guild Pickets Arrested," 19 October 1935, p. 15.

25. *New York Times*, "Newspaper Strikers Win," 25 December 1935, p. 17. Oral history, pp. 147-48.

26. On the American Newspaper Guild's affiliation with the Communist Party, see Irving Howe and Lewis Coser, *The American Communist Party: A Critical History* (Boston: Boston Press, 1957), 374. On communism and African Americans, see Nathan Glazer, *The Social Basis of American Communism* (New York: Harcourt Brace, 1961), 169, 175, 183.

27. Oral history, pp. 30-31. Benjamin J. Davis, a reporter for the Daily Worker, served on the New York City Council during the 1940s, crusading against segregated housing, overcrowded hospitals, and police brutality in Harlem and the color barrier in major league baseball. In 1949, Davis and ten other Communist leaders were convicted of advocating the overthrow of the United States government. Davis was imprisoned for three years.

28. Oral history, pp. 30-31, 73-77.

29. Oral history, p. 71. For examples of sensationalized coverage, see *Amsterdam News*, "Spotlight—Switchblade—Death," 7 January 1939, p. 1; "Death In the Evening," 7 January 1939, p. 1.

30. Adam Clayton Powell was elected to New York City Council in 1941, becoming the city's first black council member. He was elected to Congress in 1945 and was re-elected eleven times. In 1960, Powell advanced to chairman of the House Committee on Education and Labor. He sponsored civil rights legislation and piloted major anti-poverty and education bills through the House. Accused of irregularities in the use of public funds, Powell was censured and lost his seat in 1957. After returning to the House in 1961, he was stripped of his seniority. He lost the primary in 1970 and died in 1972.

31. Oral history, p. 96.

32. Oral history, pp. 93, 98. Fredi Washington starred opposite Paul Robeson in "Black Boy." Her motion picture credits included "Imitation of Life," "The Emperor Jones," and "One Mile from Heaven."

33. The *Daily Compass* began publication in 1949 as a liberal, non-Communist newspaper. Initially a sixteen-page tabloid, it later expanded to twenty-four pages, reached a circulation of 50,000, and employed a staff of 125. Editor and publisher was Ted O. Thackrey, who had been editor and general manager of the *New York Post*. I.F. Stone was a radical journalist known for his witty and polemical pieces. After the *Daily Compass* ceased operation, Stone founded his own Washington newspaper, *I.F. Stone's Weekly*, which became the conscience of liberal America.

34. Cooke, "I Was a Part of the Bronx Slave Market," *Daily Compass*, 8 January 1950, p. 1.

35. Cooke, "Bronx Slave Market: Where Men Prowl and Women Prey on Needy Job-Seekers," *Daily Compass*, 9 January 1950, p. 4.

36. Cooke, *Daily Compass*, "'Paper Bag Brigade' Learns How To Deal With Gypping Employers," 10 January 1950, p. 4; "'Mrs. Legree' Hires Only on the Street," 11 January 1950, p. 4.

37. Cooke, *Daily Compass*, "Bronx Slave Market; A Personal Experience," 10 January 1950, p. 1; "Bronx Slave Mart: $3.40 a Day," 11 January 1950, p. 1. Ted O. Thackrey, "Modern Slave Market," *Daily Compass*, 9 January 1950, p. 13. *Daily Compass*, "Expose Brings Move To Rid New York Of 'Slave Market,'" 18 January 1950, p. 6.

38. Cooke, *Daily Compass*, "Occupation: Streetwalker," 16 April, 1950, p. 2. See also Cooke, *Daily Compass*, "Katie, 'Given Away' at 3, Turned to Streets at 15," 17 April 1950, p. 2; "Katie's 'Not Ashamed Any More'—She Just Feels Helpless Now," 18 April 1950, p. 2; "Katie Is Sent To The Reformatory On Her 1st Arrest," 19 April 1950, p. 4; "How 'Vice Squad' Operates," 20 April 1950, p. 7; "Police Oldtimers Become Cynical About Prostitution," 21 April 1950, p. 7; "'I Was Framed' Is Universal Cry In Woman's Court," 23 April 1950, p. 7; "How Women's Court Works," 24 April 1950, p. 6; "It's Drab, Tawdry In Women's Court," 25 April 1950, p. 7; "Chaneta's New Home: A Dingy, Heatless Flat," 26 April 1950, p. 3; "The Judge is King In Women's Court," 27 April 1950, p. 7; "A Trip Through Women's Prison," 28 April 1950, p. 7.

39. Cooke, *Daily Compass*, "A Plan To Deal With Prostitution," 30 April 1950, p. 6; "What Can New York Do About Prostitution?", 1 May 1950, p. 6.

40. Cooke, *Daily Compass*, "What Can Happen to YOUR Child—A Study in Narcotics Addiction," 20 May 1951, p. 13; "'My Son, 20, Is a Hopeless Addict,'" 21 May 1951, p. 4; "Southeast Bronx Narcotics Peddlers Found Wherever Children Gather," 22 May 1951, p. 4; "Dope Area in Bronx Suddenly 'Quiet' As *COMPASS* Expose Turns Heat On," 23 May 1951, p. 4; "Case History of a Teen-Age Addict," 24 May 1951, p. 4. *Daily Compass*, "3-Way Battle on Dope Proposed," 21 May 1951, p. 18.

41. The transcript of the 8 September 1953 hearing was published by the United States Government Printing Office in 1953. A copy is available at the National Archives in Washington, D.C., Legislative Division, Record Group 287. See pp. 2-4.

42. Oral history, pp. 82, 131. Author's interview with Cooke, 9 January 1991. Hearing transcript, pp. 4-5.

43. C.P. Trussell, "Stevens Will Review McCarthy's Demand," *New York Times*, 9 September 1953, p. 1; *New York Daily News*, "Stevens Talks With McCarthy, Delays Answer," 9 September 1953, p. 13; Murrey Martier, "Stevens Promises McCarthy To Review Army Ban on Data," *Washington Post*, 9 September 1953, p. 3; Robert K. Walsh, "McCarthy's Army-Leak Probe Turns to Columnist's 'Leg Man,'" *Washington Evening Star*, 9 September 1953, p. A-3.

44. Oral history, pp. 126, 146. Arthur Miller won a Pulitzer Prize for *Death of a Salesman*. Among his other plays were *The Crucible*, *A View from the Bridge*, and *After the Fall*. He also wrote the screenplay for the

motion picture, *The Misfits*. John Randolph is a stage, motion picture, and television actor whose career began in the 1940s. In 1990 he joined the cast of the television series "Grand."

45. Author's interview with Cooke, 9 January 1991. Angela Y. Davis is a civil rights activist. In the 1960s she was charged with murder, kidnapping, and conspiracy following an alleged attempt to kidnap three San Quentin prisoners from the Marin County Civic Center. Four persons were killed during the incident. In 1972, after spending sixteen months in jail, Davis was tried and acquitted of the charges.

46. Author's interview with Cooke, 9 January 1991.

47. Oral history, p. 84.

8. CHARLOTTA A. BASS

1. On the significance of Malcolm X, see David Gallen, *Malcolm X: As They Knew Him* (New York: Carroll and Graf, 1992); Peter Louis Goldman, *The Death and Life of Malcolm X* (Urbana: Univ. of Illinois Press, 1979); Alex Haley, *The Autobiography of Malcolm X* (1965; reprint, New York: Ballantine, 1992); Eugene V. Wolfenstein, *The Victims of Democracy: Malcolm X and the Black Revolution* (Berkeley: Univ. of California Press, 1981).

2. Charlotta A. Bass, "On the Sidewalk," *California Eagle*, 31 January 1946, p. 1.

3. Major sources on Bass's life are her self-published book, *Forty Years: Memoirs from the Pages of a Newspaper* (Los Angeles: 1960), and the Charlotta A. Bass Papers and Manuscript Collection at Southern California Library for Social Studies and Research, in Los Angeles, which consists of six boxes of Bass's personal correspondence, speeches, campaign literature, and book manuscript. For information on Bass's early years, see Bass, *Forty Years*, 27-30; Bass Papers, Box 2, Folder 13. Other sources of information about Bass are Sharynn Owens Etheridge, "Charlotta Spears [sic] Bass," in Smith, *Notable Black American Women*, 61-64; Gerald R. Gill, "'Win or Lose—We Win': The 1952 Vice Presidential Campaign of Charlotta A. Bass," in Sharon Hartley and Rosalyn Terborg-Penn, eds., *The Afro-American Woman: Struggles and Images* (Port Washington, N.Y.: National University Publications, 1978), 109-18; Lerner, *Black Women in White America*, 342; Barbara Sicherman and Carol Hurd Green, eds., *Notable American Women, The Modern Period: A Biographical Dictionary* (Cambridge, Mass.: Harvard Univ. Press, 1980), 61-63.

4. Bass, *Forty Years*, 31-32.

5. *California Eagle*, "Editor J.B. Bass Passes," 2 November 1934, p. 1; "Hundreds Mourn Death of Editor J.B. Bass at Impressive Funeral," 9 November 1934, p. 1; "*Eagle's* Directors Hosts At Dinner," 3 May 1935, p. 1; "Remarkable Reception To *California Eagle* All Over The State," 5 April 1914, p. 1; "Another Trip to Central and Northern California," 27 June

1914, p. 1. After she married, Charlotta Spear retained her maiden name in both bylines and the masthead of the *Eagle*; not until 1925 did she begin using the name Charlotta Bass.

6. Bass, "Fight Against 'The Clansman' Lost by City Council And Many Citizens of both Races," *California Eagle*, 13 February 1915, p. 1.

7. Bass, *California Eagle*, "The Afro-Americans of Los Angeles Demand the Clansman in Motion Pictures be Denied Admittance," 30 January 1915, p. 1; "In the Civic Walk," 6 February 1915, p. 1; "Fight Against 'The Clansman' Lost by City Council And Many Citizens of both Races," 13 February 1915, p. 1; "A Fight for Justice," 13 March 1915, p. 4. Bass, *Forty Years*, 35.

8. Bass, *California Eagle*, "Managing Editor Welcomed Home," 22 September 1917, p. 1; "Editor's Last Lap of Great 'On the Wing' Trip," 29 November 1919, p. 1. Bass, *Forty Years*, 41.

9. Etheridge,"Charlotta Spears [sic] Bass," 62; Theodore G. Vincent, *Black Power and the Garvey Movement* (San Francisco: Ramparts, 1972), 56, 130.

10. Bass, *California Eagle*, "Why Has Not the Board of Supervisors," 8 March 1919, p. 4; "Colored Girls Enter County Hospital," 13 September 1919, p. 1; Helen Taylor, "It's the *California Eagle*'s 70th Birthday," *Daily People's World*, 29 September 1949, p. 5.

11. Bass, *California Eagle*, "KKK Attempts to Burn Edward Grubbs Home," 28 January 1922, p. 1; "Klan Operations," 4 July 1924, p. 1. Bass, *Forty Years*, 102, 58.

12. Bass, *California Eagle*, "Chief Mogul of Ku Klux Klan Procures Warrant for Editor and Managing Editor of 'Soaring *Eagle*,'" 15 May 1925, p. 1. See also Bass, *California Eagle*, "Ku Klux Monopolizes Watts," 10 April 1925, p. 1; "Ku Klux Case Set for 18th of June," 22 May 1925, p. 1; "Ku Klux Complaint Against *Eagle* Editors," 5 June 1925, p. 1; "Taming the KKK," 12 June 1925, p. 6.

13. Bass, "Judge Chambers in Notable Decision Finds Defendants in KKK Case Not Guilty," *California Eagle*, 26 June 1925, p. 1.

14. Bass, *Forty Years*, 58-59.

15. Taylor, "It's the *California Eagle*'s 70th Birthday," p. 5.

16. Bass, *California Eagle*, "Negro Hanged in Effigy; Editor of *Eagle* Menaced," 20 March 1947, p. 1; "Editor Attacked in Student Riot," 22 April 1948, p. 1; "Publisher Goes to Jail," 29 July 1932, p. 1.

17. Bass Papers, Box 2, Folder 10.

18. Bass, "On the Sidewalk," *California Eagle*, 14 September 1934, p. 1; 21 September 1934, p. 1; Bass Papers, Box 2, Folder 10; Taylor, "It's the *California Eagle*'s 70th Birthday," p. 5.

19. Bass, *California Eagle*, "The Boulder Dam," 15 July 1932, p. 12; "Situation At Boulder Dam Clearing Up," 29 July 1932, p. 1; "Negro Labor Called to Boulder Dam," 9 September 1932, p. 1; "Unfair Discrimination," 25 August 1917, p. 4; "Is the Council Mesmerized," 15 September 1917, p. 4; "The Welfare Department," 13 October 1917, p. 4; "Civil Service Commission Bans Jim-crow Lists," 24 November 1917, p. 1; "Notable

Victory for Justice and Fair Play—Council Backs Civil Service," 7 December 1917, p. 1; "300 Cars, Buses Out in L.A. RY. Job Bias—1,500 Threaten 'March,'" 18 December 1942, p. 1; "On the Sidewalk," 22 January 1943, p. 1; "LARY HIRES NEGRO—Conductors, Motormen!" 29 January 1943, p. 1.

20. Bass, "On the Sidewalk," *California Eagle*, 14 February 1946, p. 1.

21. Bass, *California Eagle*, "Hold Negro Girl as Peon 11 Years," 3 October 1930, p. 1; "Southern Cracker Gets Jolt Of California Justice," 31 October 1930, p. 1.

22. *California Eagle*, "The West's Greatest Journal," 4 April 1924, p. 10; Bass, *Forty Years*, 38, 42.

23. *California Eagle*, "*Eagle* Editors Returned 13th," 19 October 1934, p. 1; "Editor J.B. Bass Passes," 2 November 1934, p. 1; "*Eagle's* Directors Hosts At Dinner," 3 May 1935, p. 1.

24. Bass, "Support of Laws Case Urged By Home Owners Association," *California Eagle*, 25 October 1945, p. 1; Bass, *Forty Years*, 110.

25. Bass, *California Eagle*, "Celebrities Set For 'Sugar Hill' Covenant Fight," 1 November 1945, p. 1; "Celebrities in Spotlight As 'Sugar Hill' Trial Begins," 6 December 1945, p. 4; "Defense Attorney Analyzes Historic 'Sugar Hill' Decision," 13 December 1945, p. 1. See also *Los Angeles Times*, "Negro Property Owners Protest," 6 December 1945, p. B-2.

26. Bass, *California Eagle*, "Laws Case Postponed Again; New Trial Date November 13," 1 November 1945, p. 1; "Hearing Denied; Family Ordered To Vacate Home," 13 December 1945, p. 1; "Laws Case Postponed Again," 1 November 1945, p. 1; "Citizens Urged to Fight Laws Case Verdict," 29 November 1945, p. 1.

27. Bass, *California Eagle*, "On the Sidewalk," 20 December 1945, p. 1; "Hearing Denied; Family Ordered to Vacate Home," 13 December 1945, p. 1; "On the Sidewalk," 20 December 1945, p. 1; "This Is Your Fight!" 3 January 1946, p. 1.

28. Bass, "Race Covenants Ban by High Court Wins Wide Approval," *California Eagle*, 6 May 1948, p. 1; *New York Times*, "Anti-Negro Pacts on Realty Ruled Not Enforceable," 4 May 1948, p. 1.

29. Bass, "GI Slain in Cold Blood by Officer," *California Eagle*, 29 November 1945, 1.

30. *California Eagle*, 8 and 29 November 1945.

31. *California Eagle*, "Huge Mass Rally Demands End to Police Brutality," 13 December 1946, p. 1.

32. On the federal government's relations with the black press during World War II, see Patrick S. Washburn, *A Question of Sedition: The Federal Government's Investigation of the Black Press During World War II* (New York: Oxford Univ. Press, 1986), especially pp. 3-10.

33. "Report of Trends in the Negro Press," Office of the Assistant Secretary of War, 1940-47, Record Group 28, file no. 103777, Box 223, National Archives, Washington, D.C. See also *California Eagle*, "Washington To Hush Negro Press," 28 May 1942, p. 1.

34. *Pittsburgh Courier*, "Cowing the Negro Press," 14 March 1942, p.

6; report dated 2 October 1944, Charlotta A. Bass file, no. 100-297187, United States Department of Justice, Federal Bureau of Investigation, Washington, D.C. Bass's file was declassified in 1981 and obtained through a Freedom of Information request.

35. FBI file, report dated 5 April 1944.

36. Records of the United States Post Office Department, Office of the Solicitor, Record Group 28, file no. 103777, E-440, folder labeled "California Eagle," National Archives, Washington, D.C.; Office of the Solicitor letter to Department of Justice, 5 November 1943. Bass, "Downtown Disorders," *California Eagle*, 14 October 1943, p. 1.

37. Bass, "On the Sidewalk," *California Eagle*, 15 November 1945, p. 1.

38. Letter by Tom C. Clark, Office of the Solicitor, to Calvin W. Hassell, Assistant Solicitor, Post Office Department, 15 November 1943, Records of the United States Post Office Department.

39. Bass, "On the Sidewalk," *California Eagle*, 4 April 1946, p. 1.

40. *California Eagle*, "Editor One of 19 to Grand Jury in 1943," 29 January 1943, p. 1; Bass Papers, Additional Box 1, Folder marked "Articles and Editorials, 1940s"; *Los Angeles Sentinel*, "NAACP Board Members," 18 January 1945, p. 1. Bass christened the U.S.S. James Weldon Johnson, named for a leading figure in the Harlem Renaissance.

41. Bass Papers, Box 2, Folder 10.

42. Bass Papers, Additional Box 1, Folders marked "Congressional Campaign, 1944" and "City Council Campaign, 1945." Curtis D. MacDougall, *Gideon's Army*, vol. 3 (New York: Marzani and Munsell, 1965), 596-97; Sicherman and Green, *Notable American Women*, 62. Bass's best showing was in the Los Angeles City Council election. She finished second among six candidates in the primary and received 34 percent of the vote in the runoff. See *Los Angeles Times*, "City Election Results," 3 May 1945, p. B-1.

43. *Los Angeles Sentinel*, "City Council Winners," 3 May 1945, p. 1; Bass, "On the Sidewalk," *California Eagle*, 3 May 1945, p. 1; *New York Daily News*, "Henry and His Reds," 26 August 1948, p. 37; *Los Angeles Tribune*, "Words Fly at Burns Rally," 25 December 1948, p. 1; Bass Papers, Additional Box 1, Folder marked "Letters to C.A. Bass, 1940s," 31 August 1948 statement labeled "Notice of Libelous Statements Published and Demand for Retraction."

44. Bass, *California Eagle*, "Get American Troops Out of China," 19 September 1946, p. 6; "'Uncle Tom' Is Not Dead," 14 July 1950, 1. Sicherman and Green, *Notable American Women*, 62. Bass, *Soviet Russia Today*, "They Work for Peace—Not War: Impressions of the USSR," November 1950, pp. 19-21; *Daily Worker*, "For These Rights I Will Fight," 2 April 1952. FBI file, reports dated 11 August 1950, 15 September 1950.

45. FBI file, reports dated 14 April 1951, 6 June 1951; Sixth Report on Un-American Activities in California, 1951, p. 53; Bass Papers, Box 2, Folder 14, Marion H. Jackson letter to Bass, 14 August 1956.

46. Bass Papers, Additional Box 1, Folder marked "Letters to C.A.

Bass, 1950s." The *California Eagle* changed ownership twice during the 1950s and early 1960s. It ceased publication in 1965.

47. Black women who have followed Bass into national politics include Shirley Chisholm, who sought the Democratic Party's nomination for president in 1968; Charlene Mitchell, who ran for president on the Community Party ticket in 1968; and Angela Y. Davis, who ran for vice president on the Communist Party ticket in 1980 and 1984. Major sources of information on Bass's national race are the Bass Papers, Additional Box 1, Folder marked "Letters to C.A. Bass, 1950s"; forty newspaper and magazine articles held under her name in the Schomburg Clipping File, Schomburg Research Center on Black Culture, New York Public Library; seven articles contained in Bass's vertical file at the Moorland-Spingarn Research Center, Howard University Library, Washington, D.C. Other sources that mention Bass's campaign include Barton J. Bernstein, "The Republicans Return," in Arthur M. Schlesinger, Jr., Fred L. Israel, and William P. Hansen, eds., *The Coming to Power: Critical Presidential Elections in American History* (New York: Chelsea, 1972), 3256; Davis, *Women, Culture, and Politics*, 19; Leonard Dinnerstein, "The Progressives and States' Rights Parties of 1948," in Arthur M. Schlesinger, Jr., ed., *History of U.S. Political Parties*, vol. 4 (New York: Chelsea, 1973), 3328; William L. Patterson, *The Man Who Cried Genocide: An Autobiography* (New York: International Publishers, 1971), 180; Karl M. Schmidt, *Henry A. Wallace: Quixotic Crusade 1948* (Syracuse, N.Y.: Syracuse Univ. Press, 1960), 311-12; David A. Shannon, *The Decline of American Communism* (New York: Harcourt, Brace, 1959), 213.

48. Bass Papers, Additional Box 1, Folder marked "Letters to C.A. Bass, 1960s"; Box 2, Folder 13, brochure for Community Reading Room of Elsinore, Calif. Sicherman and Green, *Notable American Women*, 63.

49. *Los Angeles Herald-Examiner*, "Charlotta A. Bass Celebrates 40 Years as a Local Newspaper Editor," 28 April 1960, p. 17. Bass published her book herself in Los Angeles in 1960.

50. Bass Papers, Additional Box 1, Folder marked "Articles and Speeches, 1960s," speech text for "The Significance of Negro History Week in 1961," delivered in February 1961.

51. FBI file, report dated 3 July 1967; *People's World*, "Legendary Black Publisher Mrs. Bass dies at 95," 19 April 1969, p. 12; Bass Papers, Box 2, Folder 18.

9. ALICE ALLISON DUNNIGAN

1. On the opportunities that World War II brought African-American women, see Giddings, *When and Where*, 231-58. On black America during and after World War II, see Franklin and Moss, *From Slavery to Freedom*, 385-435.

2. Alice A. Dunnigan, *A Black Woman's Experience: From Schoolhouse to White House* (Philadelphia: Dorrance, 1974), 287.

3. The best source of details about Dunnigan's life is her 700-page

autobiography, *A Black Woman's Experience*. Other sources include the Claude A. Barnett Papers, held at the Chicago Historical Society; Alice Allison Dunnigan Papers, held at Moorland-Spingarn Research Center, Howard University Library, Washington, D.C.; Robert L. Johns, "Alice Dunnigan," in Smith, *Notable Black American Women*, 301-3.

4. Interview with Dunnigan by Marcia Greenlee, 7 April 1977, Black Women Oral History Project of the Schlesinger Library, Radcliffe College, p. 4.

5. Dunnigan, *A Black Woman's Experience*, 27-28.

6. Ibid., 72-74.

7. Dunnigan letter to John Hein, her boss at the President's Council on Youth Opportunity, 31 October 1969, Dunnigan Papers; Dunnigan letter to Barnett, 26 August 1947, Barnett Papers. When Dunnigan began teaching in 1924, the average teaching salary nationwide was $1,227. When she left teaching in 1942, the average salary nationwide was $1,507. See *Historical Statistics of the United States, Colonial Times to 1970* (Washington: U.S. Bureau of the Census, U.S. Government Printing Office, 1975), 375.

8. Information about Dunnigan's two marriages is contained in her autobiography, oral history, and correspondence with Barnett. Although there are two sides to every dispute, only her side of this one is documented. See Dunnigan, *Black Woman's Experience*, 182; Black Women Oral History Project, pp. 12-18; Dunnigan letter to Barnett, 26 May 1947, Barnett Papers.

9. Dunnigan letter to Barnett, 21 November 1946, Barnett Papers.

10. Dunnigan, *Black Woman's Experience*, 187. On the advantages that urban centers provide independent women, see David M. Potter, "American Women and American Character," in Don E. Fehrenbacher, ed., *History and American Society: Essays of David M. Potter* (New York: Oxford Univ. Press, 1973), 278-303.

11. Dunnigan letter to Barnett, 30 January 1948, Barnett Papers. According to census data, black women in the District of Columbia in 1949 earned an average annual salary of $1,395. The average salary for African Americans of both genders combined was $1,906. *Census of Population: 1950, Volume II: Characteristics of the Population* (Washington: U.S. Government Printing Office, 1952), 9-101.

12. Barnett letter to James H. Baker, 18 December 1946, Barnett Papers. Associated Negro Press expenses exceeded subscription revenue for every mailing distributed during its history. Fiscal problems finally forced ANP to cease operation in 1964. On ANP's history, see Richard Beard and Cyril Zoerner, "The Associated Negro Press: Its Founding, Ascendancy, and Demise," *Journalism Quarterly* 46 (Spring 1969): 47-52; Lawrence Hogan, *A Black National News Service: The Associated Negro Press and Claude Barnett, 1919-1945* (Cranbury, N.J.: Associated University Presses, 1984).

13. Barnett letter to Reid E. Jackson, 2 March 1946; James H. Baker

letter to Barnett, 18 December 1946; Barnett letter to Baker, 31 December 1946; Dunnigan letter to Barnett, 30 January 1948, Barnett Papers.

14. Dunnigan letter to Barnett, 30 January 1948, Barnett Papers.

15. Barnett letters to Dunnigan, 28 January 1948, 30 August 1947, 23 June 1948; Dunnigan letter to Barnett, 30 January 1948, Barnett Papers.

16. Dunnigan, "Liberals March In D.C., Seek Action," *Atlanta Daily World*, 5 January 1947, p. 1.

17. The Standing Committee of Correspondents determines which reporters are accredited. Committee meeting minutes are held in the Senate Press Gallery in the United States Capitol. Minutes for 22 January 1947 state that Dunnigan had requested and been sent an application. Minutes for 12 December 1946 state that Lautier had submitted his application. Minutes for 4 March 1947 state that the committee rejected Lautier's application by a 4-1 vote. Senate rules then specified that the press galleries were available only to reporters who sent their stories by telegraph. Standing Committee members rejected Lautier's application, they said, because he sent his stories by mail. Two hundred documents relevant to Lautier's application and eventual accreditation are held in the Legislative Archives Division of the National Archives in Washington. During the 18 March 1947 hearing, Lautier argued that he often sent stories by telegraph.

18. Standing Committee minutes for 17 June 1947, which list Dunnigan as being approved for accreditation, list her name under the heading: "Applications approved under the new provisions in the Senate Rules governing the Press Galleries." Dunnigan letter to Barnett, 26 August 1947, Barnett Papers.

19. Dunnigan, *Black Woman's Experience*, 209; Barnett letter to Dunnigan, 7 August 1948, Barnett Papers.

20. Frank Marshall Davis letters to Dunnigan, 29 April 1947, 20 May 1947, 30 July 1947; Barnett letter to Dunnigan, 22 February 1947, Barnett Papers.

21. Dunnigan letter to Barnett, Barnett Papers. The contents of the undated letter identify it as having been written in the summer of 1948.

22. Dunnigan, "Prejudiced MP Given Reprimand for Bias," *Washington Afro-American*, 19 June 1948, p. 3. Doris Fleeson of the *Washington Evening Star* accompanied the president as far as Omaha.

23. Jacqueline Trescott, "The Black Press: New Archive for An Embattled, Battling Institution," *Washington Post*, 18 March 1977, p. 1.

24. The *Atlanta Daily World*, *Chicago Defender*, and *Pittsburgh Courier* had correspondents in Washington at the time.

25. Dunnigan, "New York Delegation Causes D.C. Hotel To Break Down 'No Negro' Policy," *Houston Informer*, 29 January 1949, p. 3; "N.Y. Delegation Causes Washington Hotel to Breakdown Policy," *Ohio Daily Express*, 26 January 1949, p. 1. ANP newspapers available for the period at the Library of Congress are the *Atlanta Daily World*, *Norfolk Journal & Guide*, *Philadelphia Tribune*, and *Washington Afro-American*; two available at the Black Press Archives at Howard University are the *Pitts-*

burgh Courier and *Washington Afro-American*. Some clippings are in the Dunnigan Papers and Barnett Papers.

26. No coverage of the incident appeared in the *Washington Post* or *Washington Evening Star* between 22 January and 5 February 1949, the two weeks before and after Dunnigan's story was published.

27. Dunnigan, "Find Long-Lost DC Anti-Bias Law," *New York Amsterdam News*, 28 May 1949, p. 6; "New Test Case on Jim Crow Law Set," *Washington Afro-American*, 25 July 1950, p. 1; "Court of Appeals Rules Out Segregation In D.C.," *Atlanta Daily World*, 27 May 1951, p. 8; "D.C. Could Enact Valid Rights Law—Donohue," *Washington Afro-American*, 27 January 1953, p. 14; "High Court Knocks Out District Restaurant Policy," *Norfolk Journal and Guide*, 13 June 1953, p. 1. For discussion of the Thompson Restaurant case, see Marvin Caplan, "Eat Anywhere!," *Washington History* 1 (Spring 1989): 24-39.

28. Dunnigan, "D.C. Movie Houses Abandon A Segregation," *Chicago Defender*, 10 October 1953, p. 2; "Four Integrated Playgrounds Favored in D.C.," 25 April 1952, Barnett Papers; "Interracial Day Camp Opens at Rock Creek Park," *Baltimore Afro-American*, 15 July 1950, p. 7; "CAA Orders End to Race Bias at Washington National Airport," 5 January 1949, Barnett Papers; "Capitol [sic] Teacher's College To Enroll 3 Negroes," 20 October 1948, Barnett Papers; "Alphas Break Down Color Barrier In Nation's Capitol [sic]," undated, Dunnigan Papers, Box 16.

29. Dunnigan, "The Fight Is On In Industry," *Chicago Defender*, 22 August 1953, p. 2; "This Week In Washington," *Norfolk Journal and Guide*, 6 July 1957, p. 9; "On The Local Scene," *Chicago Defender*, 19 September 1953, p. 2; "National Grapevine; Community Suffers From Employment Bias," *Chicago Defender*, 22 August 1953, p. 2.

30. The Capital Press Club presented the Newsman's Newsman award. The club, founded in 1943, was composed of African-American reporters working for Washington news organizations. Dunnigan letters to Barnett, 30 June 1951 and 31 May 1952, Barnett Papers.

31. Dunnigan, *Black Woman's Experience*, 317-18.

32. Dunnigan, "National Grapevine; Worth Trying," *Chicago Defender*, 16 May 1953, p. 2.

33. Dunnigan, "Those Washington Newsgals," *Chicago Defender*, 5 September 1953, p. 2; "Covering Washington," *Oklahoma City Black Dispatch*, 5 March 1955, p. 2; "Policemen Restrain Profane Lawmaker," *Houston Informer*, 12 August 1950, p. 1; "National Grapevine; 'The Joke Is On Me,'" *Chicago Defender*, 5 September 1953, p. 2.

34. Dunnigan, "Veterans Put Out Six-Foot Burning Cross in NE Area," *Washington Afro-American*, 3 April 1948, p. 1. No coverage of the cross-burning incident appeared in the *Post* or *Star* between 24 March and 10 April 1948, the two weeks before and after Dunnigan's story was published. Dunnigan, "Covenanters Seek to Evict Family," *Washington Afro-American*, 3 April 1948, p. 2. No coverage of the eviction effort appeared in the *Post* or *Star* between 24 March and 10 April 1948, the two weeks before and after Dunnigan's story was published. Dunnigan, "'You're a Black Son-of-a-Bitch'

Shouts Georgia Congressman," *Oklahoma City Black Dispatch*, 12 August 1950, p. 1; "Policemen Restrain Profane Lawmaker," *Houston Informer*, 12 August 1950, p. 1; "'I'd Do It Again,' Says Fiery Ga. Congressman in Discussing Attack on Patterson," *Oklahoma City Black Dispatch*, 19 August 1950, p. 1. The incident took place at a hearing 11 August, but neither the *Post* nor *Star* mentioned it in 11, 12, or 13 August editions.

35. Dunnigan, *Black Woman's Experience*, 257-58; Dunnigan typed recollection, Women's National Press Club files, National Press Club Archives, Washington, D.C., p. 6. Dunnigan's personal recollections are the only documentation for the 1947 events involving her and Craig. The Elizabeth May Craig Papers at the Library of Congress do not mention Dunnigan. In general, Craig was a socially progressive woman. As a member of the Standing Committee, for example, Craig favored Lautier's accreditation. See minutes of the Standing Committee of Correspondents, 12 December 1946. *Washington Evening Star*, "Negro Seeks to Join Women's Press Club," 8 March 1955, p. C-4. For a history of the Women's National Press Club, see Maurine H. Beasley, "The Women's National Press Club: Case Study of Professional Aspirations," *Journalism History* 15 (Winter 1988): 112-21.

36. Barnett letter to Dunnigan, 1 May 1961, Barnett Papers; Dunnigan, *Black Woman's Experience*, 581. In 1960, the average Washington worker earned $3,841 per year. See *U.S. Bureau of the Census, Census of Population: 1960, Volume II, Characteristics of the Population* (Washington: U.S. Government Printing Office, 1962), 10-174. Dunnigan letters to Barnett, 21 November 1947, 6 January 1948, 21 June 1948, undated letters the contents of which identify them as having been written in the fall of 1947 and early 1948, Barnett Papers.

37. Dunnigan letter to President Harry S. Truman, 22 March 1949, Harry S. Truman Library, Independence, Mo.; Dunnigan letter to Barnett, 5 November 1948, Barnett Papers; Dunnigan, *Black Woman's Experience*, 552-60.

38. Dunnigan, *Black Woman's Experience*, 586, 588-90.

39. Ibid., 610-21, 639-40.

40. Ibid., 660; Dunnigan, *The Fascinating Story of Black Kentuckians: Their Heritage and Tradition* (Washington, D.C.: Association for the Study of Afro-American Life and History, 1979); *Washington Post*, "Reporter Alice Allison Dunnigan Dies," 8 May 1983, p. C-7; *Jet*, "Alice Dunnigan, Noted News Woman, Dies At 77," 23 May 1983, p. 42.

10. ETHEL L. PAYNE

1. George P. Hunt, "The Racial Crisis and the News Media: An Overview," in Paul L. Fisher and Ralph L. Lowenstein, eds., *Race and the News Media* (New York: Praeger, 1967). See also Emery and Emery, *Press and America*, 403-4; Folkerts and Teeter, *Voices of a Nation*, 517-18.

2. The *Chicago Defender* was founded as a weekly newspaper by

Robert S. Abbott in 1905. Publishing a national edition as well as local editions in several cities, it has been one of the leading African-American newspapers in the country. The *Defender*, which became a daily newspaper in 1956, is now the flagship of a chain of newspapers owned by the Sengstacke family, who are descendants of Abbott. On the *Chicago Defender's* history, see L.F. Palmer, Jr., "The Black Press in Transition," *Columbia Journalism Review* (Spring 1970): 31; Wolseley, *Black Press, U.S.A.*, 52-57, 97-99.

3. Interview with Ethel L. Payne by Kathleen Currie, Women in Journalism oral history project of the Washington Press Club Foundation, 25 August 1987 through 17 November 1987, Oral History Collection, Columbia University, pp. 49-50.

4. The Capital Press Club was composed of African-American reporters working in Washington, D.C.

5. Author's interview with Ethel L. Payne, 23 January 1991, in Payne's home in Washington, D.C.

6. For published information about Payne's life, see Rodger Streitmatter, "No Taste for Fluff: Ethel L. Payne, African-American Journalist," *Journalism Quarterly* 68 (Autumn 1991): 528-40; Marzolf, *Up From the Footnote*, 90-92; Grayson Mitchell, "Ethel Payne: First Lady of the Black Press," *Essence*, March 1974, pp. 66, 94, 96; Ethel L. Payne, "Loneliness in the Capital: The Black National Correspondent," in Henry G. LaBrie III, ed., *Perspectives of the Black Press: 1974* (Kennebunkport, Maine: Mercer, 1974), 153-61; Dorothea W. Slocum, "Ethel Payne," in Smith, *Notable Black American Women*, 830-33; Snorgrass, "Pioneer Black Women Journalists," 158; Jacqueline Trescott, "Ethel Payne's Lead Story," *Washington Post*, 14 June 1982, p. C-1; Wolseley, *Black Press, U.S.A.*, 259-61; Wilson, *Black Journalists in Paradox*, 74-75.

7. Author's interview with Payne, 14 February 1990, in Payne's home in Washington, D.C.; oral history, p. 6.

8. Oral history, pp. 11-14.

9. Ibid., 12-13.

10. Ibid., 118; author's interview with Payne, 7 May 1990, in Payne's home in Washington, D.C.

11. Payne, *Chicago Defender*, "Says Japanese Girls Playing GIs For Suckers; 'Chocolate Joe' Used, Amused, Confused," 18 November 1950, p. 1; "Says Japanese Girls Playing GIs For Suckers," 25 November 1950, p. 1.

12. Author's interview with Payne, 7 May 1990, in Payne's home in Washington, D.C.

13. Oral history, pp. 28, 31, 33, 118.

14. Ibid., 35; Payne, *Chicago Defender*, "Why Not Adopt A Baby?," 12 April 1952, p. 1; "Why Not Adopt A Baby?—Installment 2," 19 April 1952, p. 1; "Why Not Adopt A Baby?—Installment 3," 26 April 1952, p. 1; "Why Not Adopt A Baby?—Installment 4," 3 May 1952, p. 1; oral history, pp. 33-34; Payne, *Chicago Defender*, "The Plight Of The Unwed Mother," 7 June 1952, p. 1; "Abortionists Prey On Unhappy Girls," 7 June 1952, p. 1; "Says Education And Religion Are No Curbs For Run-Away Emotions," 14

June 1952, p. 1; "Society Stumped By Old Problem," 21 June 1952, p. 1; "Help Available For Unfortunate," 28 June 1952, p. 2; "McCarthy-Army Red Feud Rages Around Ill Widow," 6 March 1954, p. 1; "Moss Case Flops; Exit McCarthy," 20 March 1954, p. 1.

15. Payne, "Need Prodding To Get Congress To Act On Civil Rights Program," *Chicago Defender*, 3 April 1954, p. 3.

16. Payne, "Decree Labelled A Compromise," *Chicago Defender*, 11 June 1954, p. 1.

17. For other examples of Payne's civil rights coverage from Washington, see Payne, *Chicago Defender*, "Reporter Tells Why New Race Hate Group Fights Integration," 6 March 1954, p. 12; "Defer Rights Laws Says Demo Boss," 4 February 1956, p. 1; "Nixon Is Key Figure In Filibuster Fight," 5 January 1957, p. 1; "Dixiecrats Win Round In Fight On Filibuster," 12 January 1957, p. 1; "Powell Claims He Got The 'Axe,'" 2 February 1957, p. 1; "Johnson Dealt Fatal Blow To Rights Bill in Senate," 10 August 1957, p. 3.

18. Oral history, p. 127.

19. *Public Papers of the Presidents of the United States, Dwight D. Eisenhower, 1954* (Washington: Federal Register, National Archives and Records Service, General Services Administration, 1960), February 10, 1954, pp. 248-49; *Chicago Defender*, "Ike Sorry About Howard Incident, He Tells Defender," 20 February 1954, p. 1; Payne, "Bar Howard U Singers From GOP Dinner Rally," *Chicago Defender*, 13 February 1954, p. 1; *Washington Evening Star*, "'Mixup' Is Blamed For Howard Choir's Missing G.O.P. Fete," 10 February 1954, p. A-14.

20. *Public Papers of the Presidents of the United States, Dwight D. Eisenhower, 1954*, 17 March 1954, p. 323; 24 March 1954, p. 343; 7 April 1954, p. 386; 5 May 1954, pp. 453-54; 16 June 1954, p. 574.

21. Eisenhower's exact words were: "The administration is trying to do what it thinks and believes to be decent and just in this country, and is not in the effort to support any particular or special group of any kind. These opinions were sent down, these beliefs are held as part of the administration belief, because we think it is just and right, and that is my answer." *Public Papers of the Presidents of the United States, Dwight D. Eisenhower, 1954*, 7 July 1954, pp. 623-24; Edward T. Folliard, "Ike Praises Progress on His Program," *Washington Post*, 8 July 1954, p. 1; *Washington Evening Star*, "President Annoyed by Query On Travel Race Ban Support," 7 July 1954, p. 1.

22. Oral history, pp. 46-48.

23. *Public Papers of the Presidents of the United States, Dwight D. Eisenhower, 1954, 1955, 1956, 1957, 1960.*

24. Drew Pearson, "Pressure on Press Laid to Ike Aides," *Washington Post*, 27 April 1955, p. 59.

25. Pearson; *Chicago Defender*, "Hagerty Denies Probing Payne," 7 May 1955, p. 1.

26. Oral history, p. 118.

27. Payne, *Chicago Defender*, "Link Ala. Bus Boycott To Gandhi's

Technique," 18 February 1956, p. 1. See also, Payne, *Chicago Defender*, "Indict 1, Expect 20 To Face Trial In Bus Strike," 25 February 1956, p. 1; "On, On, On It Goes; Strikers, City At Impasse In Montgomery Bus Boycott," 25 February 1956, p. 3; "The South's New Hero, Clergymen Spring Forward To Lead Freedom's Fight," 25 February 1956, p. 8; "Thurgood To Defend 90 Arrested In Boycott Case," 3 March 1956, p. 1; "Here Are Names of Montgomery Heroes," 3 March 1956, p. 1; "Boycott Lawyer Freed in Court," 10 March 1956, p. 1; "Cut Sunday Bus Run In Boycott," 17 March 1956, p. 1; "Bus Boycott Spontaneous, King Says," 31 March 1956, p. 1.

28. Payne, *Chicago Defender*, "Rev. King's Own Story Of Montgomery Boycott," 31 March 1956, p. 1; "The Story Of Rev. Martin L. King," 19 May 1956, p. 18.

29. Oral history, p. 37; Payne, *Chicago Defender*, "Civil War, Lost By Bullets, Now Waged By Ballots," 21 April 1956, p. 5; "Southern Bloc Cracks Stinging Legislative Whip," 28 April 1956, p. 18; "Liberals Torn Between Loyalty And Conscience," 5 May 1956, p. 18; "South Defies High Court Bus Edict," 5 May 1956, p. 18; "Dollars Soften Dixie Resistance," 12 May 1956, p. 18; "The Tragic Story Of Dr. Lee Lorch," 12 May 1956, p. 18; "The Boycott Story And Montgomery," 26 May 1956, p. 18.

30. Payne, *Chicago Defender*, "Ethel Hears Students On Lucy Case," 18 February 1956, p. 2; "Ethel Sees Hate In Students [sic] Eyes," 18 February 1956, p. 2; "Lucy To Continue Fight, Returning to Birmingham After Medical Care, Rest," 10 March 1956, p. 1; "Autherine Lucy Shops, Small Town Girl On Spree In N.Y.," 17 March 1956, p. 8; "Little Rock 9 Still Studying," 21 September 1957, p. 3; "Ethel Payne Explains Why Faubus Called Out Troops," 21 September 1957, p. 5; "Tells Why Eckford Girl Walked Alone to School," 28 September 1957, p. 3; "Bombs Upset Racial Peace in Birmingham," 11-17 May 1963, p. 1; "Freedom March Draws 250,000," 24-30 August 1963, p. 1; "Randolph's Dream Comes True," 24-30 August 1963, p. 1; "'Not Long . . . Not Long,'" 27 March-2 April 1965, p. 1; "The Historic March To Freedom," 3-9 April 1965, p. 11; "'I's Been Climbin On, And It Ain't Been Easy,'" 3-9 April 1965, p. 14; author's interview with Payne, 20 October 1990.

31. Oral history, pp. 82, 90; author's interview with Payne, 20 October 1990; Payne, *Chicago Defender*, "Evict Prof. After He Entertains Reporter," 21 September 1957, p. 1.

32. Claudia Levy, "Journalist Ethel Payne Dies; 'First Lady of the Black Press,'" *Washington Post*, 1 June 1991, p. C-4; author's interview with Payne, 7 May 1990.

33. Trescott, "Ethel Payne's Lead Story," p. C-1.

34. Oral history, pp. 95, 97; Payne, *Chicago Defender*, "Vietnam: The History Of An Abused People," 7-13 January 1967, p. 28; "Mightiest Ship Afloat: We Visit The Enterprise," 14-21 January 1967, p. 1; "The Puzzling Adventure Of Mildred Harrison," 4-10 February 1967, p. 1; "Big Job, Paying Troops," 11-17 February 1967, p. 1; "Viet Exodus Like Noah's Ark," 25

February-3 March 1967, p. 2; "Chicago GI's Doing Their Share In Vietnam," 18-24 March 1967, p. 1.

35. Payne, *Chicago Defender,* "Ibo Leader Says Nigerian War In Final Phase," 22-28 February 1969, p. 1; "So This Is Washington," 22-28 March 1969, p. 8; "Rogers Wooing African Nations," 7-13 February 1970, p. 28; "Rogers Given Briefings On African Goods," 21-27 February 1970, p. 2; "Rogers Skirts S. Africa's Jim-Crow Practice; Sees News Policy for U.S.," 21-27 February 1970, p. 5; "So This Is Washington," 21-27 March 1970, p. 11; "Nigerian Ambassador On War, U.S. Relations," 21-27 March 1970, p. 25; "So This Is Washington," 10-16 June 1972, p. 8; "So This Is China," 17 February 1973, p. 11; "So This Is China," 24 February 1973, p. 11; "So This Is China," 3 March 1973, p. 11; "Reflections On An Odyssey In China," 10 March 1973, p. 8; "China Watching Is A Major Occupation," 17 March 1973, p. 6; oral history, p. vii.

36. Author's interview, 14 February 1990; oral history, pp. 103-10.

37. Payne, "Spectrum" scripts for 27 December 1977; 17 September 1974; "Matters of Opinion" script for 5 October 1981; "Spectrum" scripts for 22 March 1976; 1 May 1976; 22 April 1976. "Spectrum" scripts were among Payne's personal papers in her home in 1991.

38. Oral history, pp. 107-9; Marzolf, p. 91.

39. Payne's clients included the *Baltimore Afro-American, Washington Afro-American, Miami Times,* and three California weekly newspapers; oral history, p. vi; author's interview with Payne, 20 October 1990, in Payne's home in Washington, D.C.; Levy, "Journalist Ethel Payne Dies," p. C-4.

40. *Washington Post,* "Ethel Lois Payne," 2 June 1991, p. D-6; Levy, "Journalist Ethel Payne Dies," p. C-4.

41. Oral history, pp. 54, 153.

11. CHARLAYNE HUNTER-GAULT

1. On the difficulties that have plagued black America in recent years, see Franklin and Moss, *From Slavery to Freedom,* 476-511.

2. *Working Woman,* "Charlayne Hunter-Gault," July 1981, p. 60.

3. Hunter-Gault, "We Overcame Too," 35.

4. Much of the information about Charlayne Hunter-Gault's life was obtained during the author's interview with her on 11 September 1992 at the "MacNeil/Lehrer NewsHour" offices, 356 W. 58th Street, New York City. Information about Charlayne Hunter's early life also is contained in her autobiographical work, *In My Place* (New York: Farrar, Straus and Giroux, 1992). The book stresses her experiences growing up in the segregated South. It ends with her college graduation. Although there has been no previous scholarly study of the life and career of Charlayne Hunter-Gault, she has been the subject of several profiles, most of them in popular magazines. They include Judith Cummings, "The Unusual Life of Charlayne Hunter-Gault," *Savvy,* August 1980, pp. 52-56; Claudia Dreifus, "A

Talk with Charlayne Hunter-Gault," *Dial* 8 (Feb. 1987): 15-17, 45; C. Gerald Fraser, *Essence*, "Charlayne Hunter-Gault, From Front Line to Firing Line," March 1987, pp. 41-42, 110; John J. Goldman and Siobhan Flynn, "Correspondent of The Hour," *Washington Journalism Review*, September 1985, pp. 40-44; Hunter-Gault, "We Overcame Too," 32-35; Wolseley, *Black Press, U.S.A.*, 264-65; Dianne Young, "Their Southern Way With Words: Charlayne Hunter-Gault," *Southern Living*, June 1990, pp. 78-83. The *New York Times* published a profile of Charlayne Hunter when she desegregated the University of Georgia. See *New York Times*, "Breakers of a Barrier," 16 January 1961, p. 14.

5. Fraser, "Charlayne Hunter-Gault," 42.

6. Claude Sitton, "Georgia Students Riot on Campus; Two Negroes Out," *New York Times*, 12 January 1961, p. 1.

7. Ibid.

8. Sitton, *New York Times*, "Georgia U. Told to Admit Negroes," 7 January 1961, p. 1; "Georgia Students Riot on Campus; Two Negroes Out," 12 January 1961, p. 1.

9. Hunter-Gault, "We Overcame Too," 34.

10. Sitton, "Georgia Students Riot on Campus; Two Negroes Out"; *New York Times*, "Negro Student Wins on Dining Facility," 10 March 1961, p. 8; Anthony Lewis, "Robert Kennedy Vows in Georgia to Act on Rights," *New York Times*, 7 May 1961, p. 1.

11. Wolseley, *Black Press, U.S.A.*, 265.

12. Author's interview with Hunter-Gault, 11 September 1992.

13. Dreifus, "Talk with Charlayne Hunter-Gault," 45.

14. *Time*, "The Image," 13 September 1963, p. 27; *U.S. News and World Report*, "Where Integration Led to Intermarriage," 16 September 1963, p. 10.

15. Hunter, "A Hundred Fifteenth Between Lenox and Fifth," *New Yorker*, 20 February 1965, pp. 109-12; "A Trip to Leverton," *New Yorker*, 24 April 1965, pp. 95-113.

16. Author's interview with Hunter-Gault, 11 September 1992.

17. Hunter, "On the Case in Resurrection City," *Trans-Action*, October 1968, p. 47.

18. Author's interview with Hunter-Gault, 11 September 1992.

19. *Working Woman*, "Charlayne Hunter-Gault," July 1981, p. 60.

20. Goldman and Flynn, "Correspondent of the Hour," 43.

21. Hunter, "A Homecoming for the First Black Girl at the University of Georgia," *New York Times Magazine*, 25 January 1970, p. 65.

22. Joseph Lelyveld and Charlayne Hunter, "Obituary of a Heroin User Who Died at 12," *New York Times*, 12 January 1970, p. 1.

23. Author's interview with Hunter-Gault, 11 September 1992.

24. Hunter, "Many Blacks Wary of 'Women's Liberation' Movement in U.S.," *New York Times*, 17 November 1970, p. 47.

25. Hunter, "Paul Gibson In, Galiber Out As Third Deputy to Beame," *New York Times*, 17 January 1974, p. 1.

26. Hunter, "Black Muslim Temple Renamed for Malcolm X; Move

Reflects Acceptance of Slain Ex-Leader," *New York Times*, 2 February 1976, p. 1; *New York Times*, "Harlem School Will Honor A Reporter for *The Times*," 26 May 1971, p. 47.

27. Author's interview with Hunter-Gault, 11 September 1992; Cummings, "Unusual Life," 56.

28. Goldman and Flynn, "Correspondent of the Hour," 44.

29. Hunter-Gault, "MacNeil-Lehrer Report," "Black Colleges," 18 January 1979; "Busing Amendment," 23 July 1979; "Unemployment and the Black Vote," 3 July 1980; "Civil Rights Debate," 2 December 1980; "Atlanta's Children," 8 January 1981.

30. Hunter-Gault, "MacNeil-Lehrer Report," "Smoking: Fifteen Years Later," 11 January 1979; "The Hospital Cost Blues," 9 February 1979; "Shrinking Hospitals," 18 October 1979; "Marijuana Reassessment," 19 June 1980; "Competitive Medicine," 31 July 1981; "Acid Rain," 26 May 1980; "Toxic Waste," 2 July 1980; "National Energy Policy," 4 August 1980; "Natural Gas Decontrol," 26 August 1981; "Bailing Out Chrysler," 10 August 1979; "Supply-Side Economics," 18 February 1981; "Women's Rights in Iran," 19 March 1979; "Famine in Cambodia," 23 October 1979; "Refugee Policy," 20 June 1980; "Census Undercount," 25 September 1980; "ERA, Abortion and GOP," 10 July 1980; "Human Life Statute," 23 April 1981; "El Salvador," 3 March 1980; "Poland," 9 March 1981; "OPEC/Strategic Petroleum," 26 May 1981.

31. Hunter-Gault, "MacNeil-Lehrer Report," "Bishop Abel Muzorewa Interview," 11 July 1979.

32. Fraser, "Charlayne Hunter-Gault," 42.

33. Ibid.

34. Goldman and Flynn, "Correspondent of the Hour," 43.

35. Hunter-Gault, "Reflections: Dr. Death," *New Yorker*, 14 July 1986, p. 57.

36. Hunter-Gault, "South Africa: A Black American Woman's Emotional Journey through the White Man's South Africa," *Vogue*, March 1986, p. 544.

37. Clarke Taylor, "Back in Time in South Africa," *Los Angeles Times*, 28 September 1985, p. V-1.

38. Hunter-Gault, "MacNeil/Lehrer NewsHour," "Apartheid's People," 30 September-4 October 1985.

39. *Jet*, "Hunter-Gault Wins The Coveted Peabody Award," 26 May 1986, p. 5; "Univ. of Georgia Honors Its First Black Students," 7 October 1985, p. 25; "U. of Georgia Honors Its First Two Black Students It Tried To Bar 25 Years Ago," p. 23.

40. Hunter-Gault, *In My Place*.

41. Author's interview with Hunter-Gault, 11 September 1992. Hunter-Gault, "MacNeil/Lehrer NewsHour," "BCCI Scandal," 13-15 August, 5, 9 September, 22 October 1991; "Food Shortages in Iraq," 10 September 1990; "Tour of Duty," 3-4 October 1990; "Security Resolutions in Iraq," 28 November 1990; "Conversations with Soldiers Home from Iraq," 14-17 May 1991; "Making Iraq Obey," 23-24 September 1991; "Life That Failed," 18,

20 September 1991; "Campus Intolerance," 1 January 1991; "Collision Course on Affirmative Action," 3-7 June 1991; "Focus Under Scrutiny," 9 September 1991; "Day of Decision," 27 September 1991; "Can We All Get Along?" 8 July 1992.

42. Young, *Southern Way With Words*, 83.

A SYNTHESIS

1. Frederick Douglass, the most prominent African-American leader of the nineteenth century, founded or was involved with numerous journalistic enterprises. Most prominent among them were the *North Star* and *Frederick Douglass' Paper*, weekly newspapers he founded and operated in Rochester, New York, in the 1840s and 1850s; *Douglass' Monthly*, a magazine he published from Rochester in the 1860s; and the *New Era* and *New National Era*, weekly newspapers he published in Washington, D.C., in the early 1870s. T. Thomas Fortune rose to national prominence as editor of the *New York Globe* and *New York Age*, black weeklies, in the 1880s. When he joined the editorial staff of the *New York Evening Sun* in the early 1880s, he became the first African American to work for a mainstream newspaper. Heralded as the "Dean of Black Journalism," Fortune was read by politial leaders such as Theodore Roosevelt. William Monroe Trotter, a gradute of Harvard University and the first African American elected to Phi Beta Kappa, founded the *Boston Guardian* in 1901. As editor and publisher of the crusading black weekly, Trotter vehemently opposed the accommodationist philosophy of Booker T. Washington and reasserted the protest tradition among African Americans of the early twentieth century. In 1909 Trotter helped found the NAACP, and in 1915 he organized the first protest march by black Americans.

2. Author's interview with Ethel L. Payne, 23 January 1991, in Payne's home in Washington, D.C.

3. Cummings, "Unusual Life," 56.

4. Mary Ann Shadd, "The Emigration Convention," *Provincial Freeman*, 5 July 1856, 2.

5. Maria W. Stewart, "Mrs. Steward's [sic] Essays," *Liberator*, 7 January 1832, p. 2.

6. Stewart, "Lecture Delivered At The Franklin Hall," *Liberator*, 17 November 1832, p. 183.

7. Josephine St. Pierre Ruffin, "An Open Appeal to Our Women for Organization," *Woman's Era*, January 1897, p. 2.

8. Cummings, "Unusual Life," 56.

9. Gertrude Bustill Mossell, "Our Woman's Department," *New York Freeman*, 13 March 1886, p. 2.

10. Interview with Marvel Cooke by Kathleen Currie, Women in Journalism oral history project of the Washington Press Club Foundation, 3 October to 3 November 1989, Oral History Collection, Columbia University, p. 105.

11. Interview with Ethel L. Payne by Kathleen Currie, Women in Journalism oral history project of the Washington Press Club Foundation, 25 August 1987 through 17 November 1987, Oral History Collection, Columbia University, p. 54.

12. *Working Woman*, "Charlayne Hunter-Gault," July 1981, p. 60.

13. Stewart, "An Address Delivered Before the Afric-American Female Intelligence Society of Boston," *Liberator*, 28 April 1832, p. 66.

14. Shadd, "Canadian Churches fellowshiping the Pro-slavery Religious Bodies of the United States," *Provincial Freeman*, 13 December 1856, 2.

15. Ibid.

16. Gertrude Bustill Mossell, "Our Woman's Department," *New York Freeman*, 13 February 1886, p. 2.

17. Mossell, "Our Woman's Department," *New York Freeman*, 17 July 1886, p. 2.

18. Mary Ann Shadd Cary, "The Last Day of the 43 Congress," Mary Ann Shadd Cary Papers, Moorland-Spingarn Research Center, Howard University, Washington, D.C., folder 16.

19. Mossell, "Our Woman's Department," *New York Freeman*, 8 May 1886, p. 2.

20. T. Thomas Fortune, "Mr. Fortune on the West," *New York Age*, 11 August 1888, p. 1.

21. Payne oral history, p. 129.

22. Mossell, "Our Woman's Department," *New York Freeman*, 8 May 1886, p. 2.

23. On a wavelike pattern defining career development among women journalists, see Susan Henry, "Near-Sightedness and Blind Spots In Studying the History of Women in Journalism," a paper presented to the American Journalism Historians Association, October 1990, Coeur d'Alene, Idaho, p. 16. On this pattern in women's careers more broadly, see Gerda Lerner, *Female Experience: An American Documentary* (Indianapolis: Bobbs-Merrill, 1977), pp. xxvi-xxvii; Lerner, *Majority Finds Its Past*, 162-63; Hilda Smith, "Female Bonds and the Family: Recent Directions in Women's History," in Paula A. Treichler, Cheris Kramarae, and Beth Stafford, eds., *For Alma Mater: Theory and Practice in Feminist Scholarship* (Urbana: Univ. of Illinois Press, 1985), 282-83. On this pattern in the lives of African-American women, see Maxine Baca Zinn, "Family, Race, and Poverty in the Eighties," *Signs* 14 (Summer 1989): 861-68.

24. Author's interview with Hunter-Gault, 11 September 1992.

INDEX